No Shortcuts to Power

About the Series
Democratic Transition
in Conflict-Torn Societies

Series editors
Anne Marie Goetz and Robin Luckham

This three-book series explores the politics of democratic transition in conflict-torn countries in the developing South and post-communist East, focusing upon the interplay between democratic institutions and democratic politics. The different volumes in the series identify the institutional arrangements and political compromises which can assure democratic control of military and security establishments, facilitate the peaceful management of conflict, and enhance the participation of excluded groups, particularly women.

VOLUME 1
Governing Insecurity: Democratic Control of Military and Security
Establishments in Transitional Democracies
EDITED BY
Gavin Cawthra and Robin Luckham

VOLUME 2
Can Democracy be Designed?
The Politics of Institutional Choice in Conflict-Torn Societies
EDITED BY
Sunil Bastian and Robin Luckham

VOLUME 3
No Shortcuts to Power:
African Women in Politics and Policy Making
EDITED BY
Anne Marie Goetz and Shireen Hassim

No Shortcuts to Power

African Women in Politics and Policy Making

Edited by

ANNE MARIE GOETZ AND SHIREEN HASSIM

Zed Books
LONDON & NEW YORK

David Philip
CAPE TOWN

No Shortcuts to Power was first published in 2003 by
Zed Books Ltd, 7 Cynthia Street, London N1 9JF, UK and
Room 400, 175 Fifth Avenue, New York, NY 10010, USA

www.zedbooks.demon.co.uk

Published in South Africa by David Philip Publishers (Pty Ltd),
99 Garfield Road, Claremont, 7700, in 2003

Cover designed by Andrew Corbett
Designed and set in 9½/12 pt Photina
by Long House, Cumbria, UK
Printed and bound in Malaysia

Distributed in the USA exclusively by Palgrave, a division of
St Martin's Press, LLC, 175 Fifth Avenue, New York, NY 10010

A catalogue record for this book
is available from the British Library

US Cataloging-in-Publication Data
is available from the Library of Congress

ISBN   Hb 1 84277 146 9
        Pb 1 84277 147 7

South Africa
ISBN   Pb 0 86486 636 4

Contents

About the Contributors

Josephine Ahikire lectures in political science in the Department of Gender Studies at Makerere University in Kampala, Uganda. She is also a research fellow at the Centre for Basic Research in Kampala. She has researched gender in politics, labour rights issues, and popular culture and identities in Uganda. She is currently completing a PhD on gender and local government in Uganda.

Anne Marie Goetz is a political scientist and Fellow of the Institute of Development Studies, University of Sussex. She has worked on feminist political theory, and has conducted research in South Asia and Eastern Africa on the politics of promoting gender equity in development policy, and on gender and political party development. She is also studying movements of the poor to combat corruption in South Asia. She is the author of *Women Development Workers: Implementing Credit Programmes in Bangladesh* (Sage 2001); editor of *Getting Institutions Right for Women in Development* (Zed Books 1997), and co-author of *Contesting Global Governance: Multilateral Economic Institutions and Global Social Movements* (Cambridge University Press 2000).

Shireen Hassim lectures in Political Studies in the School of Social Sciences, University of the Witwatersrand. She has recently completed a PhD thesis on the political history of the women's movement in South Africa (1980–99). She has published widely in the area of gender politics including *South Africa: a Country Gender Analysis* (co-authored with Sally Baden and Sheila Meintjes) and several articles in academic journals. She was a member of the Gender and Elections Reference Group coordinated by the Electoral Institute of Southern Africa and a member of the editorial group of the *Election Bulletin* published by womensnet.org.za.

Likhapha Mbatha is a research officer with the Gender Research Project of the Centre for Applied Legal Studies at the University of the Witwatersrand in Johannesburg. She read law at the National University of Lesotho and is registered for an LLM degree with the University of the Witwatersrand.

Sheila Kawamara-Mishambi is a Ugandan women's rights activist, with a Masters of Arts in Development Studies from the Institute of Social Studies (ISS) in The Hague. She is currently a Ugandan Member of Parliament in the East African Legislative Assembly, Arusha, Tanzania. She was the Executive Director of Uganda Women's Organisations Network (UWONET) from 1996 to June 2002. Prior to that, she worked as a journalist for one of Uganda's dailies, *New Vision*, from 1992 to 1996 and was a teacher of economics in Trinity College Nabbingo, Kampala (1989–90). She is also a chairperson of the Uganda National NGO Forum, a consortium of over 650 non-government organisations in Uganda. She has written and edited several advocacy publications for UWONET. She is a keen supporter of efforts to increase the numbers of women in positions of power and decision making, and of development programmes to increase the availability of economic resources and their fair distribution between men and women.

Sheila Meintjes is a political scientist attached to the Department of Political Studies at the University of the Witwatersrand in Johannesburg, South Africa, and a Commissioner in the South African Commission on Gender Equality. Over the last 25 years she has been actively involved in women's politics. She lectures on political theory, feminist theory and politics, and African politics. She has conducted research on political violence and gender politics in conflict, post-conflict and democratising South Africa. She recently co-edited *The Aftermath: Women in Post-war Transformation* (Zed Books 2000) and has also completed a study with a number of colleagues on gender and electoral politics in South Africa, to be published by the Electoral Institute of Southern Africa. Her work in the CGE is to monitor the progress of gender equality in civil society and the state, amongst other activities.

Irene Ovonji-Odida is a human rights lawyer with a master's degree in Comparative Jurisprudence from Howard University, Washington, and various postgraduate qualifications in gender and development, advocacy and international law. She has extensive research experience, and has worked in both the public sector and civil society on gender, land and rights issues, as well as good governance, ethics and integrity. She has served in leadership positions in various NGOs including as Chairperson of the Uganda Women Lawyers' Association (FIDA) and the Coalition for Political Accountability to Women of Uganda, following public service in the Uganda Law Reform Commission, the Constituent Assembly Commission, and the Directorate of Ethics and Integrity. She is currently a (Ugandan) Member of the East African Legislative Assembly.

Preface

The Politics of Inclusion
Women in National and Local Government in South Africa and Uganda

Most transitions towards democratic governance – whether from military authoritarian systems or from civil war – are accompanied by expectations of greater social equity, broader political participation, and of course the resolution of conflict by peaceful means. This book is part of a three-book series on the capacity of political institutions to resolve deep-seated social conflict in countries in transition to democracy. This book focuses on the capacity of political institutions to address one area of conflict in social relations that is frequently neglected in good governance debates: the conflicting interests of women and men that produce gendered asymmetries in resource access and social opportunity. The reason gender-based conflicting interests are not considered by many political analysts to be as significant as ethnic or racial conflict is because they never produce the kind of ghastly civil war that ethnic, religious, regional, or racial differences can provoke. But conflicting interests based on gender do produce smouldering and socially corrosive injustices and violence that delay development and undermine any state's claim to the status of a democracy. These are injustices such as the systematic withholding from girls and women of equal rights to health care, education, and work opportunities, or under-policed and under-prosecuted forms of violence such as spousal battery, rape within marriage, and sexual assault.

Women as much as any other social group welcome peace and democracy and expect that new democratic institutions at national and local levels will be open to their participation. Yet around the world, women have found that the resumption of political competition in post-conflict democracies has left them on the sidelines. Political parties organised as 'old boys' clubs' have been hostile to their inclusion, and the straightened circumstances of capitalist market relationships in poor countries have left women with little time and few resources for political participation. This has sometimes kept them from seizing the opportunity offered by periods of regime change to renegotiate the terms of the sexual contract that has so disadvantaged them.

In Uganda and South Africa, however, this pattern does not hold. In both countries, women inserted gender equality as a core principle in the new constitution. They have also made their way in unprecedented numbers into the legislature and into local government at all levels. They have done so in different ways – in South Africa a strong women's movement has exploited the competitive dynamic of party politics to assert leverage in electoral struggles, while in Uganda women have benefited from presidential patronage and the creation of new representative offices for women-only competition. This book examines the contrasting terms of women's engagement in politics in the two countries and the consequences these terms have had for their perceived legitimacy as politicians, and for their capacity to promote gender equality in new legislation. The book seizes the opportunity offered by the unprecedented numbers of women in politics in these countries to identify conditions favouring women's political effectiveness. It looks at how the gains women have made can be consolidated and institutionalised in gender-sensitive changes to accountability systems and institutions.

This book is based on empirical research conducted under the umbrella of a research programme, Strengthening Democratic Governance in Conflict-Torn Societies, based at the Institute of Development Studies at the University of Sussex. This programme was funded by the UK's Department for International Development, and we wish to express our appreciation of this financial support. We also want to thank Aaron Griffiths for his inspired contributions as a research assistant, conference organiser and energetic copy-editor. Julie McWilliam has provided consistent and cheerful secretarial support throughout the life of this programme. We are grateful to Shahra Razavi and Maxine Molyneux for their permission to develop in Chapter 4 material published in a different form in their book: *Gender Justice, Development, and Rights* (Oxford University Press, 2002). We thank Aili Mari Tripp and Sylvia Tamale for their comments on Chapter 4. Irene Ovonji-Odida and Sheila Kawamara-Mishambi, authors of Chapter 6, wish to express their appreciation for the work of the Hon. Miria Matembe, the tireless champion of the spousal co-ownership amendment to the 1998 Land Act in Uganda, which is the subject of their chapter. They also wish to acknowledge inputs and support from women activists in the Uganda Women's Organisations Network (UWONET), the Uganda Land Alliance, and the women lawyers' association, FIDA–Uganda. Likhapha Mbatha, author of Chapter 7, wishes to thank Dira Matlatle and Constance Yose for assisting with her interviews of local government councillors and officials in South Africa. And finally, we the editors would like to thank all of the authors in this volume for the stimulating interactions and debates we have had with each other over the three years of research that gave rise to the chapters in this volume.

Abbreviations

ACFODE Action for Development
AEB Afrikaner Eensheidbeweging (Afrikaner Unity Movement)
ANC African National Congress
ANCWL African National Congress Women's League
AWEPA Association of Women in European Parliaments
AZAPO Azanian People's Organisation
CA Constituent Assembly
CALS Centre for Applied Legal Studies
CEDAW Convention on the Elimination of All Forms of Discrimination against Women
CGE Commission on Gender Equality
COPAW Coalition for Political Accountability to Women
COSATU Congress of South African Trade Unions
CSO Community service organisation
DA Democratic Alliance
DC District Council
DFID Department for International Development
DP Democratic Party
EASSI East African Sub-Regional Support Initiative
EISA Electoral Institute of Southern Africa
FIDA(U) Uganda Women Lawyers Association
FOWODE Forum for Women in Democracy
GAD Gender and Development
GAP Gender Advocacy Programme
HIPC Highly Indebted Poor Country
IDASA Institute for Democratic Alternatives (South Africa)
IEC Independent Electoral Commission
IPU Inter-Parliamentary Union
ISIS–WICCE ISIS–Women's International Cross-Cultural Exchange
LAW–Uganda Law and Advocacy for Women in Uganda
LC Local Council
LGNF Local Government Negotiating Forum
LGTA Local Government Transition Act
MLC Metropolitan Local Council
NEDLAC National Economic Development and Labour Council

NCW National Council of Women
NNP New National Party
NRC National Resistance Council
NRM National Resistance Movement
NGO Non-governmental organisation
NUDIPU National Union of Disabled Persons
PAC Pan Africanist Congress
PDS Public Distribution System
PEAP Poverty Eradication Action Plan
PMA Plan for Modernisation of Agriculture
POWA People Opposing Woman Abuse
PWDs Persons With Disabilities
PWG Parliamentary Women's Group
RC Resistance Council
RDP Reconstruction and Development Programme
RSDN Rural Development Service Network
RWM Rural Women's Movement
SABC South African Broadcasting Corporation
SADC Southern African Development Community
SALC South African Law Commission
SALGA South African Local Government Association
SANCO South African National Civics Organisation
SANGOCO South African NGO Coalition
TRC Transitional Representative Council
UDF United Democratic Front
UK United Kingdom
ULA Uganda Land Association
UN United Nations
UNDP United Nations Development Programme
UPC Uganda People's Congress
USA United States of America
UWO United Women's Organisation
UWONET Uganda Women's Organisations Network
UWOPA Uganda Women Parliamentarians' Association
WDF Women's Development Foundation
WID Women in Development
WNC Women's National Coalition
WORK Women's Movement for the Return of Yoweri K. Museveni

1

Introduction:
Women in Power
in Uganda and South Africa

ANNE MARIE GOETZ AND SHIREEN HASSIM

Uganda and South Africa stand out as trailblazers in Africa and in the world in their efforts to bring greater numbers of women into formal politics. Since the 2001 elections, Uganda's parliament is one quarter female, while women have made up nearly one third of South Africa's parliament since 1999. About one third of local government councillors in both countries are women. This puts both countries ahead of most industrialised country democracies in terms of women's presence in politics, and on a par with the most advanced of these, the Scandinavian countries. How have women been able to make their way into public life in such large numbers in societies not otherwise noted for equality between the sexes? What difference has large numbers of women in politics made in terms of advancing women's interests in legislative and policy changes? What difference has it made to the character of local and national political competition? This book answers these questions in a systematic way by examining, in both countries, the terms of women's access to local and national politics, and their impact on decision making once in office. The authors analyse the role of political parties, patronage networks and presidential support in promoting women candidates, the role of women's movements in developing policy platforms and support for women politicians, and the institutional changes that have made the public sphere more accessible to women. The book also offers a close examination of the engagement of feminist politicians of both sexes in major policy debates on matters affecting the relative rights and power of women and men in the changing economies and societies of these two countries.

This book is animated by an interest in assessing the relative impact and importance of contrasting political regimes, party systems, and affirmative action measures on the perceived legitimacy and effectiveness of women in politics. By 'effectiveness' we mean the capacity of women politicians to mobilise support in their parties and in civil society for their policy agendas. We are particularly interested in their capacities to promote gender equality in policy making and to cultivate male allies for this, though we do not make the assumption that all women politicians have feminist interests. Uganda and South Africa offer interesting case studies for examining these key factors in women's political effectiveness. Both countries have been through extended and turbulent transitions to new political regimes which have afforded women opportunities to engage in creating new political institutions. Both countries were faced with the challenge of accommodating ethnic and racial differences and preventing ethnic conflict. In both countries, women organised during the transition from authoritarian rule to ensure that the political arrangements and constitutions for the new regimes would be favourable to them. As in many other countries in the world in which women make up more than 15 per cent of elected bodies, their high representation in national and local assemblies in Uganda and South Africa is a product of affirmative action measures and quota systems under the aegis of a dominant political party.

However, the political and institutional conditions under which women's representational gains were achieved are very different in the two countries, with contrasting implications for the perceived legitimacy of women politicians and for their effectiveness in advancing a policy agenda on gender equity. Unlike South Africa's, the Ugandan transition did not produce a political system underpinned by political openness, institutional diversity and free political competition. Although it claims the status of democracy for Uganda, the ruling National Resistance Movement (NRM) has suppressed party activities under a 'no-party' system which has been variously defended as a 'consultative' and as a 'participatory' democracy offering a culturally appropriate response to the problem of preventing ethnic conflict. Rather than institutionalise competition and conflict within a common set of rules, the Movement discourages citizens from articulating political interests outside it. Women's access to politics is primarily through a system of special reserved seats for parliamentary representatives of the districts and, at the local government level, through the creation of an additional 30 per cent of reserved seats. By contrast, South Africa has a multi-party liberal democratic system underpinned by a constitution that emphasises gender equality and democratic participation in decision making. Informal mechanisms for increasing women's representation have been favoured over special seats, with women parliamentarians representing parties rather than women.

The two countries therefore offer several interesting points of comparison. First, they allow us to compare the efficacy of two different mechanisms of representation: on one hand, a constitutionally entrenched reservation system that offers women representation in a *separate* and protected arena of competition, and, on the other, a voluntary party quota system through which women compete against men for office. Second, we are able to compare the impact of two distinctly different regime contexts on the ability of women to use formal access: that is, a comparison between a political regime based on patronage – some would say this is more typical of African polities – and one based on more open political competition and a liberal rights regime. Third, while the women's movements in both countries share the familiar dilemma of defining a relationship in and against a single dominant political party, we are able to compare the difference between a relatively autonomous and diverse women's movement in South Africa (represented at the crucial moment of transition by the Women's National Coalition) and a somewhat smaller women's movement with less political space for autonomy in Uganda.

As we will show below, political parties around the world have been resistant to fronting female candidates or to championing a feminist policy platform. In Uganda and South Africa, parties remain male-dominated at all levels and have embraced gender equity concerns with reluctance and after protracted struggles of women within them and by women's organisations outside the parties. Nevertheless, political parties in South Africa and the NRM in Uganda are islands of formal democratic commitment in a sea of hostility to women's demands in civil society throughout Africa. This raises the question of whether the Ugandan rejection of multi-party competition offers a more inclusive institutional form for the entry and participation of non-élites in decision making, in this case women. Is multi-party competition simply conflict-producing, or does it offer opportunities for marginalised groups to increase their policy leverage? How effectively have women been able to use their increased representation to advance gender equality? The answer to these questions should lie in measuring the extent to which new enabling legislation for gender-sensitive policy has appeared in both countries.

This book is based on three years of research coordinated by the two editors. For each country, three sets of investigations were carried out in parallel: first, research on party systems and the role of parties in promoting both women themselves and gender issues in politics; second, research on the effectiveness of women politicians and their allies in advancing new legislation to advance women's rights, and third, research into new electoral arrangements to bring women into local government and their effectiveness in creating space for the pursuit of gender equity at the local level. The book is therefore based firmly on original empirical work, and the chapters are organised in pairs, addressing these issues in turn for each country. This comparative framework uses the contrasts between Uganda and South Africa's political regimes to help highlight matters which go beyond country-specific factors. These matters are of broader relevance when assessing women's political effectiveness in other countries – matters such as the way gender enters into patronage systems, the impact of party and electoral systems on women's capacity to exercise electoral leverage, and the extent to which affirmative action measures can challenge the power of traditional and patriarchal political élites. More generally, the concerns of this book with party systems, local government and policy debates reflect a shift in focus in contemporary feminist political studies from understanding the women's movement and its role in political transitions (Albertyn 1995; Meintjes 1996; Cock 1997; Tripp 2000) to understanding the impact of institutional variations on women's capacity to promote a gender equity agenda once in office. As Georgina Waylen argues, institutional characteristics – such as variations in the power of the executive in relation to the legislature, or different party and electoral systems – 'afford women actors different opportunities for participation and influence' (2000: 769).

This introductory chapter establishes the comparative analytical framework for the rest of the book. We begin with a section setting out key concepts which are further elaborated in Chapter 2. The objective is to justify the focus on women in politics, to explain differences between a feminine and a feminist presence in politics (or descriptive versus strategic representation), and to explain that we consider the obstacles and setbacks in advancing a gender equity agenda in politics to reveal gender biases in the accountability relationship between the state and citizens. The three following sections of this introductory chapter each contrast the findings of a pair of chapters. The section on parties and electoral systems compares chapters 3 and 4, which analyse the politics of women's access to power in South Africa and Uganda respectively. We focus on the impact of the political regime, and of political cultures, party systems, ideologies, and internal structures, as well as on the history of the engagement of the women's movement in politics. The next section contrasts the findings of Chapters 5 and 6, both of which deal with women's impact on key areas of policy making. Chapter 5 discusses the South African campaign for new legislation on domestic violence and Chapter 6 discusses the campaign to inscribe women's rights to family property in the 1998 Uganda Land Act. Here the 'political effectiveness' of women in power is compared by examining the mobilisation of the women's movement behind these issues in both countries; the nature of their arguments and strategies; the relationship between the women's movement and women politicians and their allies; and the role of the executive in both countries. The last section contrasts chapters 7 and 8, which deal with women's experiences in the new local government structures in the two countries. The very different institutional innovations to bring greater numbers of women into local office in both contexts are compared, as is the capacity of women councillors to advocate a gender equity agenda in local policy debates.

Women's political effectiveness: key concepts

A framework for assessing how far increasing numbers of women in politics will help to produce gender-sensitive policies and better public accountability to women – what we understand by 'women's political effectiveness' – is developed in Chapter 2. This aims to justify the contemporary interest in increasing women's presence in public representative institutions by suggesting conditions for moving beyond a 'descriptive' or simply numerical representation to a more substantive one: from a feminine presence to feminist activism in politics.

The starting point, however, is that this distinction between 'descriptive' and 'substantive' or 'strategic'[1] representation is misleading in two senses. It may overstate the role of political agency, encouraging a focus on women's failure to develop the electoral leverage and political skills necessary to influence policy. This detracts from the impact of political institutions on women's agency in politics. In other words, Goetz argues that the design of political institutions and the culture of competition over ideas and principles in civil society, politics and the state profoundly shapes the perceived legitimacy of women politicians and of gender equity concerns, and hence the effectiveness of feminists in advancing gender equity policy. The second reason that the 'descriptive' versus 'substantive' contrast may be overstated is that, as the studies in this book show, descriptive representation may be a necessary first step to the institutional transformation that is required if 'substantive' representation is to be achieved. Gender-sensitive institutional reform is required not just to get women through the door in politics, but also for policy making and implementation to respect gender equality. Women's movements around the world have found that such transformation is impossible without engaging with political institutions, and this, as will be shown in the next section, has sharpened the perpetual dilemma of 'integration versus autonomy' for the women's movement.

The success of the gender equity interest in policy making will depend upon three major factors and their interactions:

- *The nature of civil society* and the place and power of the gender equity lobby in civil society – its power to mobilise resources and public concern to support its demands, its power to challenge gender-biased conceptions of women's needs, roles and rights;

- *The nature of the political system* (the depth of procedural and substantive democracy) and *the organisation of political competition* (the number and nature of parties, their ideologies and memberships, the relative importance of high finance or crime in political contests);

- *The nature and power of the state* (whether it is a developmental state; the extent of decentralisation; the configuration of executive/legislative/military/judicial/administrative power and the degree to which these enable horizontal accountability institutions to function effectively; whether the top executive has the will and capacity to enforce change in the culture and practices of public bureaucracies; whether there is a professional civil service; whether the public service has internalised a commitment to poverty reduction, gender equity, etcetera).

In most societies, gender equity concerns are counter-cultural: they challenge the interests of individual men, and of groups constituted on the basis of patriarchal privilege. For instance, clan- or tribe-based power structures do not welcome the disruption to traditional property ownership patterns which women's claims to land rights represent. The demands of feminists can provoke social conflict, and a powerful and committed state is needed to see that constitutional or policy commitments on gender equity are actually implemented in policies on social services, land ownership or employment. It must, for instance, have a disciplined bureaucracy able to implement gender-sensitive policy in spite of social (and internal) resistance. Often states make commitments to advance women's rights without the means of doing so, perhaps keen to receive the plaudits associated with demonstrating gender sensitivity, yet secure in the knowledge that the domestic women's constituency is too weak to hold it to account. We argue, therefore, that the main focus of attention in efforts to increase women's political effectiveness should be on building gender sensitivity into accountability systems – improving their capacity to answer to women, and to enforce sanctions against public sector actors who have abused women's rights. In practical terms this means examining the internal democracy of civil society associations and political parties and the extent to which women have a voice within them; the extent to which opposition parties politicise gender inequalities in campaigns and in legislatures; the gender sensitivity of the legal system; the extent to which public sector budgeting and auditing exercises measure the impact of public spending (or mis-spending) on women; and the extent to which performance measures in the bureaucracy reward gender-sensitive actions.

Public sector reform and processes of democratisation around the world have introduced a wide range of efforts to improve public accountability and to broaden political participation. These measures include decentralisation, the reservation of seats in representative institutions for women and other excluded groups, and efforts to consult with civil society over new policies. These measures must be scrutinised for the quality of participation they offer women and for the rights they give women to demand answers of powerholders or to demand redress for poor decision making. Variations in the culture of politics and the design of public institutions will produce a different quality of engagement for women, and different outcomes in terms of the way policies, legal judgements and state agents in their day-to-day interactions with clients respond to women's needs and promote their interests. A distinction between three types of public engagement – access (consultation, dialogue), presence (representation) and influence (accountability) – enables us to be critical of measures that bring women into public decision-making arenas without empowering them to hold decision makers to account. We can then note that many efforts to increase numbers of women in politics tend to be oriented to supporting the legitimation project of the state, yet undermine the legitimacy and effectiveness of women as politicians because they are seen to be latecomers with artificial constituencies. This is the case in Uganda, where new seats for women have been added onto local councils to avoid a situation where women might unseat male councillors. This detaches women from normal competition for the ward councillor seats, and makes them seem lesser politicians.

Thus institutional changes designed to increase numbers of women in politics can be assessed in terms of whether they are simply a legitimation exercise for the state, enabling officials to listen to previously excluded groups but with no obligation to act upon what they hear, or whether they create the space for women to advance their needs and interests and demand policy responses. This can be assessed by checking to see whether gender equity issues are being raised by the new entrants to the system, and whether they exercise concrete influence through policy change and new accountability measures which are responsive to women. Chapter 2 reviews a wide range of contemporary experiments with political institutions to promote dialogue with the women's movement, the presence of women as representatives in politics, and their influence on policy making.

The chapters in this volume follow the framework of distinguishing between a weak form of engagement by women with the state and a more substantial form of influence. All of the chapters are attentive to the shifting fate of the gender equity interest in the three arenas of civil society, parties, and the state, and each considers the interactions between these three arenas. We ask how far new measures to bring women into public office allow for a greater influence of the women's movement on politics, for the entry of *feminists* into politics, for the forging of connections between feminists in politics and a constituency of women, and for the production of new legislation which advances gender equity.

Women in political competition – the national level

Feminist studies of political party systems have demonstrated that, around the world, parties are notoriously reluctant to put forward women as candidates in equal numbers to men – if at all (Lovenduski and Norris 1993). This is usually explained in terms of the electoral liability that women candidates are thought to constitute, given strong voter hostility to women in political office. This hostility is much stronger when voters know that they will be represented by one person – in other words, in single-member, first-past-the-post electoral systems. The persistent unpopularity and perceived high social and financial cost of many feminist policies also appear to prevent politicians and parties from making them central to their party platforms. It is now apparent that particular types of parties and party systems, combined with particular kinds of electoral systems, are more amenable to women's representation (though not necessarily to feminist policies). While parties are the key gatekeepers to elected office, certain types of parties – those on the left of the political spectrum – are more likely to accommodate women's representational claims and to incorporate concerns about gender equality into their electoral platforms and policy priorities (*ibid.*). Parties of the left have tended to be more receptive to women's demands for representation, and have been more willing to take on board women's redistributive concerns as an appropriate matter for social policy (Dahlerup 1986). Nevertheless, even left political parties have to be treated with caution by the women's movement. As Dahlerup (*ibid.*: 17) has shown, left parties have a tendency to 'alter feminist demands and use them for their own purpose'. This process of cooption of women's movement objectives may lead to some short-term concessions in areas that are less costly and less contentious – for example, recognising women's special needs in relation to childbirth and child rearing – while not necessarily shifting the basic gender inequalities in access to the labour market. As feminist analysts of welfare states have pointed out, this can lead to a deradicalisation of feminism (Sainsbury 1996).

In terms of electoral systems, proportional representation (PR) systems, with closed lists where parties have adopted quotas for women candidates, combined with well-institutionalised party systems which have formal, centralised rules for candidate selection (such as South Africa, the Scandinavian countries and, most recently, France) are most effective in producing what has been termed a 'critical mass' (30 per cent) of women in parliament (Waylen 2000; Lovenduski and Norris 1993; Rule and Zimmerman 1994). Similar results have been achieved by changing electoral rules to reserve seats for group-specific competition – for instance, competition between women candidates only, or lower-caste candidates only (as in India) – with a view to improving their levels of political participation. There is a growing interest among feminist political scientists in the ways in which variations in party and political systems affect women's prospects for establishing a substantial presence among elected representatives, and in promoting women's interests in policy making.[2]

At the same time, there is a strong tradition of feminist political activism and scholarship that has been sceptical of the capacity of liberal or bourgeois democracy either to include women amongst decision makers, or to permit meaningful representation of their interests. This has led to a feminist interest in alternatives to liberal representative democracy, and particularly in measures that support the principle of group representation for women in politics. The most prominent among these measures has been the notion of affirmative action to put some minimum number of women in political and bureaucratic positions, or to give representative groups of social and political minorities some powers of review in policy making which affects their interests (Young 1990). The dismal track record of mainstream political parties in fronting women candidates or in representing women's particular interests in policy decisions has produced a tradition of antipathy to political parties in women's

9

movements the world over. As Marion Sawer (2000: 6), an Australian political scientist, observes:

> The question of the relevance of parliamentary representation to women is linked to the historical ambivalence of women's movements concerning representative democracy and the party system on which it rests. This ambivalence manifested itself in the many 'non-party' organisations created in the aftermath of suffrage to encourage women's active citizenship without being drawn into the compromised world of man-made politics.

In developing countries, this feminist antipathy to parties has become pronounced in the aftermath of liberation and democracy struggles, in which women who have contributed to independence and democratisation have often been disappointed by their marginalisation from political power (Waylen 1994; Basu 1995). Perhaps not surprisingly, this has resulted in a literature on women's relationship to the state which has proceeded from the assumption of women's exclusion from the mainstream of political power. It has tended to focus on the ways in which states have affected women's social and economic position, with little attention to the internal character of particular states from a gender perspective. Some prominent analysts of the state in Africa, such as Naomi Chazan (1989: 186), have argued that African women have played no significant role in statecraft. There is remarkably little theoretical literature on the experience of women in African political parties.

Two broad reasons can be identified for the lack of attention to a gendered analysis of political parties in newly democratising countries. First, in many African countries where nationalist movements have transformed themselves into political parties, women's secondary status in the nationalist movement has been replicated in the new political order. Women have been relegated to a feminised and marginalised 'women's wing' within political parties. The cooption of women's organisations by nationalist movements and then by the ruling parties undermines any expectations that association with political parties might lead to better policy outcomes for women (Abdullah 1993; Tsikata 1989). The mobilising styles of political parties, too, can exclude women when the costs of mobilisation are violent conflicts. In many countries, such as Uganda, Zimbabwe and Malawi, the dominance of a single party and the discouragement of politics outside of that party have limited the extent of civil society development and particularly the emergence of feminist organisations that seek to change gender relations in both the public and private spheres. This lack of political space available for civil society organisation can reinforce women's sense of exclusion from the public sphere and enhance perceptions that political parties are for men. Even where women are courted by politicians, it is not always in the interests of increasing women's political power. Tripp (2000), for example, has argued that in authoritarian systems parties have actively repressed women's autonomous associational life in the interests of co-opting women to the legitimation projects of the single ruling party. These experiences produce a profound mistrust of parties and politics and a tendency to seek disengagement from the state and from politics.

Second, parties in many developing countries are poorly developed as political institutions *per se*. In many African countries, parties are not constituted with strong rules and procedures that would allow for open and democratic internal debate and for access of rank-and-file members to leadership. Party systems, and the ruling party, may be insufficiently institutionalised for women to challenge rules which exclude women – simply because there are no firm rules and rights, only patronage systems and favours. Alternatively, where a military or theocratic power structure bolsters ruling parties, there is little scope for women's engagement because the rules of these institutions explicitly deny women's full right of participation.

Antipathy to dealing with parties in developing countries is shared by the international development establishment. Many international development agencies have, for obvious reasons, steered clear of engaging explicitly with parties in developing countries. Even the 'good governance' policy agenda that emerged in the 1990s focuses primarily on reforms in the public administration, not the political arena. Within the Gender and Development (GAD) sector of the development establishment, an antipathy to political engagement is reflected in the scant attention assigned to political party development in the declarations and platforms of the UN conferences on women, and in Women in Development (WID) and GAD policy prescriptions for promoting gender equity in development. Instead, the focus has been on 'bureaucratic representation' – for instance, dedicated bureaucratic 'machinery' for women (women's ministries, gender or equal opportunity commissions, or women's desks in important ministries) and affirmative action measures to place more women in bureaucracies. The structures have been seen as the route to increasing women's presence in the state and offering women some degree of participation in policy formulation. However, national machineries, usually starved of resources and isolated from the arena of politics and competition, have rarely made

11

much of an impact on policy making. This approach represents what might be described as not just an apolitical discourse of inclusion, but indeed an *anti-political* discourse of inclusion. The stress is on avoiding politics and competition, except perhaps within a more narrowly defined field of contestants: women, and particularly urban and privileged women. In addressing the realm of parties and parliaments, therefore, we are seeking in this book to open a new set of discussions as to how women can enter and make an impact in the key institutions of representative democracy, while holding open the question of whether representation on its own can advance the democratic claims of feminism.

In broadening the political and scholarly focus of feminism in developing countries to include a focus on political parties, we are mindful of what Waylen (1994: 339–40) calls the 'dilemma of autonomy versus integration': that is, the tension between working within parties at the risk of being coopted, or staying outside parties at the risk of being marginalised. But for most women's movements in Africa, there has been little choice about whether to work with political parties. Liberation movements – precursors to parties – have been the primary vehicles for women's political participation. In the post-liberation period, whether they institutionalise as parties, as in South Africa, or cling to the more amorphous 'movement' form, as in Uganda, they remain the central mechanism for channelling political demands. Rarely are women activists – or oppositional social movements in general – able to build a successful movement outside the ruling party, and, where they do, it is against enormous resistance from the party. As Chigudu and Tichagwa (1995: 3) ask, 'Do [women] have an alternative power base [to the party]? Would they survive if they relied solely on the alternative power base? To both questions the answer is probably no!!'

Under what conditions, then, can feminists successfully engage political parties? We can identify four key variables: political party commitment to increasing women's representation, the existence of strong left political parties; the degree of organisation of women's structures within parties, and a strong women's movement outside of the parties. The research conducted for this book shows that while at least some of the same favourable conditions exist for making the representative system in Uganda and South Africa more responsive to women's demands, there are also revealing differences between the two countries that account for the variance in outcomes of the inclusion of women in the state. In both countries a formal commitment has been made to increasing women's representation and this has expanded women's numerical presence in the state. In both cases, centralised leadership has

12

been key to the effectiveness of affirmative action measures, which would otherwise have fallen victim to opposition to women's presence from traditional interests within the ruling parties.

Women were important to the ANC to demonstrate its continued commitment to social inclusion, and to the redress of social inequities, in the face of criticism that it had abandoned its revolutionary ideals. In Uganda, the NRM hoped that the incorporation of women as a new political group would demonstrate possibilities of non-ethnic models of group identification and political participation. However, in South Africa, the commitment of the ANC to substantive democracy is well established; this is not true of the NRM in Uganda. The thinness of commitment to democracy has outcomes for policy approaches as well as for internal democracy within the NRM, and it has been especially difficult for women within the Movement to advance their claims on the grounds of more institutionalised rules and procedures that value inclusion, rather than by grace of the party leadership. Thus while both the ANC and the NRM have been receptive to using affirmative action mechanisms for increasing the numbers of women in formal politics, the ways in which representation is structured have very different outcomes for the gender equity agenda. In South Africa, affirmative action measures have been introduced at the party level on a voluntary basis. In Uganda, a range of new parliamentary and local government seats were created for women-only competition, thus separating women's political engagement from the mainstream of political competition.

The lack of institutionalisation of democratic procedures undermines the extent to which women can use party structures to press their demands on party leaderships. Based on Scandinavian experiences, Dahlerup (1986) suggests that one factor in ensuring that parties support feminist demands – as opposed to narrower demands for an increase in numerical representation – is the strength of activism in the women's committees within the party and of women activists within the party. Again, there are significant differences between Uganda and South Africa, despite Aili Mari Tripp's characterisation of the two women's movements as the strongest in Africa (Tripp 2000). As Sheila Kawamara-Mishambi and Irene Ovonji-Odida argue in Chapter 6, the women's structures within the NRM are susceptible to patronage, and women within the NRM have been divided at crucial strategic moments. In South Africa, while the ANC Women's League as the internal women's wing of the ANC has had success in winning broad commitments from the party, it has been pressure from *outside* the movement through structures such as the Women's National Coalition (WNC) and, as Sheila Meintjes argues in Chapter 5, the civil society movement opposing violence against women that has forced the ANC to implement its commitments. This comparative research underscores the importance of an autonomous women's movement: where women's organisations are too close to political parties, they can simply become stepping stones to party positions.

Arguments that emphasise the use of internal party mechanisms for the advancement of women therefore need to bear in mind that women in decision-making positions will only be effective and accountable to the extent that there is a strong women's movement in civil society acting as a pressure group and an accountability mechanism. This suggests that the emphasis on internal party reform (such as quotas) has to be supplemented by a focus on conditions external to the political party. We need to look at the broader political context in which parties operate to assess the extent to which they are likely to be responsive to women's demands, and the extent to which women's representational and policy demands are likely to be coopted into projects that are not of their own choosing. The relationship between parties and women's movements may be synergistic rather than purely competitive or antagonistic, but in either case it is an unavoidable relationship for Third World feminists. This is particularly true in Uganda and South Africa, where parties have been the main vehicles through which women have made political advances and where civil society is both relatively weak and relatively conservative on gender issues.

Shireen Hassim analyses South Africa's much-lauded success in bringing unprecedented numbers of women into national politics in Chapter 3. She tracks the institutional changes and the social movement struggles which made this possible. Her chapter shows that the historic closeness between the women's movement and the ANC formed the basis for demands for women's representation during the political transition and in the democratic state. Representation was understood by gender activists as a necessary, but not sufficient, condition for the advancement of the feminist agenda for substantive equality that was elaborated in the Women's Charter for Effective Equality adopted by the women's movement in 1994. In both the first and second democratic elections, electoral competition played an important role in broadening the democratic advances that were made within the ANC, the largest political party as well as the party with the strongest commitment to reducing social and economic inequalities. First, having assumed the political high ground in supporting gender equality and in instituting a quota on its electoral lists, the ANC was placed in a position where it could not back away from supporting gender equity legislation in Parliament. Second, the ANC set a standard for party commitment to gender equality that other parties with democratic pretensions could ill afford to ignore. The knock-on effects of the quota were significant; although no other party formally adopted a quota, most paid attention to gender representation on their electoral lists and included references to gender equality in their party manifestos. Third, women's organisations were able to exploit the formal commitments made by different political parties to open public debate about the values that underpinned the new democracy and to centralise gender equality as one of the key social values. In sum, the multi-party system allowed the women's movement to broaden its arenas of political action and to make its claims for substantive representation on the political system as a whole rather than only within one sympathetic party.

Comparing the different political parties, Hassim examines how differing levels of internal democracy have affected women's chances of rising to decision-making levels or gaining full party backing in elections. She alerts us to shifts within the internal culture of the ANC, suggesting that while the party has been traditionally predisposed to gender equality, greater centralisation of decision making might reduce the effectiveness of women within the party. Indeed, while quotas are a mechanism that draws directly on centralism for its effect, centralism can also have negative consequences, reinforcing the power of party élites over weaker constituencies within the party. Even where there is a democratic ethos within the party, 'democratic centralism' can erode the ability of feminists to challenge policies and processes that hamper equality, and can make women hostage to the good will of particular individuals in the party's higher echelons. In this context, Hassim argues that success in using politics to promote women's interests depends on the women's movement's carefully maintained simultaneous autonomy from and strategic engagement with parties.

Anne Marie Goetz shows, in Chapter 4, that the women's movement in Uganda has relied heavily upon the good will and positive protection of Museveni's National Resistance Movement to recover from decades of repression. Similarly, the large number of women in government results from the NRM's reservation of special seats for women. However, the institutional basis for representation has serious consequences for its effectiveness. A central institutional choice has been the suspension of multi-party competition on the grounds that parties are incapable of competing on the basis of different programmes, as opposed to ethnic differences. By ruling out pluralism, the NRM has emasculated the development of accountability mechanisms outside of the Movement, and, by extending an ever-widening net of patronage, it has neutralised oppositional energies, including those of women pushing for a legislative agenda which would challenge male rights within gender relations. On one hand, the suspension of party competition and the creation of special reserved seats for women has freed women from the need for political party backing for their candidacies as well as from competing with men in a context that is hostile to women's political participation. On the other hand, this has undermined the institutionalisation of women's presence and interests in the state, and women have been held hostage to the Movement and to Museveni in particular.

This raises sharply the question of the nature of the NRM as a political party. Goetz analyses the systems for candidate selection and promotion, internal policy debates, managing dissent, recruitment, and so on, to develop a gendered critique of this rather personalised and clientelistic 'party'. She shows how the lack of attention to democratic rules and procedures within the NRM undermines, first, its pretensions to democracy and, second, the ability of women to make sustainable gains in terms of institutionalised support for a gender equity agenda. While the system of reserved seats has increased women's representation, it has also fuelled perceptions that women can only participate in politics within circumscribed limits and by creating a separate, feminised and marginal sphere alongside the primary public domain. This approach has undermined women's legitimacy as politicians. She argues that under the current system, the women's movement is unlikely to break out of the trap of patronage if all its politics is conducted within the fold of the NRM. Individual women politicians who seek to challenge the party leadership can simply be removed or be subjected to vilification campaigns that drive them out of politics. Goetz concludes, therefore, that women's political gains in Uganda are insecure, because women have not been in a position to challenge patriarchal party systems or to develop political leverage out of their electoral strength. Her chapter highlights the dangers that obtain when institutionalised representation precedes political mobilisation and is used by the political leadership to contain and control women's activism rather than as a democratic response to the women's movement.

There are a number of important differences between the two women's movements that highlight the importance of the final variable, the nature and strength of the women's movement, in making party engagement successful. These relate, first, to the length and depth of engagement by the women's movement with and within each party, and, second, to features of the internal organisation of each party. In South Africa, the struggle to get the ANC to recognise women's interests and provide for their representation in the party leadership and on party candidate lists has a long history which predates the party's ascension to power. The women's movement was able to coalesce prior to constitutional debates in such a way as to develop views on how democracy should be conceived. It also had the opportunity to clarify for itself some of the issues about the means and meaning of women's accession to formal representative positions – in other words, linking the presence of women representatives to the project of representing women's interests. In Uganda, the women's movement was caught on the back foot, still fragmented from the years of authoritarian repression under previous regimes. By the time it recovered, the NRM had pre-empted a number of its demands for inclusion by introducing affirmative action and creating new political seats for women.

These differences in the role of the women's movement in directing the terms of women's inclusion have important implications for the capacity of women in civil society to act as a constituency holding the dominant party to account. In South Africa, the women's constituency is considerably more autonomous from and critical of the ANC than women in Uganda are of the NRM. In South Africa, women demanded inclusion as of right; in Uganda, inclusion has been extended as a favour. This has obvious implications for women's influence both within and outside the party.

The second key contrast in the two cases is in the different levels of institutionalisation and internal democracy in the two parties. The ANC is an older and more deeply institutionalised party than the NRM. The ANC has an established rural branch structure for mobilising participation and generating new leadership, clear lines of authority, and structured forms of participation within the party both for individuals and different interest groups. This has enabled women within the party, first, to establish their importance as an internal constituency, and, second, to use connections to the women's movement, to assert an 'autonomous' position for feminists and feminist policy goals in the party (not that this has been easy). In contrast, the NRM's top levels are completely impervious to democratic pressures, as indeed are many other levels of the party.

In South Africa, women were ready at the right moment to make an impact, and were able to introduce notions of women's rights to participation on the grounds of their equal citizenship. In Uganda, they were pre-empted by a powerful political association that made considerable

17

electoral mileage out of stressing women's difference as a group. These contrasting discourses of equality and difference, and the differences in the strengths of the women's movements in the two countries, go some way to explain the differences in the ways women have gained access to representative positions, and influence over policy making.

Advancing a gender equity agenda – key legislation

The key to assessing whether representation and the strategy of 'entryism' have translated into real benefits for women, or simply into creating a new élite of women in government, is to examine the extent to which principles of gender equality and institutional mechanisms for reducing inequalities are integrated into government policies and delivery. A close study of significant policy debates helps us to assess the effectiveness of new democratic institutions in amplifying women's voice (both within public institutions and in the state–civil society interface) and improving public accountability to women. The ethnographic study of the role of various actors in advancing or undermining new legislation on women's rights reveals the significance of continued civil society pressure from the women's movement, no matter how gender-friendly the new institutions are.

Research into the relationship between women's political representation and policy effectiveness in developing countries is not well established. As we argued above, there has been a tendency to measure the outcomes of various state policies, such as structural adjustment, on women without considering the particular relationships within the state that influence policy formulation. Research done in countries where women's suffrage is relatively established finds a pattern of initial upsurge in attention to women's demands at the national level and the passage of gender equity legislation, followed by a decline of women's policy effectiveness. For instance, Anna Harvey (1998) shows how in the USA women had considerable influence on national politics for the first four or five years after suffrage was extended in 1920, but the influence diminished rapidly. This diminished efficacy lasted for forty-five years, until the 1970s, when women began to have an impact on national policy debates again. In her study, Harvey argues that voters' leverage over policy requires the intermediary action of 'policy-seeking interest group activity in electoral politics'. that is, there must be a threat of 'electoral retaliation' (ibid.: 11). Her study suggests that the strategic issue that the women's movement needs to confront in the context of liberal democracy is not so much whether or not women constitute a distinct group, but rather whether electoral and policy élites *believe* that women constitute a voting bloc. This perception, and women's ability to 'retaliate' electorally, depends on the extent to which there are strong women's organisations outside political parties and Parliament. This observation underscores our own findings in this research about the importance of treating the party and electoral domain seriously while simultaneously building up a strong women's movement outside party control.

In Chapter 5, Sheila Meintjes, a commissioner in South Africa's Commission on Gender Equality, offers a case study of the politics of policy change which asks questions about the influence of women active in politics and in civil society on national decision making and long-term legislative change. The chapter highlights the importance of long-term organisation in civil society around the issue of violence against women, showing how this context provided an articulation of women's interests that was derived independently of political parties and the state. Women's organisations were able to offer concrete policy proposals at crucial stages in the policy-making process and were able to defend these through ongoing mobilisation in civil society. The chapter looks closely at the difficult process of fast-tracking progressive legislation on domestic violence through the last few weeks of the first democratic South African parliament in 1999. Meintjies finds a combination of factors to account for this successful experience. Central among these are women's strength in civil society and their capacity to threaten electoral retaliation, the development of support networks amongst women politicians and in the bureaucracy to press gender demands within the state, and the importance of a substantive normative discourse and democratic framework that value gender equality. She argues that it is crucial for the women's movement to cultivate male allies at top levels of political parties and government (including the President), and for women's movement activism to continue in parallel with strategic interventions inside government.

In Chapter 6, Sheila Kawamara-Mishambi and Irene Ovonji-Odida analyse the disappointing outcome of Ugandan women's mobilisation in 1997 to ensure that women's property rights would be respected in new legislation on land titling and ownership. The introduction of Western land tenure systems has been associated in Africa with the historical process of vesting ownership rights in men, and undermining women's productive base and rights and status within the community (Staudt 1987; Boserup 1970). Customary land tenure systems do not provide women with ownership rights either, making women temporary custodians of land passing from father to male heir, but they do provide them with the usufruct rights necessary for security in family food production. When the government proposed to regularise titling and tenure systems in Uganda, the women's movement recognised the tremendous importance of capturing this historic opportunity to secure women's land control rights. They were mindful of the need to avoid creating a land market hostile to women's land ownership rights, such as has happened in neighbouring Kenya, where the Registered Land Act has resulted in land title deeds going almost exclusively to men.

A coalition of women's groups entered into the land law reform debate by proposing a clause granting women ownership rights in spousal homestead property. This aroused enormous resistance from men in politics and civil society. The most serious opposition came from the President, who made statements suggesting that women might make a capital accumulation strategy out of serial monogamy by seizing the property of a sequence of husbands. The clause was eventually tabled and approved in Parliament, but when the Land Act was published a few days later, the clause had vanished. In the end, the President admitted that he had intervened personally to delete the amendment. Ovonji-Odida, a lawyer working for Uganda's Law Reform Commission, and the prominent women's rights activist Kawamara-Mishambi trace the politics of the promotion of this clause and demonstrate the fragility of relying on patronage and presidential goodwill to advance a gender-equity agenda. Withdrawn as easily as it is extended, top-level patronage of women in politics worked against them in their efforts to promote this important legislative change.

Women in political competition – local level

Decentralisation is one of the cornerstones of the contemporary good governance agenda. Transferring power, budgetary control, revenue generation, development planning responsibility and management control over local services to elected local councils is part of the agenda of reforming distended and under-accountable states. It is expected to promote 'greater responsiveness to citizens, improved decision making based on more accurate information and better knowledge of local conditions, and improved efficiency in service delivery' (Parry 1997: 211). A corollary expectation is that the result will be improved local accountability to more disadvantaged groups and areas, as well as improved capacities amongst poorer groups to influence local development policy. The reasoning is simple: local governance has a more immediate effect on most people than national decision making in the sense that local road maintenance, the staffing and maintenance of local health and education facilities, adjudication of local disputes over land use, and so on, will have an immediate effect on the welfare and livelihood prospects of locals, and poor service delivery will be more immediately traced to the predilections or mistakes or corruption of local decision makers than they can be at the more remote and aggregated national level. This quality of tangibility and immediacy in accountability relationships is reinforced by assigning revenue-generating responsibilities to local councils. Tax-paying locals will feel a greater sense of entitlement when demanding answers from local decision makers about how their money has been spent.

Women are supposed to benefit in the same way as all constituents from this dynamic of improved local accountability. Although nowhere fully articulated in the policy literature, there seems to be an implicit assumption that decentralisation might be a particularly efficient way of enhancing women's political participation and effectiveness. This is mainly because it is assumed that women are better able to engage in politics at the local than the national level, since constraints on their time, mobility, and financial resources are considered less severe when council offices are nearby and meetings fit into the rhythm of local productive cycles. This presumption appears to be informed by Western political experience, where women are found in greater numbers on local councils than in national parliaments (IULA 1998). This pattern, however, does not appear to hold so strongly for developing countries. Though statistics on numbers of women in local councils are less reliable or even available than those for national parliaments, it appears that in many parts of the Third World, and particularly in Africa, numbers of women on local councils are actually lower than those in Parliament (unless there are specific affirmative action measures, as in Uganda, to increase their local political participation) (ibid.). Why this might be so is not entirely clear, as there has been remarkably little cross-country research on this issue. Chapters 7 and 8 in this book discuss women's engagement in local governments in South Africa and Uganda, and put forward at least two explanations for constraints on women's political participation at local levels. First, traditional patriarchies can be more intense and immediate in their repressive effect on women's public engagement at the local level compared to the national level. Second, the women's movement's capacity to support women in local politics and help develop gender equity policy platforms can be fragmented by decentralisation.

In many contemporary decentralisation efforts there is a contradiction between the greater power enjoyed by traditional – and often culturally conservative or ethnically defined – local élites under new institutions of decentralised governance, and the notion that previously subordinated groups ought to participate in decision making. The *realpolitik* of decentralisation is that power and control over resources is usually only relinquished to local levels by the central government when there is an important pay-off in terms of purchasing the loyalties of dissident groups or diffusing ethnic or other tensions which threaten violence or secession. This is a pattern inherited from colonial administrations. In other words, decentralisation is often a way of palliating the political ambitions of sub-national, regional or ethnic political rivals; providing them with small territorial parcels to govern but in a way that 'deliberately fragments potential local power bases into smaller, weaker, non-politically significant units' (Crook 2001: 10). This has characterised patterns of decentralisation in Uganda, which have been so successful that new and smaller districts continue to be created just before each national election to reward particular localities for supporting the government. In South Africa, decentralisation was an established apartheid strategy for purchasing the collaboration and compliance of certain traditional leaders and ethnic groups. There are very strong and almost separatist tensions within South Africa's racial and ethnic mix, and for this reason the ANC ferociously resisted a strong version of federalism in the 1991–4 constitutional negotiations. This left the arena of local government up for grabs by traditional authorities, and, as Mbatha's chapter shows, there was so much tension around this issue that civil society groups were completely excluded from the local government negotiating forum in the early 1990s. Traditional leaders have been awarded protected space in local councils: 10 per cent of the seats in all rural and municipal councils that fall in areas conventionally under traditional authorities. Women's organisations have accused the Department of Local Government of placing the accommodation of traditional authorities above the interests of ordinary citizens, and have pointed out that the way traditional leaders decide on issues of land access and service delivery discriminates against women.

Running against the logic of awarding limited powers to traditional or ethnically defined local élites are the modern constitutional principles of gender equality in the two countries. Both have adopted a variety of measures to ensure that up to about one third of local councillors are women. Though not all men elected to councils will be representative of traditional authorities, the patterns of local politics in both countries ensure that traditional culture dominates public life, particularly in the more remote rural areas. This creates incentives for women councillors to conform to conservatively (racially, religiously or ethnically) defined expectations about female deportment. As Ahikire's chapter shows, voters in one region of Uganda go so far as to expect women candidates to kneel in supplication before them during political campaigns, in conformity with Ganda cultural practice. They must also assure voters of their unimpeachable sexual propriety (they must show that they are properly married or, if single, they must be widowed, not divorced or unmarried), and of their virtue as mothers (women with older and more independent children are likely to face less criticism than women who might be seen to be neglecting younger children). The salience of traditional authority and of ethnic politics at the local level also diminishes the prospect that gender equity concerns will be treated seriously. Customary law and practice tend to prevail in matters of marriage, divorce and property ownership, resulting in deeply patriarchal decisions, subordinating women's rights to those of their husbands, fathers or sons, as Mbatha shows in cases of local adjudication of land disputes in South Africa.[3]

In Uganda, another feature of the rules of local political competition compounds the emphasis on ethnicity and tradition. Because political parties are prohibited from supporting local candidates and running campaigns, competition for office is based on the 'individual merit' of candidates. Inevitably campaigns become personality-based rather than programme-based, resulting in appeals to clan or religious loyalties rather than interests and ideas (Mamdani 1988, 1994, cited in Tripp 2000: 66). Ahikire's chapter shows that this forces women candidates, like men, to emphasise whatever clan or religious identity is most likely to match that of the majority of voters. But, unlike men, they are disqualified as direct biological expressions of the local clan or ethnic body. This is because most married women will not have been born in the area, but will have moved there on marriage. The banning of parties from political competition means that women candidates, like men, lack organisational support, a problem which can be more significant for women given that their lesser exposure to politics and their relative lack of resources for campaigning mean that they have less experience than men and a greater need for institutional backing. The absence of an associational arena in which policies can be debated and defended also limits women's capacity to introduce gender equity issues to campaigns, and to shield behind the party platform if these matters arouse a social backlash. The result is that older, more conservative and wealthier

23

women who do not threaten clan, religious, or ethnic interests will tend to be more successful in the polls, and carry their conservatism into office. Women in South African local politics do not suffer from the same lack of institutional support – though, as Mbatha shows, almost all say that their parties are biased against women candidates. The involvement of parties in local politics, and the fact that half of local councillors are selected through a closed-list PR system instead of a ward-based system, enables women to campaign on policy platforms, raise controversial issues like gender equity concerns, and use party resources for developing policies or support bases.

The second constraint on women's effective political engagement is the dispersing effect that some forms of decentralisation have on the women's movement and its capacity to support women candidates and councillors. Local government is meant to open up new public space for the expression of political interests – and in the case of Uganda, it is the one arena in which a free play of political energies is encouraged. Ironically, however, the concentration of the political energies of ordinary Ugandans at this level has worked as a means of dispersing and limiting autonomous associational energy in the country and within the NRM. Mamdani has argued that local councils operate to postpone the evolution of interest-based or broader programmatic patterns of civil and political association. Because rights to participation are based on residence, limits are placed on the capacity of outside interest groups to engage in local politics and generate enthusiasm for non-local issue-based politics. The very remoteness and isolation of local arenas can fragment the political potency of poorer groups and make them even less able to influence decision making than they are at higher levels of political aggregation. While this problem can affect all types of civil society groups, women's associations have tended to benefit more than others from working at a national and international level because of the distance this gives them from local and intimate tyrannies.

Ahikire's chapter shows that even in a fairly wealthy and cosmopolitan district like Mukono, local women's associations in Uganda are relatively weak, and have not coalesced either to support women councillors or to lobby them. Women councillors have been unsuccessful in forming a women's caucus and liasing with women's associations, possibly because of the shortage of resources for women's associational activities at the local as opposed to the national level. This same lack of connection between women councillors and women's associations is evident in South Africa, although there was more gender-based civil society activism evident in the two councils studied in Mbatha's chapter.

In both countries, national women's associations are making efforts to build the strength of local women's groups and to forge connections between them and local women councillors. Organisations like the Gender Advocacy Programme and the Rural Women's Movement in South Africa, and the Forum for Women in Democracy in Uganda are training women councillors and civil society groups not just in lobbying and policy-making techniques, but also in collaborative methods for analysing local spending from a gender perspective – something which can help build local councils' accountability to women constituents.

The two chapters on women's experience of local government show the gender-specific consequences of particular forms of institutional design in local government. Seemingly gender- and class-neutral institutional changes affecting electoral rules, delineation of local council boundaries, and devolution of control over land or services may favour traditional authority structures. A possible outcome is the intensification of traditional patriarchal prescriptions regarding the proper role of women in public, *even if* simultaneous arrangements have been made to enhance women's participation. One of the most interesting contrasts between the two countries is in the electoral arrangements in local government. Uganda continues to use an exclusively ward-based system, obliging women to run the gauntlet of notorious voter hostility to women representatives. South Africa has mitigated this effect of the ward-based system by assigning local voters two votes – one for their ward representative, and one for their party. The party vote is based on a PR system using closed lists. The result in the local council elections of 1995 and 2000 has been that more women have won seats through the closed-list party vote. Uganda's response to the challenge of increasing numbers of women councillors has been unusual. It has not followed the pattern of women's reservations in other purely ward-based systems, such as in India or Bangladesh, which involves demarcating a certain proportion of wards for women-only competition, thereby obliging voters to select a female representative. Instead, local councils have now been *expanded* with new seats for women added until the new seats make up 30 per cent of the council. Elections for these new 'women's seats' are held a good two weeks after the regular ward elections. The electorate for each seat is an artificial entity created out of a clustering of two or three established wards. This arrangement sends out a number of negative signals about women councillors: they are an afterthought, an add-on, their constituencies are unmanageably big, and in any case they are superfluous since the wards they cover already have representatives. Voter reactions to this new arrangement are evident in the widespread failure to achieve quorum in the women councillors' elections.

Conclusion

The ruling parties in South Africa and Uganda have taken important steps to bring unprecedented numbers of women to power, and they share a recognition of the importance of the female electorate for the legitimation project of liberation governments. But it is the differences, rather than the similarities, in the ways women have come to power in South Africa and Uganda that are instructive for appreciating the institutional variations that produce more effective representation of women's interests. These differences also illuminate the political conditions under which representative politics might be used to advance a feminist agenda. In South Africa, women have made the transition from a liberation struggle to Western-style multi-party politics in such a way as to retain and indeed consolidate feminist policy ambitions. In Uganda, where a 'no-party' system is in operation, the political gains women have made have been impressive, yet highly dependent on presidential patronage. There have been setbacks in advancing a gender equity agenda in new legislation, notably in the new land law and in the perpetually postponed domestic relations bill. The main differences between the two countries inhere mainly in the political regimes — in the fact that multi-party competition in South Africa has enabled women to exploit political competition by emphasising their electoral importance. A liberation discourse based on equal rights has enabled women to politicise their concerns using the same language as was used in the struggle for racial equality. Women would not have been able either to assert electoral leverage or politicise their rights to equality in the absence of the large and autonomous women's movement that has developed in the country since the 1950s. New political space for women has become a springboard for a driving gender equity agenda in politics and policy. In Uganda, without a strong women's movement or the pressure of party competition to hold the government to account, the government has used new political space for women as a means of accommodation and control of women's political energies.

The conclusion is not that pluralism and conventional liberal democracy is the key to advancing women's interests in politics. It is probably indispensable, but we know from other countries in Africa and elsewhere with multi-party politics and strong women's movements (Tanzania, Kenya, Ethiopia) that pluralism does not by any means assure effective political voice for women. The comparison between South Africa and Uganda in this book shows that a range of conditions make for building women's effectiveness in politics: civil society strength, institutional reforms which facilitate women's access to politics without stripping women politicians of legitimacy or of connections to the women's movement, a supportive and powerful party – all these combined with, indispensably, political skills in identifying allies, getting the timing right for pressing demands, and asserting electoral strength.

References

Abdullah, H. (1993) 'Transition Politics and the Challenge of Gender in Nigeria', *Review of African Political Economy*, 56.

Albertyn, C. (1995) 'National Machinery for Ensuring Gender Equality', in S. Liebenberg (ed.), *The Constitution of South Africa from a Gender Perspective*, Cape Town: David Philip.

Basu, A. (ed.) (1995) *The Challenge of Local Feminisms: Women's Movements in Global Perspective*, Boulder: Westview Press.

Boserup, E. (1970) *Woman's Role in Economic Development*, London: George Allen and Unwin Ltd.

Chazan, N. (1989) 'Gender Perspectives on African states', in J. L. Parpart and K. A. Staudt (eds.), *Women and the State in Africa*, Boulder: Lynne Rienner.

Chigudu, H. and W. Tichagwa (1995) 'Participation of Women in Party Politics', Zimbabwe Women's Resource Centre and Network Discussion Paper No. 9.

Cock, J. (1997) 'Women in South Africa's Transition to Democracy', in J. Scott, C. Kaplan and D. Keats (eds.), *Transitions, Environments, Translations: Feminism in International Politics*, New York: Routledge.

Crook, R. (2001) 'Strengthening Democratic Governance in Conflict-Torn Societies: Civic Organizations, Democratic Effectiveness and Political Conflict', Institute of Development Studies Working Paper 129, University of Sussex.

Dahlerup, D. (1986) 'Introduction', in D. Dahlerup (ed.), *The New Women's Movement: Feminism and Political Power in Europe and the USA*, London: Sage.

Harvey, A. L. (1998) *Votes without Leverage: Women in American Electoral Politics, 1920–1970*, Cambridge: Cambridge University Press.

IULA (International Union of Local Authorities) (1998) *Women in Local Government*, The Hague: IULA.

Khadiagala, L. S. (2001) 'The Failure of Popular Justice in Uganda: Local Councils and Women's Property Rights', *Development and Change*, 32: 55–76.

Lovenduski, J. and P. Norris (eds.) (1993) *Gender and Party Politics*, London: Sage.

Mamdani, M. (1988) 'Democracy in Today's Uganda', *New Vision*, 16 March.

Meintjes, S. (1996) 'The Women's Struggle for Equality during South Africa's Transition to Democracy', *Transformation*, 30.

Molyneux, M. (1985) 'Mobilization without Emancipation? Women's Interests, the State, and Revolution in Nicaragua', *Feminist Studies*, 11, 2: 227–54.

Parry, T. R. (1997) 'Achieving Balance in Decentralization: a Case Study of Education Decentralization in Chile', *World Development*, 25, 2.

Pitkin, H. (1967) *The Concept of Representation*, Berkeley: University of California Press.

Rule, W. and J. Zimmerman (eds.) (1994) *Electoral Systems in Comparative Perspective: Their Impact on Women and Minorities*, Westport, Connecticut: Greenwood Press.

Sainsbury, D. (1996) *Gender Equality and Welfare States*, Cambridge: Cambridge University Press.

Sawer, M. (2000) 'Representation of Women: Questions of Accountability', paper presented at the International Political Science Association Conference, Quebec City, August 2000.

Staudt, K. (1987) 'Women, Politics, the State, and Capitalist Transformation in Africa', in I. L. Markovitz (ed.) *Studies in Power and Class in Africa*, New York: Oxford University Press.

Tripp, A. M. (2000) *Women and Politics in Uganda*, Oxford: James Currey.

Tsikata, E. (1989) 'Women's Political Organizations 1951–1987', in E. Hansen and K. Ninsin (eds.), *The State, Development and Politics in Ghana*, Dakar: CODESRIA.

Waylen, G. (1994) 'Women and Democratization: Conceptualizing Gender Relations in Transition Politics', *World Politics*, 46 (April).

—— (2000) 'Gender and Democratic Politics: a Comparative Analysis of Consolidation in Argentina and Chile', *Journal of Latin American Studies*, 32: 765–93.

Young, I. M. (1990) *Justice and the Politics of Difference*, Princeton: Princeton University Press.

Notes

1 Terms used here for qualifying the role of women in representative politics as being 'descriptive' (i.e. 'standing for' a particular group as their literal biological copies in public) versus 'substantive' or 'strategic' ('acting for' or in the interests of a particular group) draw from a number of discussions in political science. Hannah Pitkin made the distinction between 'standing for' and 'acting for' (Pitkin 1967: 232), and Maxine Molyneux has distinguished feminist interests as 'strategic' gender interests in contrast to 'practical' interests women have in their sex-typed roles (Molyneux 1985).

2 An excellent example of comparative political analysis which demonstrates the impact of variations in constitutional frameworks and party and electoral systems on women's political effectiveness is Georgina Waylen's analysis of women's political gains from democratic transitions in Argentina and Chile (Waylen 2000).

3 For accounts of gender-biased patterns in land dispute settlements in Uganda at the local level, see Khadiagala (2001).

2

Women's Political Effectiveness: A Conceptual Framework

ANNE MARIE GOETZ

What difference do institutions make in advancing women's interests? What difference does politics make? This chapter reviews current knowledge about how different ways of structuring democratic political institutions affect the degree to which women and men participate in these institutions as citizens, the extent to which they gain access to positions of authority, and the extent to which these institutions are differently accountable to women and men. These issues are discussed in relation to the impact of political institutions on poor women's prospects of influencing decision making in developing countries. 'Women's political effectiveness' is understood as the ability to use voice to politicise issues of concern to women, to use electoral leverage to press demands on decision makers, to trigger better responsiveness from the public sector to their needs, and better enforcement of constitutional commitments to women's equal rights.

This 'voice-to-representation-to-accountability' relationship is not linear, a matter of women in civil society mobilising around issues of concern to them, advancing them through the political process, and implementing solutions to women's problems through the legal and administrative system. Indeed, the whole point of investigating the impact of institutions and politics on women's political effectiveness is to understand why there is so often no such direct 'voice–to–representation-to-accountability' process in politics in the case of women and other socially excluded groups. Why, for instance, do strong women's movements sometimes fail to produce large numbers of women in politics (as in the USA)? How is it that even in the absence of widespread feminist mobilisation, some states have imposed radical legal requirements on political parties to adopt quotas of 30 to 50 per cent women candidates (Argentina and France)? Why did women's engagement in

29

the liberation struggle in South Africa subsequently result in large numbers of women in formal politics, whereas similar levels of engagement elsewhere in Africa did not? Why is it that women's ministries or other forms of dedicated bureaucracy in many developing countries fail to promote women's interests?

This chapter – illustrated with examples from around the world – offers a conceptual framework for synthesising new evidence on the impact of institutional arrangements on women's political prospects. Many states are currently making considerable efforts to augment dialogue and consultation between state actors and women in civil society, and also to increase the numbers of women within public institutions. Whether these efforts promote improved policy outcomes for women, however, depends very much on whether attention has been paid to setting up accountability mechanisms that make authorities answer for meeting standards of gender equity in policy and service delivery. Very often poor women, like other socially excluded people, are welcomed as participants in policy review forums – indeed, they are treated as virtual trophies because of the immediate aura of grassroots authenticity that their presence seems to impart. But these opportunities for 'dialogue' do not provide women with legally actionable rights to demand answers from public officials for poorly managed policy or corrupt activities, nor with the means of enforcing punishment of errant officials, nor even with the basic information about decision making and policy implementation which is needed in order to assess whether official commitments to gender equity or poverty reduction are being implemented properly.

Thus, to the contemporary interest in increasing women's public participation and representation this chapter adds a concern with accountability to women. This chapter asserts that the success of the gender equity interest in policy making and policy implementation will depend upon the interaction of three major factors: the strength of the gender equity lobby in civil society, the credibility of feminist politicians and policies in political competitions, and the capacity of the state to enforce commitments to gender equity. It goes on to show how variations in institutions of civil and political society and the state will produce different degrees of access to public space for women, different qualities of participation and control, and different outcomes in terms of the way policies, legal judgements, and state agents in their day-to-day interactions with clients respond to women's needs and promote their interests. It thus distinguishes between three types of public engagement: access (consultation, dialogue), presence (representation), and influence (accountability). First, however, the chapter makes conceptual clarifications about the terms 'accountability', 'gender equity interests', and the relationship between agency and institutional structure in determining women's political effectiveness.

Gendered accountability failures

'Accountability' has two dimensions: the notion of 'answerability', where powerholders are obliged to explain and justify their actions, and the notion of 'enforceability', where powerholders suffer sanctions for mistakes or illegal behaviour (Schedler 1999). Accountability mechanisms generally operate along either a vertical axis (the 'bottom-up' electoral process, external to the state, enabling citizens to hold politicians to account), or a horizontal axis (institutional supervision, checks and balances internal to the state) (O'Donnell 1999). The primary accountability relationship is that of the state to citizens: the vertical accountability functions, such as the periodic vote, and the work of civil society institutions in monitoring the actions of representatives. Horizontal accountability refers to the ways in which different parts of the state – the legislature, the judiciary, the audit office and the public administration – monitor and hold other parts answerable.

These accountability institutions are commonly scrutinised – particularly in contemporary 'good governance' debates – from the point of view of their effectiveness in preventing corruption or promoting efficiency in service delivery. Accountability institutions are not commonly analysed from the point of view of their gendered nature and effects. We know, however, that there is a systemic failure across institutions of accountability to make the state answer for its gender equity commitments.

In terms of the vertical relationship where politicians answer to citizens through the electoral process, the organisation of voting (as we will see below) does not necessarily enable women to politicise matters of concern to them, to mobilise a 'feminist constituency' across geographically delineated constituencies, or to be elected to office in equivalent numbers to men. Outside of the voting process, civil society and political associations frequently fail to advance matters of concern to women.

In the horizontal dimension of accountability relationships, the failures of state institutions to answer to women, or of systems of sanction to detect and punish gender biases in public actions, help to reinforce the conditions of women's subordination. Government and opposition parties may fail to promote *political accountability* to women by refusing to problematise gender biases in existing and proposed legislation, by failing to back up national commitments to gender equity with budgetary commitments, and by failing to consult with women's interest groups when formulating policy. Gender biases can be detected in all manner of social and economic policy which reinforces the domestic ideal of the dependent wife and provider husband, when such policies assign women to a secondary recipient status for development resources, or fail to tackle discrimination against women in the market.

Fiscal accountability functions do not include 'gendered audits' of public spending to assess whether the distribution of public resources has been gender-equitable. In *administrative accountability* systems public workers are neither assessed nor rewarded according to whether they advance the interests of women clients or ensure gender equity in their work. Few systems exist to detect or check gender-specific patterns of discrimination in the treatment of women by public officials, particularly at the grassroots level at which service providers most directly interact with women clients.

And finally, *legal accountability* institutions are often the biggest defaulters when it comes to answering to women. Around the world, judicial systems fail to criminalise or prosecute offences against women such as domestic violence, rape within marriage, gender-based violence, and violations of women's property, inheritance and child custody rights. Police forces in some countries not only fail to assure the physical security of women, but are among the agents denying it through crimes such as rape in protective custody.

The gendered accountability failures briefly listed here do not fall neatly into the category of 'capture' of public resources – or corruption – which is how accountability failures are often discussed. But arguably there are gender-specific forms of corruption which ought to concern us. While women, and especially poor women, will suffer along with the rest of the poor when resources for development are thinned out *ex ante* through high-level corruption, corruption at the level of resource delivery may affect them more than men in two possible ways. First, it may be that money destined for women's development – whether it be a subsidised loan, a minimum-wage job on a drought-relief public works programme, or investment in improving reproductive health care – may be more easily pilfered by state agents because women are seen as less aware of their rights, less willing to challenge authorities and demand that they account for missing monies, than men. This is an untested proposition, as levels of corruption have not, so far as I am aware, been compared between services targeting women and more 'mainstream' programmes. Second, we can think of sexual 'currencies' of corruption, for instance, when sexual services instead of money bribes are demanded of – or forcibly seized from – women by state agents.

At a more general level, if corruption is understood as the abuse of public office for private gain, and private gain may include advantages for a particular social group, then arguably it is possible to identify implicit or explicit collusion between male state officials, politicians, and male citizens in denying women access to some development resources or human rights in order to advance men's social and economic position individually and as a group. An example of this is the apparent (but unarticulated) male collusion in defending masculine sexual prerogatives sometimes seen when judges and lawyers undermine the legitimacy of the testimony of women victims of sexual assault.

This last way of conceptualising gendered patterns of corruption, however, overstretches the notion of 'capture' of public office, and obliges us to introduce a second category of accountability failure: 'bias' (Goetz and Jenkins 2001a). This is helpful for the analysis of the many forms of accountability failure that afflict women. Masculine – but also class, caste, racial, and ethnic – biases in the formulation and implementation of public policy and legislation, in the review of government spending patterns, and in the criteria for rewarding or punishing public service providers, and, above all, in the functioning of electoral systems and political processes, have become institutionalised over time. Bias can be institutionalised in two ways which produce gendered (or class-based) patterns of accountability failure: first, accountability institutions may simply have *no remit* for punishing officials whose actions produce a pattern of bias against women. In other words, their terms of reference – or the standards of justice and of probity in the performance of duties – focus on procedural correctness rather than the achievement of positive outcomes for women.

Second, gender and anti-poor biases may be built into the mechanisms through which disadvantaged people are entitled to use accountability mechanisms directly, such as literacy or official language requirements for access to the legal system, or norms for presenting evidence which disqualify women's testimony in rape cases (*ibid.*). These biases prevent poor women from taking the first step in activating accountability systems: the step of demanding a justification from officials for their neglect or subversion of women's rights and needs. There may be neither a remit for advancing gender equality, nor a basic understanding that gender injustices are socially intolerable.

33

Mutual determinations of voice and accountability: the mystery of political effectiveness

It is important to understand how power relations can distort account-ability institutions in order to avoid making the assumption that ampli-fied 'voice' for a particular group (for instance, stronger civil society associations representing women) will automatically strengthen the moral and social claims of the powerless on the powerful and produce better accountability to that group. Eliciting a broader expression of the voices of women will not produce changed policies, nor will it change the behaviour of bureaucrats, the police, or politicians, without some changes in the norms and procedures of accountability institutions.

Looking at the 'voice' or 'demand' side of the question of women's political effectiveness is a politics-centred approach. If more effective interest articulation and representation were all that there was to the accountability struggle, then the focus of our concern with women's political effectiveness would be to better understand how women's political interests are expressed, how these interests are brought into political institutions and brought to bear on decision-making processes, and how women and their allies can best monitor government actions. Too exclusive a focus on 'voice', however, can produce an excessively voluntarist, and classically liberal, perspective on how disprivileged groups can advance their interests. It is worth remembering that 'voice' is also determined, in part, by the state and civil and political institu-tions – by the rights the state extends to citizens, the electoral rules which either facilitate or restrict the representation of diverse interests, the types of social or development policies on offer and the ways these enhance the human and physical capital of women. Women's political effectiveness can therefore also be scrutinised from this 'supply' side, looking at public institutions and the rights they provide to women, gender biases in the spaces for public participation, and in the means available to citizens to demand answers from policy makers or to enforce punishments for poor decision making. Effective public institu-tions of accountability may help build 'voice', in the sense of creating a point of access to the state for groups of citizens who may discover, and then act upon, shared interests (Joshi and Moore 2000). In other words, the creation of institutions to make holders of state or non-state power more directly accountable to women may foster more effective engage-ment with the state by women.

A focus on the 'supply' side of political effectiveness helps to illumi-nate obstacles to gender equity in political institutions which will inhibit even feminist politicians from working in women's interests (assuming, that is, they make it past these obstacles to get into power in the first place). But important as is the gender-sensitive reform of public institutions, too narrow a focus on institutions is as limiting as is the excessively voluntarist focus on women's politics. It can produce a narrow concern with bureaucratic solutions and affirmative action exercises at the expense of a focus on advancing women's interests as a gender through the political process. One consequence of the neglect of politics is that these dedicated bureaucratic 'machineries' frequently have few tools for holding the state to account (no veto powers over public spending plans, no rights to comprehensive policy overview, no rights to press charges or demand information when gender-related malpractice is suspected). Also, these bureaucracies have weak autonomy (which is essential for accountability functions) in relation to other parts of the state, particularly the executive.

Considering the demand and the supply side of political effectiveness together enables us to understand that 'voice' does not easily and simply lead to better outcomes for women, because public institutions can have strong gender biases which undermine the impact of women's voice and presence in public. At the same time, the 'voice leads to accountability' relationship can work the other way around: equity-sensitive changes to accountability institutions may have the effect of creating new opportunities for the expression of voice, or can make the voice of previously excluded groups more effective. By keeping 'voice' in mind when reviewing changes to political institutions that are intended to produce better participation and presence for women, we can avoid the 'anti-political' problem of promoting bureaucratic changes in isolation from the politics which would make new bureaucracies and procedures work effectively for women.

Constraints on women's 'voice' – are there gender equity interests?

The capacity of any social group to advance its interests in civil society will depend upon its wealth and social status *vis-à-vis* its opponents, the unity and sheer size of its membership, the social legitimacy its cause enjoys, and points of leverage in social or policy bargaining (for instance, the capacity to threaten work stoppages to disrupt production processes, or protest action to disrupt urban life). Four structural characteristics of women's position in social relations make their associations and 'the women's movement' score poorly on many of these points.

35

First, gender-based divisions of labour and power in most societies create practical and psychological constraints on women's civil society engagement. Women's double duty of work in production and reproduction limits their time and energy for activism, especially where party meetings or local and national government assemblies are held at anti-social hours, far from home. Assigned to roles as wives, mothers, and homemakers, women can develop sex-role-limited perceptions of their interests, linking their concerns primarily to household well-being. This does not rule out effective ways of engaging in politics by politicising traditional gender identities. For instance, the famous Madres de Plaza de Mayo in Argentina exposed human rights violations and contradictions in official policy by manipulating imagery of conventional mothering roles (Feijoo 1989). However, sex-role-limited forms of interest identification can pose a tremendous challenge for efforts to mobilise women behind aspirations to gender equity.

A second feature of gender relations which influences the nature of women's civil and political engagement is women's lower human and physical capital resource base stemming from disparities between the sexes in access to resources. These disparities are often legally sanctioned. The consequences of this include a tendency for women's engagement in civil society to centre on projects that support household survival, a tendency to focus associational energies at the local level where there is a risk of losing sight of the bigger picture (Razavi 2001), and a lack of socialisation for political competition. The low-resource constraint, combined with the time constraint, can sometimes mean that women's civic and political engagement is *ad hoc*, unsustained, or else can show a preference for loose organisational forms that can accommodate women's diverse responsibilities. These loose organisational forms can prove a positive advantage where repressive regimes have outlawed formal party political organisation and, indeed, have proved effective in the struggle for democracy against Pinochet's military regime in Chile in the mid-1980s. However, women's associations were subsequently left out of the process of identifying leaders and political candidates in the new democratic era, partly owing to the fact that their structureless organisation proved unequal to the job of backing candidates and debating policy (Jaquette 1989).

A third feature of women's position in social relations that shapes the way they engage in politics is that as a social category women are not clustered or grouped by class or caste, ethnicity, race or geography. On the contrary, they are evenly distributed both physically across a territory, and across social categories. This not only makes them a challenge to organise because constituencies cannot be targeted using class-, region- or ethnicity-specific language and concerns, but it also accounts for the phenomenal diversity of women's interests – and consequently of women's associations – according to the salience of other social cleavages besides gender in their lives.

Because of this, many feminists have insisted that sex is not a sufficient basis for assuming common interests (Molyneux 2001: 152).

Molyneux has suggested that one can distinguish between 'women's interests' and 'gender interests', the latter arising specifically from the social relations between the sexes. 'Strategic gender interests' would be those oriented to transforming gender relations in the direction of justice and equity between the sexes – what I call 'gender equity interests' in this chapter.

It is important not to assume that most associations of women are based upon the kind of feminist social analysis which would produce a set of gender equity interests. On the contrary, usually just a minority are, because of the limited social legitimacy of feminist condemnations of inequalities in relations between the sexes. In many societies this is seen, even by the majority of women, as a radical challenge to social relations which are still considered to be a matter of nature, not human choice and social design. Thus women's associations do not share an analysis of the causes of women's problems or of solutions to them. Some women's groups take a decidedly conservative perspective on gender relations, seeking to preserve, rather than challenge or change, unequal sexual relations.

The fourth and unique feature of women's position in social relations that determines the quality of their civic and political lives is men's control over women's sexuality. No other social category is systematically and often legally made subject to the sexual prerogatives of another. Symptomatic of this are the difficulties women have experienced around the world in criminalising rape within marriage, or policing domestic violence. Consequences of this for politics include women's diminished physical security in public arenas, and the fact that their sexuality becomes an object for public discussion and attack when they are in public life.

At a more profound level, this sexual subordination undermines women's political 'voice'. 'Voice' and 'consent', are key principles animating representative democratic institutions. We use voice to articulate interests and complaints; we use consent to indicate our agreement to being governed by particular people. However, the terms of the 'sexual contract' in many societies are such as to establish that women's consent to social and political arrangements may be *assumed*, not elicited. According to Pateman, what women putatively consent to in the marriage agreement are not the terms of a negotiable contract, but 'to a status which in its essence was hierarchical and unalterable' (1988). Men have no obligation to be accountable to married women for their behaviour in the family and in relation to women's property rights because women have freely surrendered these rights to men. By the consenting to women to a *loss of power and rights*, the value of women's consent is undermined; indeed, their 'voice' becomes unreliable. This has always made them secondary citizens in the public arena, and accounts in part for the indifference and even hostility shown to women and their concerns in certain key political institutions, particularly parties.

Another political consequence of women's sexual subordination to men, in combination with their economic dependence on them, is that women lack effective 'fallback' positions to use as leverage in policy debates in the way that organised workers can do in industrial disputes. They lack the institutional survival alternatives to the family which would provide them with the income and social support required to enable them to effect a 'strike' from domestic work.

Thus one may identify (and, inevitably, overgeneralise) three main impacts on women's civil society and political engagement flowing from characteristics of gender relations in many contexts. First, resource constraints limit their time for and leverage in politics, and encourage a focus on local issues and survival projects, as well as a preference for loose organisational forms. Second, because gender-based inequalities are often seen as 'natural', the gender equity interest usually enjoys only a narrow social support base, and the feminist cause frequently lacks social legitimacy. And, third, women's sexual subordination to men undermines the value of their consent or 'voice' in politics. The point of this review of the consequences of unequal gender relations for the ways in which women articulate 'voice' and mobilise in civil society is to suggest that any attempt to improve women's political effectiveness must compensate for the constraints women face. Sometimes this involves creating conditions of disproportionate – if temporary – advantage, through affirmative action measures to bring women into politics, for instance.

The determinants of women's political effectiveness

The success of the gender equity interest in policy making will depend upon gendered politics, and the way women and men's interests are institutionalised, in the following three arenas:

Civil society: The place and power of the gender equity lobby in civil society, its power to mobilise resources and public concern to support its demands, its power to challenge gender-biased conceptions of women's needs, roles, and rights – in other words, the strength and autonomy of the women's movement – will influence the way issues are framed for social and political debate. The strength of the women's movement will be influenced by the general political and cultural environment for associational activity.

The political system: The number and nature of parties, their ideologies and memberships, the relative importance of high finance or crime, or discourses of ethnic particularity versus national unity in political contests, will shape the prospects that feminists can advance their interests through the political process. So too will variations in the electoral system and, of course, in the depth and breadth of democracy in the political regime.

The state: The commitment of the state to democracy and to development, the welfare orientation of the state, the extent and nature of decentralisation, the configuration of executive/legislative/military/judicial/administrative power and the degree to which this enables accountability institutions to function effectively, will determine its openness to feminist claims. These factors will also affect the state's capacity to enforce gender-sensitive change in the culture and practices of its bureaucracies.

Other important institutional arenas might have been included here: notably the market and the family, as women's economic prospects in the first, and bargaining power in the second, are important determinants of their social power. The point of excluding these other institutional arenas from this framework, however, is to train our sights on specifically *political* institutions, thereby isolating features of politics and the bureaucracy which can advance women's interests. The arena of international economic institutions and international rights regimes might also have been included, but space constraints forbid it here.

When assessing the usefulness of institutional changes designed to enhance women's political effectiveness in each of these arenas, we must not only consider whether they enhance both the voice of and accountability to women, but to what degree they do so: do they provide just for 'consultation' and 'dialogue' between women and state officials, parties, and civil society associations? Or do they give women direct or indirect powers to demand answers from officials, and to trigger sanctions for inappropriate or corrupt actions? We should therefore distinguish three types of engagement and control: *access*, *presence* and *influence*.

39

Access involves opening arenas to women (or other socially excluded groups) for dialogue and information sharing, and can vary in form from one-off consultative exercises, to ongoing participatory efforts to monitor government services, and to citizens' juries, or even surveys. Access can range in intensity from a public relations exercise in which decision makers, whether in civil society associations, parties or state bureaucracies, seek to endow decisions which have in effect already been taken with an aura of legitimacy by demonstrating that they have been found acceptable to a wide range of clients. Access opportunities can be a form of 'barometric' consultation, where decision makers test public reactions to various policy options before selecting the one most likely to meet widespread approval. Alternatively, if access opportunities endow participants with real powers to obtain information about official actions, or power to pursue grievances or issue dissenting accounts to public authorities, then a more decisive and accountable form of participation is possible.

The second step, *presence*, involves institutionalising women's participation in decision making (for instance, through quotas in local government). Here the focus is on a numerical presence of women, but variations in approaches to bringing more women to office can strongly influence the capacity for this numerical presence to translate into a more meaningful representation of gender equity interests in decision making. Of great importance is the relationship between women in official positions and their constituencies, whether that be the members and clients of a civil society association, voters supporting a politician, or the clients of a public service provider.

The third step, *influence*, brings women's engagement with civil society, politics and the state to the point where they can translate access and presence into a tangible impact on policy making, the operation of the legal system, and the organisation of service delivery. This can happen when accountability mechanisms incorporate women's concerns and preferences, by, for instance, engaging women in financial audits at local levels, or incorporating gender-sensitive client satisfaction measures into performance indicators for bureaucrats. This last stage is the point at which improved accountability to women may be achieved. Table 2.1 provides a matrix in which institutional changes in civil and political society, and in the state, might be evaluated according to whether they promote better consultation with women, whether they institutionalise a presence for women, or whether they institutionalise mechanisms to provide for more direct and effective accountability to women.

The distinctions between consultation, representation, and influence

Table 2.1 Dimensions of the political effectiveness relationship

	Access (from 'barometric' to decisive)	Presence (from simple numbers to strategic presence)	Influence (accountability to a gender equity constituency)
The nature of civil society			
The nature of the political system and of political competition			
The nature of the state and its bureaucracies			

are designed to emphasise that opportunities for consultation do not lead, on their own, to policy influence. Nor do opportunities for excluded groups to be represented in political forums or in the administration (through advocacy structures such as special bureaucratic units for women, for example) mean actual influence and power.

The nature of civil society and the power of the gender equity lobby

Defining civil society and, in particular, finding ways of distinguishing it meaningfully from informal community politics and more formal political competition, has become a popular sub-industry in political science and in good governance debates (Crook 2001; Jenkins 2001; Goetz and Lister 2001). Civil society is commonly defined as an associational realm located somewhere between the family/community and the state, seeking engagement with the state to pursue social and economic changes. This definition is critiqued by feminists for excluding the wide range of informal community-based associational activities in which women engage. It also obscures the fact that, in some contexts, women's groups may avoid any engagement with the state for fear of cooption and exploitation (Tripp 2000). It risks completely ignoring the social and political significance of a range of politically unconventional forms of

41

expression and protest which women may adopt in the absence of access to (or as a deliberate critique of) formal associations and public arenas (Hirschmann 1991: 1688–90; Molyneux 2001: Chapter 6; Feijoo 1989). Students of paternalistic politics, particularly in Africa, have also pointed out that the standard distinctions between the state and civil society are hard to apply in contexts where the boundaries between the state, the economy, society and the family are blurred by patronage politics and neo-patrimonial relationships (Crook 2001; Tripp 1994). To respond to these problems, a sociological and descriptive definition is used here: civil society is all manner of self-chosen group-based activities that grow out of interest divisions in society, and which are not formally part of the state (Goetz and Lister 2001: 3). Though this definition includes opposition political parties, they will receive particular attention in the next section.

Civil society is the key proving ground for establishing the legitimacy of gender equity policy goals, and for building a feminist constituency. Factors shaping the effectiveness of women and feminists in advancing a gender equity interest in civil society include:

- the environment for associational life created by the state, the 'thickness' or diversity of civil society, and the level of social conservatism in civil society;

- the nature of women's associations, their number, social leverage, and capacity to unite behind a common agenda;

- the position and number of women (members and leaders) within other (not gender-defined) civil society associations, and the extent to which they and other groups can politicise matters of concern to women and see gender equity espoused and advanced as part of their association's goals.

The environment for associational life

A key influence on the nature of associational life in any context is the capacity of the political regime to tolerate openness and variety in civil society. While feminists therefore clearly have a stake in democratic politics for this reason, democracy alone will not facilitate feminist mobilisation. Much depends upon the prevailing social and cultural environment. Cultural negativity to activism which challenges narrow gender roles for women and men is found around the world. Religion tends to be a powerful depresser of feminist (though not women's) associational life, particularly where it is promoted by a theocratic state, but even democracies in religious societies see strong patterns of exclusion of women from many associational arenas, and intolerance for feminist politics (Reynolds 1999: 4–5; AbuKhalil 1994; Geisler 1995). Thus women's interests and gender equity interests will not automatically find expression even in the most democratic of societies. What may be more significant than diversity is the existence of civil society space for socially progressive groups. For instance, an environment of support was created for the women's movement in South Africa during the period of democratisation by the commitment of most liberation associations, including trade unions and even church groups, to notions of substantive democracy and social equality.

The nature, number, leverage, and unity of women's associations
It is hard to identify a coherent 'women's movement' in any country, simply because women's interests are so diverse, and they are pursued in such radically different ways in civil society. In making an assessment of the strength of the gender equity lobby in civil society, however, the most significant factor is the nature and strength of the women's movement. This can be assessed by 'mapping' the number of women's associations and the range of interests they promote (feminist?/Islamist?/ 'family values'?), and the nature and size of their memberships (urban professionals?/rural farmers?/church-going mothers?). An assessment can be made of their relative presence in public debates on matters of importance to women, and of the divergence between them on gender equity concerns. The relationship between women's associations and other civil society groups, political parties and state bureaucracies can also be mapped to determine the relative influence and importance of the gender equity lobby. This can be contrasted to the relative social and political influence of other important groups which may be opposed to gender equity, such as conservative religious or ethnic associations. Finally, an assessment can be made of the willingness and capacity of diverse women's associations to unite, and to identify points of leverage over decision makers. For instance, certain issues – such as rape and domestic violence in South Africa, or statutory rape in Uganda (known as 'defilement') – have served as catalysts to unite very diverse women's associations, and to galvanise women into threatening to use their electoral strength to oppose non-responsive governments.

Autonomy or integration?
A longstanding challenge for feminist activists is that of maintaining autonomy from sexist institutions in order to avoid corruption of the

gender equity interest, yet at the same time infiltrating, or 'mainstreaming' the gender equity interest into other social and political institutions. Failure to do the latter can result in political isolation and irrelevance, yet mainstreaming has often compromised feminist gender equity ambitions by subordinating them to other goals. Molyneux identifies two organisational principles characterising non-autonomous female collective action: 'associational linkages', and 'directed mobilisations'. The first sees autonomous women's associations in negotiated alliances with other organisations in ways that enable women to retain control over their agendas. In the second, women's collective action is directed by interests outside of the women's movement. This is the case with women's wings of political parties or ethnic and religious associations (Molyneux 2001: 150–1). This kind of 'manipulated political participation' (Chazan 1982) is often dismissed as 'irrational', exhibiting false consciousness on the part of women. Hirschmann makes a plea for treating it very seriously. In some contexts, this may be the only form of civic or political engagement open to women, and attention must be paid to the subtle or unconventional means they use to express their concerns (1991). He gives an example from Malawi of the sharp social commentary and complaints about the behaviour of officials that were insinuated in women's songs of praise for the then President Banda (ibid.: 1688–90).

Molyneux's distinctions refer mainly to social movements, but what is the nature of women's participation in other forms of civil society – business associations, trade unions, professional groups, sports clubs, developmental NGOs, or neighbourhood associations? When assessing the strength of the gender equity interest in civil society it is worth conducting an inventory of the female membership, clientele, and leadership of these kinds of civil society associations. Are women found as leaders of powerful business and labour associations? Or are they more likely to be leaders of less politically significant neighbourhood associations or school support groups? What kinds of organisations have a large female membership? What are the terms of this membership? Are women paid-up members of, say, a trade union, with rights to vote for leaders and debate policy? Are women a minority, and if so, does that limit their capacity to select leaders and influence decision making? Are they a majority yet not proportionally present among its leaders (for instance in teachers' and nurses' unions), and does this have an impact on the representation of their concerns?

In the context of mainstream civil society, we can, following Molyneux, distinguish different degrees of female participation, ranging from equal participation with formal accountability to clientilistic forms with weak accountability. In the former category are associations in which there is self-selected formal membership and members have rights to vote for the leadership and participate in decision making. This would include trade unions, professional associations and business associations. Of interest here would be the proportion of the membership and leadership which is female, the nature of concerns raised by women, and the extent to which gender equity is advanced by women and men in decision making. In the second category would be associations which assume a mandate to represent certain groups without cementing this through a formal membership. This happens frequently with development NGOs aiming to assist socially marginalised groups which may not have the social or political resources to represent themselves effectively – children, for instance, and many groups of poor people. Frequently the form of representation and assistance offered by such organisations is paternalistic, in the sense that there are few formal channels for the putative beneficiaries of such organisations to complain about the services offered, influence service delivery, or participate in decision making.

Access, presence and influence in civil society

We can now fill in the top row of the matrix in Table 2.1. This framework (see Table 2.2) allows us to ask questions about the quality of women's participation not just in mainstream civil society organisations (CSOs), but in women's associations and the women's movement also. The access, presence and influence of women will differ by class, race, age and many other factors. These will be critical questions to pose of women's associations, particularly feminist groups claiming to advance the rights of all women.

This framework enables observation of whose 'voice' is promoted and represented by CSOs, and scrutiny of the often murky area of accountability in CSOs. Gender-sensitive accountability systems in civil society must be scrutinised from two vantage points: the *internal accountability* of CSOs to their memberships or clients, and the engagement of CSOs in holding public office holders to account – in other words, their role in animating *external accountability* systems. Issues to examine with regard to internal accountability include the rights of the female membership of CSOs to challenge the leadership, and to demand reviews of decision-making processes and outcomes from the perspective of their impact on gender relations. This can include rights to scrutinise spending patterns, or to activate internal investigations of poor decision making.

As for the role of civil society in animating external accountability systems, the scope for introducing gender sensitivity is considerable.

Table 2.2 Civil society dimension of the political effectiveness relationship

Access	Presence	Influence
Nature of the women's movement: its size, resources, internal democracy, diversity, and capacity for unity. Its 'depth' – how socially established is it? Its 'breadth' – how is diversity accommodated, how are conflicting perspectives on women's interests debated and resolved? In both women's associations and 'mainstream' civil society, assess: • The level and type of female membership (social categories, and proportion of women in relation to men); • Access barriers to the participation of women of different social categories, and how these are overcome; • Quality of membership or client status – formal, rights-bearing? Or informal, lacking rights to vote for leadership or to activate internal inquiries?	**Leadership systems in women's and feminist associations:** • Existence of apprenticeship systems for emergent leaders. • Clear selection methods for leaders. • Nature of relationship between leaders in women's movement and leaders of other social movements, CSOs, political parties, state officials. **Structure of women's movement:** does it produce clearly identifiable leaders and disciplined members? Is it collective and loosely organised? (Associations with clear leadership structures and disciplined membership integrate better to party systems and lobbying politics. But collective, fluid organisations are also effective in certain forms of public protest.)	**Internal accountability** within the women's movement to its various constituencies – what legally actionable rights do members have to dismiss the leadership or activate internal inquiries into decision making, spending patterns, etcetera? Is the women's movement constituted as a watchdog on the state to monitor state performance? Or as an autonomous self-help and survival network? Are accountability systems in CSOs responsive to the grassroots membership or to financial supporters? Do accountability systems compensate for gender-specific obstacles to articulating complaints and acting upon them? **Citizen initiatives to hold the state accountable** (*external accountability*):

- Mechanisms used to consult with women members and women outside the organisation about their needs and interests;
- Mechanisms to inform leaders of other CSOs, political parties, and state officials about women's needs/interests.

Outside the women's movement:
Proportion of women leaders in CSOs

- Are they a token minority?
- Are they segregated into sex-typed roles or associations (nursing, teaching, children's charities)? What are their structural connections to the women's movement? To women clients or members?

('report cards' on services, social audits, public hearings, media, lobbying, protests) – where and how do women's interests get expressed? Are such mechanisms limited to information provision (see column 1) or linked to powers to hold officials to account (right to information, right to litigate)?

47

Civil society associations are crucial to the vertical accountability relationship between citizens and the state: they politicise neglected issues and injustices; their critical analysis of government decision making helps to form public opinion and shape voting behaviour; and their protest actions help to focus public energies on righting public wrongs. These activities very often pay insufficient attention to politicising matters of concern to women, or developing a critique of official actions from the perspective of their failure to contribute to gender equity.

Around the world, civil society associations in recent years have insinuated themselves as the state's *horizontal* accountability institutions in an effort to improve their functioning and responsiveness to citizens' concerns (Goetz and Jenkins 2001b). Examples of citizen engagement in such institutions include public interest litigation, in which civil society associations engage the judiciary in investigating government actions seen to have wronged particular groups, or citizen's 'report cards' on the quality of urban amenities which act as alternative performance indicators for service providers. Another example is public participation in formulating municipal budgets, as in some parts of Brazil (Abers 1998), or public auditing of the way local government officials spend funds on development projects. This latter process engages ordinary people in the formerly closed and official arena of financial auditing and can be a highly effective method of exposing corruption. But these innovations rarely highlight gender-specific concerns about corruption or gender-biased service delivery.

The nature of the political system and the organisation of political competition

Politics is the intervening variable between voice and accountability. The relative strength of oppositional political energies in society will shape civil society strategies. For instance, where there is robust multi-party competition, civil society groups may pursue confrontational, high-visibility strategies in the hope of interesting opposition parties in taking up their concerns. This worked to spectacular (if short-lived) success in the case of poor women fighting for prohibition in Andhra Pradesh, India, in the early 1990s, where their anti-alcohol campaign was championed by the opposition party that won the state elections. If, on the other hand, parties are weak, lack programmatic platforms and rely on appeals to identity politics, emancipatory groups will see little point in engaging with parties. Women may instead seek to institutionalise their interests directly in specialised bureaucratic units, or withdraw from politics altogether.

Political systems have a critical impact on the calculations civil society groups make about the value of engaging with the state. Formal democracy and the protection of basic civil and political rights are crucial preconditions for virtually any kind of critical engagement by women with the state. But for all the obvious stake that feminism, like any other emancipatory project, has in democracy, studies have found that the degree of democracy – measured as length of experience with multi-party elections, and extent of political and civil rights and freedoms – is not a good indicator of the likelihood of women reaching high political office in significant numbers (Reynolds 1999).[1] Regardless of the political system, the percentage of women in national parliaments around the world is low – averaging 13.8 per cent in 2000 (Inter-Parliamentary Union 2000).

The low numbers of women in office even in established democracies (such as the USA, where their participation in Congress only recently inched close to the global average), has led feminists to conclude that women's exclusion is not just a 'deficit' of democracy but indicative of fundamentally gendered conditions for political participation which are 'intrinsic to politics, not an extraneous, additional concern' (Phillips 1993: 98). There is a significant body of critical feminist analysis of conventional liberal democratic institutions which has demonstrated that these institutions frequently neither enable more women to participate equally with men in public decision making, nor produce policies which benefit women and men in equivalent ways. In part, this has to do with problems inherent to the organisation of political competition in representative democracies: the geographical, not issue- or identity-based (gender-based, for example) organisation of constituencies for representation, and with the time lags between voting for and dismissing politicians (Mansbridge 1998), a problem which distorts accountability in the electoral system and affects all citizens.

But feminists have pointed out that at a deeper and constitutive level, liberal democracy – particularly in its role as a handmaiden to capitalism – relies upon and reproduces a gendered division between public and private worlds. In the capitalist economy, women's private and invisiblised labour subsidises the costs of reproducing the household. In democratic politics, the gendered public/private split limits the range of issues which can be politicised legitimately, with authoritarian relations between women and men (and parents and children) often deemed beyond the remit of politics. Beyond the practical implications of this for women's time for political engagement, the gendered public/private split is deeply internalised in notions of legitimate political agency, creating marked public hostility to women politicians. Internalisation of gendered norms of political participation is also evident in the most important institutions for articulating citizen voice: political parties. These are notoriously closed arenas to women's participation in any but a highly sex-typed support role for the male leadership.

A vibrant debate in political science is currently identifying the most significant institutional determinants of the numbers of women who make it to public representative positions.[2] Most observers agree that key determinants of the level of women's presence in formal politics are variations in:

* electoral systems;
* quotas or reservations to boost numbers of women in office;
* levels and types of party organisation;
* the political culture.

These features of political institutions will be reviewed here with a view to assessing how far institutional engineering affects the perceived legitimacy of women representatives (as politicians in their own right), and second, how it affects their effectiveness in supporting gender equity policy (working as politicians in women's rights).

Women-friendly electoral systems

The electoral system is 'the basic electoral formula that determines how votes are cast and translated into seats allocated to parties' (Squires and Wickham-Jones 2001: 6). There is broad consensus that systems with multi-member constituencies and proportional representation with party lists are much more likely than majoritarian-plurality systems to overcome voter reluctance to select women candidates, as well as party reluctance to field them (Norris and Lovenduski 1995; Inter-Parliamentary Union 1997; Rule and Zimmerman 1992; Matland 1999). Where more than one person can represent a constituency, and any party can have more than one candidate winning in any constituency, all parties have an incentive to embrace greater diversity, and so the resistance to women candidates drops. Majoritarian systems create incentives to front the one candidate likely to appeal to a sweeping majority in a voting district, a 'lowest common denominator' (Reynolds 1999: 8) candidate who will not be a woman or a class, ethnic, or racial outsider. The British electoral system, which has influenced political institutions in so many countries, is one of the most deeply resistant to the introduction of social newcomers. It combines the constraints of the first-past-the-post, single-candidate constituency with an absence of term limits and a huge number of safe seats, making candidate selection by parties a zero-sum game in which insiders – rarely women – have a huge advantage (Lovenduski 1999: 204).

PR systems return more women to office than do majoritarian systems. For instance, a review of 53 national legislatures in 1999 found that national assemblies in PR systems were composed of on average nearly 20 per cent women, compared to nearly 11 per cent in majoritarian systems (Norris 2000). But PR alone does not produce gender-balanced legislatures. Although almost all of the few countries in which women are one quarter or more of the national assembly have PR systems, they also share at least one of the following characteristics: an egalitarian political culture (the Scandinavian countries), strong socially egalitarian or left-of-centre dominant parties which have voluntarily adopted quotas of women on their electoral lists (Scandinavia again, and South Africa, Namibia, Mozambique), or, in a few cases, laws to institutionalise female quotas on party lists (Argentina, France).

What impact does the electoral system have on the ease with which feminist issues can be politicised, and on the accountability of politicians to voters concerned with gender equity? One of the chief differences between electoral systems is whether they encourage voters to focus upon the candidate or the party in making their selection, and this can affect the willingness of candidates to champion controversial causes. In PR systems this distinction is clear in the differences between 'open list' and 'closed list' systems. In the former, voters influence the party by making their own selection among the candidates put forward by the party. In closed list systems, voters simply select the party, and accept the party's list of candidates. They are prevented from reordering the list in ways which would worsen the position of women candidates on those lists. Closed-list systems are seen to have some advantages in delivering larger numbers of women to office (provided the party supports women's candidacies), and they are also seen to offer a form of protection to women who wish to campaign on electorally risky feminist policy platforms appealing to a cross-section of the electorate. But there are concerns about democratic deficits in closed-list systems, for instance the way they detach representatives from the citizens they are supposed to represent, making them accountable not so much to voters as to party bosses. This problem is exacerbated in highly centralised parties, as will be seen shortly.

Reservations and quotas

In almost every case where women exceed 15 per cent of elected representative bodies, this is the result of the application of special measures
to advantage some women candidates over men. In Africa, for instance,
while countries with PR systems have legislatures in which women
represent an average of 11.65 per cent of representatives, only those
with party quotas of women candidates rise above this average
(Mozambique, with a 30 per cent female parliament, and South Africa,
with a 29.8 per cent female parliament)[3] (Yoon 2001: 181). Of the
African democracies with a majority-plurality system the average proportion of women in legislatures is 5.46 per cent, and only Tanzania
rises above these because it reserves 17.5 per cent of parliamentary
seats for women. Reservations of seats for women-only competition, or
quotas for women candidates in political parties, are seen as non-democratic tampering with political institutions and therefore as necessarily
temporary measures. Political parties in a growing number of countries
have voluntarily adopted quotas – in 1997 some or all parties in 36
countries had done so according to the Inter-Parliamentary Union (IPU)
(1997: 67) – while constitutional amendments in Argentina and France
have obliged all parties to adopt them (the French system requires that
50 per cent of party lists for local elections be female, on pain of with-
drawal of state campaign financing). Five countries have national legislation reserving seats either in national or local government for women
(Bangladesh, Burkina Faso, Uganda, India and Tanzania).

The way reservation or quota systems are applied makes the difference between a token 'presence' of women in politics and a more legitimate and substantial form of participation. Least valuable for advancing
women's interests are reserved seats filled by appointment by the ruling
party – these become an additional vote bank for the government, as
has been the case in Bangladesh. In Tanzania, each political party ranks
female candidates for the reserved seats and sends a list to the National
Electoral Commission. Each party's share of women's seats is proportional to its vote share in parliament. This makes female legislators
beholden to their party, not to a feminist or indeed any constituency of
citizens (Killian 1996). As shown in chapters 4 and 8 of this book, the
addition of reserved seats for women in local government in Uganda,
and the fact that elections for women councillors are separate in time
and space from elections for 'normal' ward representatives, creates a
secondary and redundant status for women local councillors.

But even democratically agreed party quotas do not, as Sawer points out, 'put an end to resistance to women within the party or to associated fears that only "tame" women loyal to male-controlled factions would ever benefit' (2000: 371). To build the accountability of women politicians to a gender equity constituency, other measures are needed to establish connections between the women's movement and growing numbers of women who enter politics through quotas. In some countries feminist party activists have set up a body independent of party control to provide financial and moral support to feminist politicians. The best-known of these is 'EMILY's List',[4] set up in the USA to raise funds for pro-choice women Democrat candidates. These kinds of measures are designed to hold feminist politicians accountable for advancing equity commitments. In other countries, notably South Africa, the women's movement has done this through more informal means, encouraging women from their number to enter politics, and hoping that their historical commitment to the women's movement will hold its own against the call of party loyalty once in office.

Party structure – level and type of institutionalisation
Norris suggests that differences in the organisational structure of parties, in their hierarchies and recruitment patterns, and in their internal democracy, influence women's engagement with parties, their relative voice within them, and success in winning party backing for their candidacies (1993). When assessing the effectiveness of positive discrimination measures for women in parties, Norris distinguishes between levels of institutionalisation (high, or formal, versus low, or informal), and between levels of command and control (centralised versus localised). These distinctions draw attention to the existence and relative clarity of rules about candidate selection or the identification of policy priorities, on the one hand, and to the relative control that top leaders exercise over these processes on the other. Norris finds that in formal-centralised systems top leaders decide upon who will be electoral candidates, and gender equity will have to rely in this process on the gender sensitivity of the leadership. More productive for gender equity are formal-localised systems: women are considered better able to mobilise politically at the local level and therefore build support at the branch level, yet overcome potential hostility of local party bosses through the knowledge that formal rules on candidate selection will be respected (Norris 1993: 326). This will only be effective if the formal rules have been changed to support women's candidacies. Also, the assumptions made here about women's greater propensity to organise at the local level may not hold true for deeply patriarchal rural communities. The least productive

model, in terms of promoting women's interests, of party organisation is the 'informal-centralised' model which relies mainly on patronage systems and a dominant individual leader, not transparent rules (1993: 323). This describes Uganda's ruling National Resistance Movement, as shown in Chapter 4. While this kind of 'benevolent autocracy' (*ibid.*) can promote women quickly, enabling the centralised leadership to overcome conservative opposition to women's presence, it can just as easily be eroded when that patronage is withdrawn. In this situation, there is little point in seeking to change party rules, as women did in the South African case, because: 'since the process is not rule-governed, changing the rules will not alter the outcome' (*ibid.*).

Political parties are considered to be institutionalised when they have, and respect, rules about candidate selection and identification of policy concerns, when they have an organisation that is distinct from the personal connections of their leaders, and when their elected members form a distinct and coherent group in the legislature (Moore 2002). Party institutionalisation is considered essential for the consolidation of democracy in developing countries, for only when parties are stable and predictable in their membership and policy positions can voters make informed choices secure in the knowledge that their votes will influence the policies of the government. However, not only are parties often poorly institutionalised in developing countries, but in many contexts the rise of identity politics or else the prevalence of violence and crime in political competition is bringing about a de-institutionalisation of parties. As one frustrated feminist observer of politics in India complains:

> [Parties in India] have no proper organisations or proper offices or definable ideologies or identifiable issues and long-term programmes. They seem to be interested only in seeking chairs for the sake of collecting benefits and privileges accruing from different positions. In such [a] chaotic situation, even if women entered decision-making apparatuses of the party, they would have a bleak future. They would affect very little – either the party system or the political system as a whole (Sharan 2000: 143).

Parties may be such blatantly hollow vehicles for kleptocratic families or ethnic groups, lacking any but the flimsiest organisational structures, decision-making processes, and ideologies, that they simply offer no purchase for an internal democratisation project designed to promote gender equity. There may be no discernible party platform if politics is a matter of appealing to ascriptive loyalties rather than broad ideas and policy programmes, and therefore no political space to raise gender equity concerns.

As Waylen observes, it is not 'that hyper-institutionalisation is good, but rather that low levels of institutionalisation produce problems and make lasting change difficult to achieve'. In contrast: 'in an institutionalised system there is stability in the rules of competition and party organisations matter: therefore rules, for example over quotas and candidate selection, can be enforced more easily' (2000: 790–1). Comparing women's political gains in Argentina and Chile, she notes that while the President's patronage of women in Argentina has brought them some gains, it is also capricious, and that weakly institutionalised parties are ill-equipped to defend women's political gains from erosion. She notes that: 'the absence of institutionalisation allows for the dominance of élites, patrimonialism and clientelism that may favour individual women, but does not generally facilitate a long-term increase in the total number of women active in conventional politics' (Waylen 2000: 791).

Critical factors to consider when assessing the impact of party structure on women's access, presence and influence, are recruitment strategies (how are women encouraged to join?); branch structure (how democratic are local branches, how high is women's representation as members and as local leaders?); information generation mechanisms (how are women in civil society consulted about their needs and interests?); the nature of the women's wing, if there is one (is it a tea-making brigade for the leadership?); systems of mentoring and leadership development (do promising young women enter into leadership apprenticeship relationships with senior leaders the way young men do?); and the procedures by which party activists make it to the national executive committee (are they elected democratically or selected personally by the leader?). Variations in these aspects of party structure will affect the ways women within the party organise to influence party policy, and the extent to which they can build links to the autonomous women's movement.

The nature and culture of political competition

Similar electoral systems and party systems in different countries have produced different outcomes for women, and the somewhat vague variable of 'political culture' is invoked to explain this. Jane Jaquette, for instance, argues that 'political cultures intersect with democratic institutions to produce different kinds of connections between the state and civil society, and these in turn can promote or curtail women's involvement in politics' (2001: 121). Among the factors she considers important are: the persistence of patriarchal ideology, the importance of identity politics, the adoption of pluralist forms of social organisation and more transparent decision making, the degree of religious opposition to gender reforms, and, in some post-communist countries, the association of women's equality with the negative legacy of communism (*ibid.*: 120). Reynolds concurs, noting that: 'Variations in women's electoral success across democracies are better explained by the ideological orientation of dominant political parties, and the numbers of women who have held office in the past – in other words, the political culture' (1999: 2). As suggested in Chapter 1, left-wing parties around the world have been more willing (usually after prolonged internal struggles by feminist party activists) than conservative parties to extend egalitarian ideologies to embrace a commitment to gender equality, and to take affirmative action steps to give women an advantage over men in political competitions (Norris 1993; Caul 1997). Post-materialist parties advancing a 'green' or a 'peace' or even a 'new left' agenda also tend to be more gender-friendly than the old-style machine politics of class-based parties.

Other variables to add to the grab-bag of political culture that have implications for women's engagement include the number of competing parties, the nature of campaign financing systems, and the level of violence and intimidation in political campaigns. Party fragmentation can increase the chances that women candidates and gender equity concerns are backed by parties because new and smaller parties will see new electoral niches to exploit in the gender equity cause. Where significant resources are required for political campaigns, and campaign financing rules are inadequately policed by the state, women candidates are worse off, not just because of their weaker resource base compared to men, but because they are less likely to start out as incumbents and to use the resources of office to promote their re-election. Growing levels of violence and active criminal elements in campaigns not only compromise the physical security of women candidates, but they masculinise the political arena because it is young men that are mobilised to add 'muscle' to efforts to intimidate the opposition.[5] Even the culture of political debate in parliaments can be so antagonistic as to silence newcomer women. For instance, Sawer notes that women in Australia 'perceive themselves as doing less well in the adversarial chamber politics characteristic of majoritarian Westminster systems, contending, for example, with a hostile wall of sound from the benches on the other side' (2000: 369). For this reason, when women move from being a small to a large minority in politics their first efforts often centre on making themselves more 'at home' in the public arena, modifying political cultures to better accommodate their time constraints and behavioural preferences. This involves the introduction of crèches in Parliament, family-friendly sitting hours, and doing more preparatory work in parliamentary committees.

Women's access, presence, and influence in party political competition

Table 2.3 outlines some of the main institutional variations that affect the prospects of improving women's engagement in political debates, their formal presence in political institutions as representatives, and their substantial influence over politics. The main object of Table 2.3 is to identify *gender-sensitive changes in political accountability systems*. Does the introduction of a closed list system make representatives accountable to their constituencies or to the party? Do party financing systems make candidates responsive to top leaders or to branch members? Does the party relegate women members to a secondary women's wing, or can women within the party maintain links to the autonomous women's movement? Do systems of party discipline and policy debate prevent women and feminists from working across party lines with feminist allies in other parties to advance women's rights?

Simply increasing the numbers of women politicians will not change the fact that incentives and accountability systems in politics make politicians responsive primarily to their parties, or to geographical constituencies, not to women as a social group, or to counter-cultural and electorally disastrous concerns with gender equality. As Anne Phillips notes, 'accountability is always the other side of representation, and, in the absence of procedures for establishing what any group wants or thinks, we cannot usefully talk of their political representation' (1993: 99). Most experiments to bring more women into office are designed to overcome profound voter hostility to women representatives, and to subvert 'old boys clubs' in many political parties that make them such unfriendly spaces for women, but these efforts are not designed to forge connections between women politicians and feminist male politicians and a feminist constituency. Encouraging such connections is not unimaginable: parties can engage in open and transparent policy debates with constituents and can encourage cooperation between sections of the party and external autonomous associations. Opposition parties can make parliamentary committees on women's rights more effective in reviewing the legislative agenda from a gender equity perspective, and can foster better methods of encouraging civil society

Table 2.3 *Political competition dimension of the political effectiveness relationship*

Access	Presence	Influence
Accessibility of party policy debates to women's input and participation depend on: **a) Party characteristics** • Party ideologies; • Branch structure of parties and degree of local democracy or centralised control; • Recruitment and mentoring strategies; • Presence, nature, and power of a women's wing of the party, and its relationship with the autonomous women's movement; • Mobility inside the party – based on patronage and personal connections? • Leadership selection methods and mentoring networks; **b) Nature of political competition** • Degree of violence associated with political engagement. • Campaign financing – does the need for big money in elections rule out women candidates or buy influence	**Electoral system:** impact on women's electability: • PR versus first-past-the-post majority systems. • Closed lists versus open lists **Reservations and quotas** **a) Method** • Legally mandated or voluntary? • Introducing women into competition for existing seats or for newly created ones? • Introducing women to direct competition with men within and outside the party for open seats? Or to women-only competition for reserved seats? • Electoral college for reserved seats: universal adult suffrage? Or governing party élites? These characteristics affect the perceived legitimacy of women politicians. **b) Mandate** • Functional reservation 'acting for' –	**Electoral system:** impact on accountability: are elected representatives accountable to the party (closed-list PR system), to the ward or geographical constituency (single-member majoritarian system) or to a broader group-defined constituency – for instance of women, poor women, black women, etcetera? **Party type** • Centralised and informal: women not likely to have much influence as a group but rather depend upon patronage of leader. • Decentralised and formal: provided there are affirmative action measures, women are likely to have influence at local levels. • Centralised and formal – provided the executive is gender-friendly, more influence likely for women at top levels, but accountability systems also likely to encourage answerability to the party chief, not the grassroots.

for interest groups hostile to gender equality?
- Competition between parties to demonstrate commitment to gender equality and attract women's vote?

Voting mechanisms

Measures to enhance women's engagement such as gender-sensitive civic education, secret ballots to enable married women to keep their preferences secret from husbands.

Consultative forums

How do parties generate information on voter's needs and interests? Surveys? Citizen juries? Are women included equally in these processes?

e.g., reserved seat on local government for a 'secretary for women' (Uganda).
- Reservation on grounds of biological characteristics 'standing for' – e.g., one woman representative per district in Uganda, addition of 1/3 new seats for women in local councils.

This distinction may affect women politicians' perceived mandate and relationship with women's associations.

Political culture

Many small parties or just two large ones? Adversarial and aggressive styles of debate and competition?

Campaign financing

Do campaign financing systems indebt politicians and push them into corrupt behaviour in order to recover their losses? Are parties less willing to finance women candidates?

Accountability systems in the legislature

- Women's cross-party caucuses in Parliament – can they coordinate efforts to advance gender equity in new legislation?
- New standing committees on equal opportunities or women's rights – do they scrutinise government decisions and whistle-blow on decisions damaging to women?
- Does the opposition keep a watching brief on government commitments to gender equality, or does it view women's rights as secondary concerns in politics?

submissions to these committees. Electoral systems such as closed-list PR systems, that detach representatives from particular constituencies, create space for campaigning on controversial issues like gender equality; if combined with single-member ward-based systems, as in local government in South Africa (see Chapter 7), they can counteract the tendency for closed-list systems to exaggerate loyalties to the party leadership.

The nature of the state

State institutions influence the effectiveness and impact of citizen voice. The legal framework created by the state, the rights it extends to citizens, the human and productive resources it helps to build, and the opportunities it creates for participation in policy debates are part of the constitution of citizens' capacities and identities. This institutional framework influences civil society choices about ways of influencing authority. For instance, authoritarianism in Argentina encouraged the symbolic, ethical and non-negotiable nature of the women's movement demands – because the political environment made bargaining impossible (Waylen 2000: 776). Authoritarian regimes in Africa pushed the women's movement in a different direction because, as Jaquette shows, there was little point in making demands on a state that could not deliver: 'In Africa, autonomy has been seen as an 'exit' strategy made necessary by states that are weak in delivery capacity but coercive in their modes of control' (2001: 116).

The state, as the general regulator of society and the market, can challenge as unjust the rules that undermine the rights of relatively powerless parties in market or domestic institutions – hence its importance for gender equity projects. Its capacity to challenge gender-inequitable rules and change them, however, is highly dependent upon the coherence of the bureaucracy (are top-level legislative commitments to gender equality translated into changed performance measures, new targets for service delivery, and sanctions against bureaucratic behaviour that abuses women's rights?), the engagement of the judiciary and the security system (is a national commitment to gender equality internalised by judges and magistrates in their sentencing patterns; is it reflected in policing patterns, in the ways lawyers prosecute crimes, and so on?), and the public expenditure system (are gender equity concerns reflected in the allocation of public funds?). The state's capacity to enforce gender equity policies also depends on the extent to which the state penetrates society (are there still areas in which the state's authority is not recognised – for instance in traditional social organisation like clans, tribes, or certain ethnic or religious groups?).

These aspects of state authority – the extent of its penetration of society, the coherence of the bureaucracy, the probity of the justice system, the extent of civilian control over the military, the integrity of the public revenue-raising and expenditure system – are all components of what is loosely called state 'capacity'. States are considered to have low capacity in many developing countries. Ironically, many of these countries have gone far beyond more efficient, high-capacity or 'hard' states in making constitutional commitments to gender equality. But considerable control over the bureaucracy, policy coordination capacity across all state institutions, and power in society are needed for states to bring gender equity into the delivery of social and economic services or the administration of justice.

This is because gender equity goals, just like other important goals such as poverty reduction, arouse considerable social resistance. They challenge the rights – and sometimes threaten the resource base – of powerful social actors. The difference between gender equity goals and others like poverty reduction is that resistance may be located not in just one sector of society (the wealthier classes) but in every single household in the land where men and some women benefit from power asymmetries in gender relations. Thus, for the state to be an effective champion of women's rights it must be able to achieve a certain amount of autonomy from the interests of dominant and conservative social groups, indeed, autonomy from patriarchal interests. It may, for instance, have to act against the interests of individual men in assigning women inheritance or custody rights, or against the interests of groups of men in supporting women's employment rights in sectors previously the preserve of men.

The degree to which public institutions will be responsive to the interests of women will depend upon:

- the institutional make-up of the state, as indicated in constitutional provisions on the extent to which the administration, the judiciary, the military, and the legislature limit the powers of the executive;

- the capacity of state institutions to translate a gender equity policy commitment into new performance indicators for staff, changed procedures, new or changed laws, changed spending priorities, women staff and 'femocrats' (bureaucrats mandated to promote gender equity – see Sawer 1995), and changed behaviour in relation to female citizens or clients of state services;

- the level of administrative and political decentralisation.

Constitutional framework:
the organisation of power in the country

The first distinction to make when assessing the prospects that a particular state will successfully implement gender equity goals is between different models of organising public authority. Beside the obvious contrast between democratic and authoritarian states there are a range of important distinctions about the relationship between the executive and other branches of government. This is usually specified in the constitution, and it will affect the impunity with which the executive takes decisions, and the effectiveness of accountability systems.

Presidential and prime ministerial systems differ in the extent to which they generate an authoritative drive behind new policy initiatives. If the President is supportive of gender equity concerns, a bold initiative to support women's rights can avoid the dilution that comes through extended debate and interest-group lobbying in a parliamentary system. The Argentine case shows how dramatic changes can be promoted in this way. It was Menem's presidential decree that established the national women's machinery there – the Consejo Nacional de la Mujer, and supported the Ley de Cupos (the quota law) in 1991 that obliges parties to ensure that 30 per cent of closed party lists are female, and in winnable positions on the list.

But while strong, centralised leadership can build popular mandates for wide-ranging and long-term social equity projects, it is a close cousin to authoritarianism or non-participatory 'delegative democracy' (O'Donnell 1994). Waylen shows how the Argentine case exhibits the impact of arbitrary populist presidentialism – all of women's gains in politics were hostage to the good will of the President. By 1995 he was becoming more pro-Vatican – and was particularly uneasy about the success of women in politics in excluding anti-abortion principles from new reproductive rights legislation. He attacked the Consejo's budget and dismissed the leader. In contrast, the position of the Servicio Nacional de la Mujer in Chile appears more secure, 'in part', says Waylen, 'because it was established after pressure from women activists and by law rather than presidential decree' (2000: 789).

A second distinction to be drawn in distinguishing models of the state is based on the way citizens' relationship to state agents is mediated. In centralised state models with majoritarian political systems, citizens assign responsibility for monitoring the behaviour of the executive and the government, and for reviewing the quality of public services, to representatives. This implies that they surrender the option of direct engagement with state agents, and this is often supported by civil service cultures that stress impartiality and equity, as is the case in the relatively efficient bureaucracies of the north of Europe. For this to work to citizens' benefit, tight party discipline is required to channel citizens' concerns to the legislature. For this to work to women's benefit, dominant parties must have internalised gender equity concerns.

Corporatist state models establish 'categoric representation' for certain groups of citizens – normally business and labour groups. These usually result in greater responsiveness to their interests, but at the expense of the interests these groups do not represent. Some new democracies have made attempts to incorporate non-governmental associations, including women's associations, to corporatist arrangements – a good example is the fourth chamber provided for NGOs in South Africa's corporatist negotiating forum (NEDLAC). However, in this case NGOs do not have the same rights of veto in negotiations as do government, business, or labour. The effectiveness of corporatist arrangements in advancing gender equity concerns is contingent on the capacity of the main partners to broaden their social base and embrace women's economic concerns.

Contemporary neo-liberal models of the state assign citizens rights to engage directly with the state to individually prosecute inequities in service delivery or other forms of state action. In this model of the 'supermarket state' (Olsen 1988: 241–2) that is currently being exported to developing countries, citizens are constructed as consumers with rights to a direct relationship to public agents, particularly service providers. The latter, as far as possible, are distanced from central state political-administrative controls and are made to function like market-driven institutions. But accountability relationships can be weakened in this model, first because 'consumers' have fewer rights than 'citizens', and, second, because the socially fragmenting effect of markets in services means that the influence of consumers on services can be limited, particularly if they act individually. In this customer-oriented vision of public services, there are few common standards by which to hold the performance of organisations up to a standard of 'the common good'. The resort to market mechanisms to weed out poor service providers can be devastating for efforts to introduce new performance standards based on gender equity, and new (but sometimes loss-making) services responsive to women's needs. Women may not act effectively as a consumer lobby because their individual and collective 'voice' in relation to service providers may be weaker than that of consumers with better resources and greater capacity to 'exit' to private providers.

Another factor to consider when analysing the gendered implications of the organisation of public authority is the presence of women in top executive positions, and their prominence as a group in the legislature. Reynolds finds that, in Africa at least, the strongest determinant of the number of women in Cabinet is the ideology of the ruling party or coalition (1999: 19). Women who make it to these levels, or to the office of the chief executive,[6] are less likely to be independent-minded feminists than party stalwarts. In addition, women ministers are very often assigned sex-stereotyped portfolios.[7] But even if this is the case, significant numbers of women in Cabinet send signals that the executive values their contribution.

In legislatures, women parliamentarians in a number of countries have taken steps to raise the profile of gender equity matters in debates, either forming women's caucuses to work across party lines, or establishing standing committees on women's rights or on equal opportunities – both measures have been used to great effect in South Africa, as Chapter 3 shows. Though parliamentary committees on women's rights may not have automatic rights of review over fresh legislation, they can be influential in politicising government business of relevance to women. These committees can be assessed in terms of their relative accessibility to women in civil society – in some countries, parliamentary committees hold hearings away from the capital city in order to cut travel costs for rural women. They can also look inwards and challenge gender biases in the working of parliament, the family-unfriendly sitting hours, the lack of childcare and so on, and thereby build the effectiveness of women MPs. However, parliamentary committees tend not to provide civil society representatives with any substantial accountability rights, rights to answers, to official information, or to demand investigations of poor decision making on the part of women parliamentarians or any other members of the government.

Administrative capacity

The centre piece of most contemporary good governance reforms are civil service reforms designed to promote responsiveness in the relationship between public service providers and their clients, and to eliminate corruption. There is not as yet much understanding of the ways in which the public administration could be reformed to better promote gender equity. Key areas for consideration include actions to ensure a stronger presence of women at all levels of the bureaucracy, the introduction of gender equity concerns to performance measurement exercises, the existence of bureaucracies dedicated to advancing women's rights, measures to consult with women clients of public services, and measures to respond to their complaints.

Some states have advanced the presence of women in public bureaucracies through quotas for women recruits. Bangladesh, for instance, has a 15 per cent quota of women staff in the bureaucracy. These quotas, like quotas of candidates in political parties, have been effective at edging women past barriers to public space, but can also act as ceilings on further recruitment, and can undermine the perceived merit of the women who are hired to fill quotas. Just as significant as the problem of low numbers of women in the public administration is their skewed distribution within the state. As Connell points out, the only places in the public service in most countries where women are found in significant numbers are education and health, and even there they are rarely in senior positions (1990). Women tend to be particularly scarce in the sectors of importance to economic development policy: finance, industry, infrastructure or agriculture. It is for this reason that there can be a gender-specific effect when civil service reform programmes set targets for 'trimming the fat' in public sector employment through job cuts. Often the weaker bureaucracies – those in the social sector – are targeted for the deepest cuts, and across the public administration, the staff with the weakest unions, the most tenuous job security, the part-time workers, are fired first. These are more likely to be women than men, although the gender-specific impact of retrenchment in the public sector in developing countries has not yet been the subject of systematic study.[8]

Lately, the puzzle of how to improve the capacity of public institutions to perform effectively, efficiently, and honestly (let alone to develop a particular receptivity to the interests of the poor) has ignited a renewed interest in the ways incentive structures and performance measures affect the performance and commitment of bureaucrats (Grindle and Hilderbrand 1995; Thomas and Grindle 1990), and the responsiveness of lower-level staff to the clients with whom they interact daily (Tendler and Freedheim 1994). In this literature on the perspectives and influence of development administrators on policy outcomes, there is relatively little attention to gender issues. In the competitive environment of reform efforts that urge a market-like response in public service provision, there are few incentives to encourage staff to invest in the wide range of time-consuming and potentially socially unpopular acts that might contribute to the empowerment of women clients. To take the example of micro-finance programmes, there are rewards for staff to rapidly disburse loan funds and recover interest payments, creating incentives to target better-off borrowers who represent less of a credit risk. This rules out precisely the category of poorer women most in need of loans. It also rules out investment in helping women address problems in other areas of their lives that make it difficult for them to invest loans profitably.

Few performance measures or standards for monitoring the work of staff are gender-sensitive. One problem is that actions to promote gender equity are not always easily quantifiable – they may involve a deep investment in gaining the trust of women clients, and engaging with them on matters not directly related to the service in question. Tendler and Friedheim's study of women community health workers in Northeast Brazil, for instance, showed that one key to the high-quality performance of these women was their investment in gaining the trust of women clients, and their willingness to spend time in non-health-related activities, helping women cook, bathe children, and so on (1994). But these efforts are not recorded or rewarded in official performance-related pay systems or quality monitoring systems.

Contemporary measures to enhance the responsiveness of public service providers include new means of consulting directly with clients. These exercises include citizens' juries, participatory needs assessments, participatory planning exercises, social audits of existing policy or services, and conventional surveys or opinion polls.

Obvious gender-related concerns to raise in relation to new consultative mechanisms include: are women involved equally and appropriately? For instance, in relation to services and policies that affect them most directly, there should be a stronger representation of women. A good example of this was a short-lived experiment in 1992–4 in joint monitoring of the Public Distribution System (PDS) in Mumbai, India. The Regional Controller of Rationing invited civil society representatives to participate in an official monitoring and clean-up effort, and gave a central role to a city-wide network of women's groups who had been informally monitoring the 'leakage' of subsidised commodities onto the black market. In this case, however, no formal rights to be present in the monitoring exercise, to have access to official information on the flow of PDS commodities, or to lodge complaints about corruption were extended to the women participants. As a result, when the sympathetic Controller left, the experiment dissolved (UNRISD 1998). Thus consultative 'access' exercises must be assessed in terms of whether women (and other) participants are given an institutionalised place in policy discussions, whether they have formal rights of redress or at least the right to issue a dissenting report to higher authorities, whether they have the right to official information about the policy or service in question, and whether they have the right to litigate against the public authority if necessary.

The importance of establishing a formal presence for women in the public administration has produced thirty years of experimentation in bureaucratic representation. Different types of 'national women's machinery' have been dedicated to the promotion of women's interests – these range from bureaux in the office of the chief executive, to ministries, and to women's units in key ministries such as agriculture, health or education. A recent comparative analysis of women's political effectiveness across Europe finds that these women's units are one of the key factors in promoting gender equity in policy making (Squires and Wickham-Jones 2001: 43). Studies of women's units in developing countries have been more equivocal, suggesting that these women's units have often been appropriated by the ruling party to serve its legitimation agenda, starved of resources, and denied effective access to, or veto power over decision making (Goetz 1995). Key questions to ask about the role of women's bureaucratic units in advancing the gender equity project, therefore, are about their resources in staff and funds, their location within the bureaucracy and their capacity to influence policy making, particularly in public expenditure planning, and their powers to review and if necessary veto all legislation likely to have an impact on gender relations.

Horizontal accountability systems

Horizontal accountability institutions like the justice system, the reporting relationship between the administration and the legislature, parliamentary committees, or the audit office, are not designed to encourage public authorities to answer directly to women or to any other social group. They are designed to enable different branches of the state to demand answers of each other, and to enforce sanctions if necessary. The first concern in reviewing the gender sensitivity of any of these mechanisms is to assess whether standards of accountability are gender-sensitive. In other words, are public authorities made to answer for perpetrating injustices against women? The second concern is to see whether these horizontal institutions can be made to answer more directly to women. Recent years have seen greater levels of citizen engagement in horizontal accountability institutions in holding governments to account – for instance, participatory auditing of local development spending. In addition, a range of new 'overarching' accountability institutions such as offices of ombudspersons or public prosecutors, commissions on human rights or gender equality, and anti-corruption commissions are designed precisely to enable citizens to trigger formal investigative processes. Earlier I distinguished between two types of accountability failure: 'capture' and 'bias', and noted that the forms of accountability failure that afflict women fall more readily into the category of 'bias'. This can be either unintended gender blindness in the terms of access to public institutions or in their procedures for gathering information and setting priorities, or else intentional bias – outright sexism or misogyny – in the practices of state agents or the rulings of law makers. An example from Egypt of a gender-specific access barrier is the requirement of an identity card for the poor to access subsidised goods, social welfare services, or to get their children into school. Identity cards, however, are not evenly distributed by gender. Because a woman's name can be added as a dependant on her father's and later her husband's identity card, girls and women tend not to be issued them. Great care is taken to ensure that all boys and men, however, have ID cards, as the state monitors ID cards to ensure that all eligible men are drafted into the army, and men are penalised if they do not have their ID cards in order. The registration of women as dependants on their fathers' and husbands' ID cards has two implications for their capacity to access public services. First, it means that their engagement with public service providers is mediated by male relatives, thus reproducing aspects of female subordination to men within the family. Second, in cases of separation or divorce where women have left husbands or their natal families, they are left without their own identity card, and thus are stripped of an essential access requirement to the very public services for which they now have the greatest need (Bibars 2001).

Where women overcome access barriers to public services, or access barriers to the accountability institutions that are supposed to control for these biases, they often encounter a fresh set of problems: contemptuous treatment by service providers, or else discrimination in service provision that endows them with less of the public resource which is their due. Examples abound of high-handed, patronising, rude, or outright abusive nurses, teachers, police, and local government officers. For instance, girls in many schools in Africa and elsewhere are the targets of sexual harassment and even rape by male teachers (Leach and Machakanja 2000: 17–20). In Benin, élite and peasant women receive radically different types of care from the same overworked nurses and midwives in the same service (Sargent 1989). Accountability institutions tend not to punish this behaviour because they have internalised the same gender and class biases that produce it in the first place. Gender-blind and gender-biased disciplinary and reporting systems within the public administration are the greatest culprits for the many exclusions, humiliations and poor quality services endured by women. Performance standards used to assess quality in public services may fail to detect gender biases in access requirements, or whether women's particular needs in relation to services such as health, education, housing and so on are addressed. Regulatory supervisory bodies and licensing systems run by independent or government-supported professional bodies are very unlikely to report to the disadvantaged female clients of services. Their reporting patterns are oriented towards the top levels of the bureaucracy and government. Informal accountability institutions that cultivate quality controls amongst service providers, like the peer reviews and self-regulation that are provided by medical associations or teacher training systems, may not only fail to encourage professionals to address the particular problems and needs of women, but usually also function to preserve the interests of professionals over their clients.

Gender-sensitive reforms to these systems therefore focus on improving the quality of information about women's needs and interests that informs priority setting and decision making, and introducing incentives to respond to women. Women in civil society around the world have been piloting means of engaging more directly with accountability systems. A good example are exercises in gender-sensitive budget analysis, some of the best of which are conducted in South Africa. These involve civil society groups working in partnership with parliamentarians and officials in the Ministry of Finance, analysing the national or local budgets to demonstrate gender biases in funding patterns, and to predict gender-differential impacts of spending plans.

Few of these exercises have moved to the more challenging accountability exercise of actually auditing public spending from a gender perspective – an exercise resisted by the state as it would empower citizens to identify corruption. There are some examples, however, of citizen auditing initiatives that have done just this, to great effect. In Rajasthan, India, a rural social movement has conducted public audits of local government spending throughout the 1990s. It has exposed corruption in the use of funds destined to pay poor women for their labour in drought relief programmes, and, in the process, has challenged inadequate accountability systems in local government (Jenkins and Goetz 1999). For citizens to take such initiatives and provoke investigations into corrupt or biased official actions, they require at least two rights: a right to information (for instance access to official accounts), and a right to litigate against the state. Few states are willing to concede such powers. The judicial system is the key to the effectiveness of accountability institutions; the system's legitimacy, and the capacity of the judiciary to enforce the law will determine whether women's groups use the law to challenge gendered obstacles to accountability in other government institutions. However, there are two significant barriers to women's capacity to appeal to the judicial system. The first is the fact that in many countries gender biases are built into the letter and practice of the law. The second are the serious gender biases and even misogyny built into the culture and practices of the police and other providers of services necessary to the investigation and prosecution of crimes against women.

In many countries, perpetrators of sexual and domestic violence against women count on and receive impunity from the justice system. Laws are simply not framed to cover many of the abuses that women face in the privacy of their homes. Certain types of violence or discrimination against women are not actually illegal. For instance, forcible and violent intercourse within marriage is not, in many countries, interpreted as rape. A Human Rights Watch report on domestic violence in Brazil found that women faced a criminal justice system so biased against them that even a crime as serious as wife murder was excused by the courts as a legitimate defence of male honour. Such acts were considered consistent with the rule of law, to the degree that the law recognised male authority in the private sphere and relegated women to a subordinate status to men (Thomas 1999: 183). In countries where family and personal law is based on religious ordinances, legal discrimination against women may be even more explicit.

Even where laws have been reformed to embrace new norms regarding women's right to physical autonomy and bodily integrity, effective policing and prosecution are undermined by gender biases in the application of the law, that, for instance, discount the testimony of women victims of sexual assault, or subject women victims to humiliating courtroom exposures of their sexual histories. The disdain of courts for the integrity of women victims of sexual assault is supported by the poor treatment of women victims in other public services, particularly the medical professionals responsible for preparing forensic evidence of sexual assault for the courts, and the police responsible for investigating charges of sexual assault or domestic battery.

A gender bias against a fair hearing for women is built into procedural aspects of some legal systems. Language and informational barriers may keep women, with a lower educational endowment than many men, away from the courts. Another access barrier that keeps women and the poor from prosecuting abuses against them more effectively is raised by laws of legal standing, which make it impossible for them to sue the government collectively in civil suits (for instance in public interest litigation) and thus overcome informational, financial, and psychological barriers to holding officials to account.

These access and attitudinal barriers point to a form of accountability failure which operates through collusive practices based on gender. In other words, there can be both tacit and explicit cooperation between male offenders and male police, lawyers, prosecutors, and judges to ensure that the legal system defends men's sexual rights over women.[9]

Gender-sensitive access, presence and influence reforms within the judicial system, therefore, have to begin with comprehensive legal reform, particularly in matters having to do with women's rights in domestic relations. These reforms would have to involve removal of gendered access barriers. They would involve cultivating a greater feminine presence within judicial institutions including the police, magistrates, judges, lawyers and court officials, particularly the lower-level clerks who act as gatekeepers to access to the legal system. And they would have to involve the extension of new rights to collective representation so that women can overcome mobility and resource constraints in public interest cases.

Decentralisation

Levels of decentralisation influence the immediacy of citizens' access to the state. Enthusiasts of democratic decentralisation hope that multiplying opportunities for political competition and representation will make local government more responsive to socio-economic and cultural diversity. By extension, the poor and women are expected to better engage in politics and better make their views and needs known. But decentralisation alone cannot affect the persistent problem of the political weakness of women or other socially excluded groups. Away from the scrutiny of central authorities, local class, ethnic, racial or patriarchal tyrannies can be more extreme. The very remoteness and isolation of local arenas can fragment the political potency of poorer groups and make them even less able to influence decision making than they are at higher levels of political aggregation. There is a strongly gendered dimension to this problem, as élites in control of local government can also be more overtly and defensively patriarchal than at national levels, with obvious consequences for women's efforts to participate in local politics.

In recognition of the overwhelming strength of traditional authority in local government, some contemporary decentralisation experiments

71

institutionalise special measures to ensure that women participate in policy debates, are formally represented as councillors, and have access to local development funds. For instance, in India, a number of states have supported the 1993 constitutional amendment mandating political devolution by adding inducements to local communities to encourage women's participation. Beyond the reservation of 30 per cent of seats for ward councillors (and 30 per cent of council chairperson positions) for women-only competition, the states of Madhya Pradesh and Kerala require that one third of participants in the regular open village meetings be female before they can be considered to have reached quorum. Kerala obliges local councils to earmark at least 10 per cent of the development funds they receive from the state for 'women's development', and representative all-female sub-groups of the village assembly are in charge of planning for the spending of this money. All of these measures have been criticised because they are so open to abuse: women may be fronted as candidates for election by husbands frustrated that they cannot run themselves, who govern using their wives as proxies. Local councillors may ensure that only a certain class of women – their supporters – attend village assembly meetings to make up the required 30 per cent female presence. And in Kerala, there are cases of women being coerced into diverting the 'women's development' fund into spending that brings them no advantage, or cases of women being harassed by local councillors for asking to know how the earmarked funds were spent (Chatukulam 2000).

When assessing the quality of women's access, presence, and influence in local government, then, we need to see whether there are provisions to encourage women's participation in public assemblies, to encourage their caucusing on matters of importance to women, to earmark funds for them to allocate, and to ensure that local accountability mechanisms are geared to answer to women (in other words, are stripped of gendered access barriers, and include gender equality in standards of performance and justice).

Women's access, presence and influence in the state ☆

In the end, women's access, presence and influence in decision-making forums is shaped by public constructions of women's rights as citizens. If women are not seen as making a contribution to society and the economy of equivalent importance to men, they will not be seen as having equivalent rights to pronounce upon the way public monies are spent, the way laws are framed, and the way standards of accountability are set. Legal frameworks are key to establishing women's citizenship rights, and for this reason have been the target of much feminist activism. But, as we have seen, gender biases in the way the public administration creates access opportunities, allocates resources, and implements policy are also important targets of efforts to make states more responsive to women. Table 2.4 summarises the above discussion, indicating the features of accountability systems in the public administration, judiciary, legislature, and audit office that have an impact on women's enjoyment of equal rights, and that can be reformed to enhance public accountability to women.

Conclusion

In democratic transitions around the world, women have realised that a failure to attend to details of post-conflict or post-authoritarian institutional design can inhibit their chances of participating in politics and policy making. This chapter has argued that when assessing the usefulness of institutional changes designed to enhance women's political effectiveness, we must consider not only whether they enhance both the voice of and accountability to women, but also to what degree they do so: in other words, do they provide just for 'consultation' and 'dialogue' between women and state officials? Or do they give women, directly or indirectly, powers to demand answers from officials, and to trigger sanctions for inappropriate or corrupt actions? Reforms to accountability systems that empower women to demand answers of public agents, and that enable a gender equity constituency to demand punishments for violations of women's rights – and to see them enforced – is taken as the indicator that a gender equity lobby has gained influence in the state.

The conceptual framework developed here enables analysis to look at both 'voice' and accountability processes in tandem, when considering how changes to democratic institutions might affect women's political effectiveness. This enables us to understand that 'voice' does not easily and simply lead to better outcomes for women, because political institutions can have strong gender biases which undermine the impact of women's 'voice' and presence in public office. At the same time, keeping 'voice' in mind when reviewing changes to political institutions which are intended to produce more accountability to women helps us to avoid the 'anti-political' problem of promoting bureaucratic changes in isolation from the politics which would make these new procedures work effectively in promoting gender justice.

Table 2.4 The state dimension of the political effectiveness relationship

Access	Presence	Influence
Accessibility of official policy process to women's participation: • number and types of forums for consultation over policy making and the terms and conditions for access (state–civil society forums for joint policy making, analysis, monitoring – e.g. the Poverty Action Group in Uganda – with NGO, political, and bureaucratic representation to monitor spending of funds saved under the Highly-Indebted Poor Countries (HIPC) initiative); • technical obstacles to participation (technically difficult language, poor distribution of or secrecy around policy drafts, etc.); • financial obstacles to participation (cost of obtaining or reproducing policy information, cost of travel, etc.); • urban bias in location of policy-making forums;	**Corporatist arrangements:** do they include representation of civil society and of the women's movement? **Affirmative action** in state bureaucracies (high-level appointments of women in Uganda, 15 per cent reservation for women in Bangladesh's bureaucracies). **National women's machinery** (bureaucratised representation) and its power, placement and resources: • review/veto power over Cabinet decisions? • Located in powerful ministry or with good access to the state directorate? • High-quality staff with resources to create incentives for compliance with gender equity policy goals?	**Constitutional framework:** presidential versus parliamentary systems – relative powers of executive to support women in politics: controls on power of executive to make women's presence permanent as opposed to contingent. **Legal and regulatory framework (judicial accountability):** gender equity in family law, criminalisation of abuses of women's rights, effective prosecution of sexual offenders, violent spouses, etc., resolution of contradictions between customary and civil law in respect of women's rights. Gender sensitivity throughout the legal system – from law enforcement agents (police) to the courts and judges. **Administrative capacity from a gender perspective (administrative accountability):** • independent and autonomous civil service capable of resisting particularistic class, race and patriarchal interests;

- Do technical, financial, and location-specific obstacles affect women more than men?
- Is consultation linked to concrete decision making or is it a form of policy market research?

Parliamentary standing committees on women's rights – do ordinary women have access to these? How are meetings and debates advertised? What NGOs attend? How is account taken of civil society inputs?

In decentralised government structures:
Nature of consultative and participatory mechanisms at local level – e.g.:
- Existence of open local forums in which all citizens participate to review policy and spending;
- requirement of at least 1/3 presence of women villagers for quorum to be reached in the general assemblies of local councils (Madhya Pradesh).

Earmarking or **ring fencing of funds** for gender-related programmes (particularly at local levels).

Women in the executive: how many women in the Cabinet, and what portfolios do they hold?

Local government: measures to reserve seats for women-only competition, or combinations of PR and ward systems to encourage voters to select more women councillors.

- integrity and transparency in policy-making and spending decisions;
- incentive systems for lower-level state agents supporting implementation practices which address women's needs (and do not exclude or denigrate women clients);
- performance-related pay or monitoring which rewards non-sexist performance.

Budgetary transparency from a gender perspective (financial accountability):
- women's budgets (likely impact of public expenditure decisions on women);
- gender audits of actual spending (especially effective at local levels);
- requirement that representative sub-groups of women make decisions on spending of local funds which are earmarked for women's needs (Kerala);
- involvement of women in targeting government anti-poverty programmes (e.g.: women's groups determine which families are in the Below Poverty Line category and monitor this over time – Kerala).

References

Abers, R. (1998) 'From Clientelism to Cooperation: Local Government, Participatory Policy, and Civic Organising in Porto Alegre, Brazil', *Politics and Society*, 26, 4: 511–38.

AbuKhalil, As'ad (1994) 'Women and Electoral Politics in Arab States', in W. Rule and J. Zimmerman (eds.), *Electoral Systems in Comparative Perspective: Their Impact on Women and Minorities*, Westport, Connecticut: Greenwood Press.

Benninger-Budel, C. and A-L. Lacroix (1999) *Violence Against Women: A Report*, World Organisation Against Torture [OMCT], Geneva.

Bibars, I. (2001) *Victims and Heroines: Women, Welfare, and the Egyptian State*, London: Zed Press, 2001.

Caul, M. (1997) *Women's Representation in Parliament: the Role of Political Parties*, Research Monograph Series, Centre for the Study of Democracy, Irvine, California.

Chatukulam, J. (2000) 'Institutional Reform and Movements for Right to Information and Anti-corruption: the Kerala Situation', mimeo, Centre for Rural Management, Kottayam.

Chazan, N. (1982) 'The New Politics of Participation in Tropical Africa', *Comparative Politics*, 14, 2: 169–90.

Connell, R. W. (1990) 'The State, Gender, and Sexual Politics: Theory and Appraisal', in *Theory and Society*, 19: 507–44.

Crook. R. (2001) 'Strengthening Democratic Governance in Conflict-Torn Societies: Civic Organisations, Democratic Effectiveness and Political Conflict', Institute of Development Studies Working Paper 129, University of Sussex.

Edwards, M. and D. Hulme (eds.) (1995) *Non-Governmental Organisations – Performance and Accountability: Beyond the Magic Bullet*, London: Earthscan Publications.

Feijoo, Maria del Carmen (1989) 'The Challenge of Constructing Civilian Peace: Women and Democracy in Argentina', in J. Jaquette (ed.), *The Women's Movement in Latin America: Feminism and the Transition to Democracy*, Boston: Unwin Hyman.

Geisler, G. (1995) 'Troubled Sisterhood: Women and Politics in Southern Africa', *African Affairs*, 94: 545–78.

Goetz, A. M. (1995) 'The Politics of Integrating Gender to State Development Processes: Trends, Opportunities, and Constraints in Bangladesh, Chile, Jamaica, Mali, Morocco, and Uganda', Occasional Paper No. 2, United Nations Research Institute for Social Development, Geneva.

—— (2001) *Women Development Workers: Implementing Rural Credit Programmes in Bangladesh*, Delhi: Sage Press.

Goetz, A. M. and J. Gaventa (2001) 'Citizen Voice and Client Focus in Service Delivery', Institute of Development Studies, Working Paper 138, University of Sussex.

Goetz, A. M. and R. Jenkins (2001a) 'Voice, Power and Accountability: the Emergence of a New Agenda', background chapter for the UNDP Human Development Report, mimeo.

Goetz, A. M. and R. Jenkins (2001b) 'Hybrid Forms of Accountability: Citizen Engagement in Institutions of Public-Sector Oversight', *Public Management*

Review, 3, 3: 363–83.

Goetz, A. M. and S. Lister (2001) 'Civil Society Engagement with the State: a Comparative Analysis of Uganda and South Africa', Institute of Development Studies, University of Sussex, May.

Grindle, M. S. and M. E. Hilderbrand (1995) 'Building Sustainable Capacity in the Public Sector: What Can Be Done?', *Public Administration and Development*, 15: 442–63.

Hirschmann, D. (1991) 'Women and Participation in Africa: Broadening the Scope of Research', *World Development*, 19, 12: 1679–94.

Inter-Parliamentary Union (1997) *Democracy Still in the Making: Men and Women in Politics*, Geneva: IPU.

—— (2000) *Politics: Women's Insight*, Geneva: IPU.

Jaquette, J. (ed.) (1989) *The Women's Movement in Latin America: Feminism and the Transition to Democracy*, Boston: Unwin Hyman.

—— (2001) 'Regional Differences and Contrasting Views', *Journal of Democracy*, 12, 3 (Special Issues on Women and Democracy): 111–25.

Jenkins, R. S. (2001) 'Mistaking Governance for Politics: Foreign Aid, Democracy and the Construction of Civil Society', in Sudipta Kaviraj and Sunil Khilnani (eds.), *Civil Society: Histories and Possibilities*, Cambridge: Cambridge University Press.

Jenkins, R. and A. M. Goetz (1999) 'Accounts and Accountability: Theoretical Implications of the Right-to-Information Movement in India', *Third World Quarterly*, 20, 3: 603–22.

Jewkes, R., N. Abrahams and Z. Mvo (1998) 'Why Do Nurses Abuse Patients? Reflections from South African Obstetric Services', *Social Science and Medicine*, 47, 11: 1781–95.

Joshi, A. and M. Moore (2000) 'Enabling Environments: Do Anti-Poverty Programs Mobilize the Poor?', *Journal of Development Studies*, 37, 1: 25–56.

Killian, B. (1996) 'A Policy of Parliamentary Special Seats for Women in Tanzania: Its Effectiveness', *Ufahamu*, 2–3: 21–2.

Khadiagala, L. S. (2001) 'The Failure of Popular Justice in Uganda: Local Councils and Women's Property Rights', *Development and Change*, 32: 55–76.

Leach, F. and P. Machakanja, with J. Mandoga (2000) *Preliminary Investigation of the Abuse of Girls in Zimbabwean Junior Secondary Schools*, Department for International Development, Serial No. 39, London.

Lovenduski, J. (1999) 'Sexing Political Behaviour in Britain', in S. Walby (ed.), *New Agendas for Women*, London: Macmillan.

Lovenduski, J. and P. Norris (eds.) (1993) *Gender and Party Politics*, London: Sage.

Mansbridge, J. (1998) *The Many Faces of Representation*, Kennedy School of Government Politics Research Group Working Paper, Harvard University, Cambridge, Massachusetts.

Matland, R. E. (1993) 'Institutional Variables Affecting Female Representation in National Legislatures: the Case of Norway', *Journal of Politics*, 53, 3: 737–55.

—— (1999) *Women in African Legislatures and Executives: the Slow Climb to Power*, Electoral Institute of South Africa.

Molyneux, M. (2001) *Women's Movements in International Perspective: Latin America and Beyond*, London: Palgrave.

Moore, M. (2002) 'Elites Oppose the Development of Political Parties (Russia)',

Governance and Development Review, January 2002. www.ids.ac.uk/gdr/reviews/review-01.html

Mukarasi, L. (1991) *Post Abolished: One Woman's Struggle for Employment Rights in Tanzania*, London: The Women's Press.

Norris, P. (1993), 'Conclusion: Comparing Legislative Recruitment', in J. Lovenduski and P. Norris (eds.), *Gender and Party Politics*, London: Sage.

—— (2000) 'Breaking the Barriers: Positive Discrimination Policies for Women', in J. Klausen and C. S. Maier (eds.), *Has Liberalism Failed Women? Parity, Quotas and Political Representation*, New York: St Martin's Press.

Norris, P. and J. Lovenduski (1995) *Political Recruitment*, Cambridge: Cambridge University Press.

O'Donnell, G. (1994) 'Delegative Democracy', *Journal of Democracy*, 5, 1: 55–69.

—— (1999) 'Horizontal Accountability in New Democracies', in A. Schedler *et al.*, *The Self-Restraining State: Power and Accountability in New Democracies*, London: Lynne Reinner.

Olsen, J. P. (1988) 'Administrative Reform and Theories of Organization', in C. Campbell and G. Peters (eds.), *Organizing Governance: Governing Organizations*, Pittsburgh: University of Pittsburg Press: 233–54.

Pateman, C. (1988) *The Sexual Contract*, Cambridge: Polity Press.

Phillips, A. (1991) *Engendering Democracy*, Cambridge: Polity Press.

—— (1993) 'Must Feminists Give Up on Liberal Democracy', in D. Held (ed.), *Prospects for Democracy: North, South, East, West*, Cambridge: Polity Press.

Prud'homme, R. (1998) 'The Dangers of Decentralization', *World Bank Research Observer*, 10, 2: 201–20.

Rao, A., R. Stuart, and D. Kelleher (1999) *Gender at Work: Organisational Change for Equality*, West Hartford, Connecticut: Kumarian Press.

Razavi, S. (2001) 'Women in Contemporary Democratization', *International Journal of Politics, Culture and Society*, 15, 1: 201–24.

—— (2002) 'Women and Democracy', in S. Razavi and M. Molyneux (eds.), *Gender, Justice, Democracy and Rights*, Oxford University Press, Oxford.

Reynolds, A. (1999) *Women in African Legislatures and Executives: The Slow Climb to Power*, Electoral Institute of South Africa.

Rule, W. and J. Zimmerman (eds.) (1992) *Electoral Systems in Comparative Perspective: Their Impact on Women and Minorities*, Westport, Connecticut: Greenwood Press.

Sargent, C. (1989) *Maternity, Medicine, and Power: Reproductive Decisions in Urban Benin*, Berkeley: University of California Press.

Sawer, M. (1995) 'Feminism in Glass Towers? The Office of the Status of Women in Australia', in D. Stetson and A. Mazur (eds.), *Comparative State Feminism*, London: Sage, pp. 22–39.

—— (2000) 'Parliamentary Representation of Women: From Discourses of Justice to Strategies of Accountability', *International Political Science Review*, 21, 4: 361–80.

Schedler, A. (1999) 'Conceptualising Accountability', in A. Schedler *et al.*, *The Self-Restraining State: Power and Accountability in New Democracies*, London: Lynne Reinner.

Sharan, S. (2000) 'Women in Decision-Making Positions in Political Systems', in N. Sinha, (ed.), *Women in Indian Politics*, New Delhi: Gyan Publishing House.

Simmons, R. and C. Elias (1993) *The Study of Client–Provider Interaction: a Review of Methodological Issues*, The Population Council, Working Paper No. 7, Washington, DC.

Squires, J. and M. Wickham-Jones (2001) *Women in Parliament: a Comparative Analysis*, Equal Opportunities Commission, Research Discussion Series, Manchester.

Tendler, J. and S. Freedheim (1994) 'Trust in a Rent-Seeking World: Health and Government Transformed in Northeast Brazil', *World Development*, 22, 12: 1771–91.

Thomas, D. Q. (1999) 'Comments on Acosta', in J. E. Mendez, G. O'Donnell and P. S. Pinheiro, (eds.), *The (Un)Rule of Law and the Underprivileged in Latin America*, Indiana: University of Notre Dame Press.

Thomas, J. W. and M. S. Grindle (1990) 'After the Decision: Implementing Policy Reforms in Developing Countries', *World Development*, 18, 8: 1163–81.

Tripp, A. M. (1994) 'Rethinking Civil Society: Gender Implications in Contemporary Tanzania', in J. Harbeson, D. Rothschild, and N. Chazan (eds.), *Civil Society and the State in Africa*, London: Lynne Reinner.

—— (2000) *Women and Politics in Uganda*, Oxford: James Currey.

UNRISD (1998) 'For a Handful of Grain', occasional paper case study by YUVA and the Action Committee for Rationing (RKS), Geneva.

Waylen, G. (2000) 'Gender and Democratic Politics: a Comparative Analysis of Consolidation in Argentina and Chile', *Journal of Latin American Studies*, 32, 3: 765–94.

Weyland, K. (1997) '"Growth with Equity" in Chile's New Democracy?' *Latin American Research Review*, 32, 1: 37–67.

Yoon, Mi Ming (2001) 'Democratisation and Women's Legislative Representation in Sub-Saharan Africa', *Democratisation*, 8, 2: 169–90.

Notes

1 The weak relationship between democracy and numbers of women in office should not be taken as an indication that women do not enjoy democratic freedoms. Global statistical comparisons of the sort that produce these observations are distorted by the fact that many of the democracies under observation are barely consolidated, and by the use of affirmative action strategies in non-democracies to place larger numbers of women in politics than are elected in most democracies.

2 For just a few contributions to this debate see Norris 2000; Matland 1993; Yoon 2001; Reynolds 1999.

3 One party in Equatorial Guinea, which has a PR system, has adopted quotas, but it is a minor party – the People's Social Democratic Convergence, winning just 6 of 80 seats in 1993 and just one in 1999 – and it has not persuaded the dominant parties to follow suit (Yoon 2001: 180).

4 An acronym for Early Money Is Like Yeast – a reference to the centrality of campaign finance in US politics.

5 This is not to suggest, of course, that female politicians are incapable of participating in violence or criminal behaviour. Not only have a number of women politicians at high levels shown themselves fully capable of enthusiastic engagement in corruption, but they have been implicated either directly

or indirectly in violent attacks on opponents or on people considered threatening. Recent examples include Winnie Mandela in South Africa, or Jayalalitha in Tamil Nadu, India.

6 In 1999–2000, only 3.7 per cent of presidents and 1.6 per cent of prime ministers were women (IPU 2000: 130).

7 In 1999–2000, for instance, women provided the Minister of Defence in just four states, Minister of Finance in nine, Minister of Home Affairs in one, and Minister of Trade and Industry in 14 – but the Minister of Social Affairs in 44, Minister of Health in 30, Minister of Family/Children (etc.) in 26, and Minister of Women's Affairs in 47 (IPU 2000: 130–2).

8 For a personal account of a gender-biased retrenchment exercise in a Tanzanian parastatal, see Mukarasi 1991.

9 Female court and police officials have also been known to participate in the persecution of women victims of sexual assault or domestic battery. That they do so is evidence of the power and pervasiveness of male biases built into the legal system.

3

Representation, Participation and Democratic Effectiveness: Feminist Challenges to Representative Democracy in South Africa[1]

SHIREEN HASSIM

> Let us ... say: I am woman; my concerns, my problems, my difficulties, my achievements are an integral part of our new society. No-one will succeed in marginalising them or me. I am woman, I am South African, I am me. I go to Parliament but I am woman (Frene Ginwala, speech at the national conference of the Women's National Coalition, February 1994).

These stirring words by Frene Ginwala, as she stepped down from leading the Women's National Coalition (WNC), the largest national women's organisation that South Africa had ever seen, to take up her position as the Speaker in South Africa's first democratic parliament, capture the optimistic mood of that phenomenal moment in the country's transition to democracy. For Ginwala, as for most other women activists who had been in the forefront of pro-democratic politics, moving into parliament was not a break with the women's movement but a continuation of women's struggles in a new domain – one, moreover, in which women had to fight to gain entry as full citizens. Her speech promised more than continuity; it also promised to retain accountability to women, to act politically *as* a woman, and to refuse marginalisation or domination by other political interests.

The inception of a democratic state in 1994 reshaped the terms under which women engaged in politics. As in other new democracies, women's organisations turned to electoral strategies to achieve at least some of their goals (Jacquette and Wolchik 1998). The shift to electoral strategies had far-reaching consequences. It eclipsed – even undermined – the cross-party mobilisation among women that had characterised the approach of the Women's National Coalition during the transitional period. The departure of the leadership of the WNC for positions on party lists exacerbated the organisation's difficulties in defining a new role for itself in the democratic era. The core of its leadership shifted its concern to intra-party imperatives of ensuring that gender featured in party manifestos and that women were represented on party lists. The shift to electoral and bureaucratic politics has been a common pattern in post-authoritarian transitions and opened new sets of issues for South African feminists as it did in other contexts. As Jacquette and Wolchik (1998: 6) have shown, in Latin American countries

> The return to democratic politics created unexpected problems for the women's movements and for social movements in general. The politics of the transition had been intense, with a strong emphasis on rhetoric and mass mobilisation. Democracy meant that brave concepts had to be turned into workable legislation, that sustained organisational effort would be needed to ensure that women's issues would be taken up by the political parties, and that legislation would be implemented and monitored.

Comparative literature suggests that all too often the shift to engaging the state from within is accompanied by the jettisoning of earlier concerns with the achievement of substantive equality (Alvarez 1990; Jacquette and Wolchik 1998). In this chapter, I explore the extent to which the demands for substantive gender equality articulated by the women's movement in South Africa have been inscribed within political party principles and in political institutions. The chapter examines the debates about representation of women as a constituency in the new democracy, and explores the extent to which political parties were amenable to the presence and interests of women members. In particular, it assesses the extent to which feminists have been able to turn political presence into policy leverage.

Women's organisations' demands for greater participation and representation in liberation movements, political parties and politics generally came into sharp relief with the advent of representative democracy. Women's organisations on the left had, since the 1980s, questioned the idea that the formal right to vote would necessarily lead to better policy outcomes for women. Formal membership of political parties and liberation movements had not increased women's political power to any significant degree. However, the increased representation of women in elected offices and demands for greater visibility of 'women's concerns' in national political debates were seen by the women's movement as strategically necessary. Initially, this led to an intense focus on numbers – that is, on getting as many women into parliament as possible, across all political parties. By the 1999 elections, however, the *quality* of women's participation re-emerged as a central concern. The interventions of women's organisations in electoral politics by 1999 reflected a concern with specific policy issues and party manifestos, and with the relationship between elected women representatives and women voters. While these shifts suggest a maturing of women's electoral politics, and a consolidation of women as an electoral constituency, the extent to which women's policy leverage has been increased as a result of representation remains the key question. By the June 1999 national elections, the conception of constituency among women's organisations – the perception that there were a set of political concerns that women shared regardless of race and class position or party ideology – advanced significantly beyond broad formulations. While representation and participation remained key concerns, there was a much deeper consideration of the strategic uses of political leverage. This was facilitated by a dense network of organisational initiatives in civil society to pressurise political parties to consider *which* women they put on their party lists, to challenge parties on the gender implications of their policy platforms and to engage in interest group politics around specific policy initiatives. The process of constituency building among women intensified during both electoral periods although, as this chapter will show, electoral outcomes were not solely responsible for increasing women's political leverage in the representative sphere.

Drawing on ideas elaborated by Anne Marie Goetz in Chapter 2, this chapter argues that limitations on women's political effectiveness in South Africa are set by two factors, both relating to the political universe within which women act. The first is the rules and procedures of institutional engagement within which parties operate and over which women have had little influence. As Goetz argues, these rules and procedures are not only the formal characteristics of the political system but also include deeply entrenched patterns of power and authority that shape political behaviour. The second limitation is the dominance of a single party, albeit one sympathetic to notions of gender equality, within the electoral system *and* within civil society. The women's movement has tended to privilege the leadership of women within the ANC. Indeed, this factor was a prime reason for women's movement successes in the transitional period and, as this chapter will show, also drove the feminist agenda within Parliament. However, by the end of the first democratic parliament, it became evident that representation even within a majority party committed to the principles of gender equality offered no guarantees for women, and that a broadening of democratic commitment in the political system as a whole and the strengthening of the women's movement outside the state are also needed if women are to be effective in the formal representative realm.

Descriptive representation: the first step

The idea that women, as a group, constituted an electoral constituency entered South African politics in the early 1990s.[2] The interests that were seen to hold this constituency together, however, were narrowly defined in terms of a common exclusion from the processes and forums of public decision making. The focus on 'getting women in' – that is, onto party lists – to a large extent regardless of political ideology, provided the glue which held together a diverse range of women's organisations and gender ideologies in the run-up to the 1994 elections. Debate focused on mechanisms to achieve women's representation, most notably a quota, rather than on the particular interests of different groups of women.

Accompanying the drive to 'get women in' was a concurrent emphasis on 'getting women's vote out' (Zondo 1994: 57). Women's organisations and, to a lesser extent, political parties, were concerned that women's higher levels of illiteracy, poverty and spatial marginalisation would prejudice women's right to exercise their votes. Many feared that a combination of political violence and patriarchal control would keep women out of the electoral process. A significant proportion of women's organisations' efforts (and donor funding) was therefore devoted to voter education campaigns directed at women. In addition, demands made by the WNC for women's representation in decision-making structures finally found support among political parties, especially within the ANC. Within these terms, the strategic approach of the women's movement was successful. Just over 1.5 million more women than men registered to vote in the 1999 election, reflecting the success of campaigns to ensure that women were informed citizens with regard to the mechanics of voting. At least at the procedural level, women were not disadvantaged. As appendices 1 and 2 to this chapter (see page 105) show, women constituted nearly 30 per cent of all parliamentarians elected, placing South Africa in the ranks of the top ten democracies in the world on this indicator (Ballington 1998: 82). This statistic was widely used locally and internationally to signal the extent to which the new democracy was inclusive. Although not all parties used a quota for women, for reasons outlined below, the extent of women's representation emboldened women activists and engendered a sense of optimism about the possibilities for shaping legislative and policy priorities.

Representation: a good in itself?

It is not surprising that women's organisations pursued a strong representational strategy in advance of the 1994 election, despite the long history of demanding substantive equality. An obvious reason is that the liberal democracy crafted by negotiators demanded that feminists derive a strategy appropriate within the context of a multi-party electoral system; that is, the political context required that feminists interrogate the possibilities for increasing women's representation in the conventional institutional sites. In any case, there was some continuity with earlier struggles within the ANC, in which women pursued representation in the highest decision-making structures of the ANC. In relation to the new democracy, women activists sought to hold representative democracy – or government by elected leaders – to the promise that it offered citizens the opportunity to select the representatives they preferred, and to remove them from office should they fail to 'perform'. Pursuing representation, women activists were equally concerned that it should offer the opportunity for enforcing accountability to constituencies of women through proper institutional mechanisms.

A strong body of feminist literature has been concerned with the ways in which representative democracy might be enhanced to ensure women's equal participation (Phillips 1991; Young 1990; Williams 1998). This literature has shown that for women citizens in most democracies, there is a problem of *both* representation and accountability. The possession of formal political equality, the vote, does not necessarily translate into representation even in the broadest sense of the presence of women in representative institutions. Even if representation is significantly increased, some analysts argue that representative democracies fail to deliver accountability (Hirst 1990: 2). Elections which are free and fair in the procedural sense do not necessarily produce outcomes which reflect either the diversity of interests or identities in societies. Anne Phillips regards this as a fundamental weakness in democracies and suggests that without representation in legislatures, women citizens have a diminished ability to hold governments accountable (1991). Although not explicitly drawing on such theoretical frameworks, women activists in South Africa saw demands for representation as a necessary step in creating accountable and responsive government. There was, furthermore, an explicit view that increasing women's representation in parliament would improve policy outcomes for women. This view was strongly held among women activists in the ANC who had lobbied to ensure that policy proposals developed in the ANC's electoral platform of 1994 (the Reconstruction and Development Programme) took gender equity concerns into account.

The formal commitment to equality in both the interim constitution of 1994 and the final constitution ratified in 1996 has been used by gender activists to argue that the under-representation of women in Parliament is undesirable.[3] However, there is no consensus among South African feminists as to how equality could be achieved, and there are major differences over the use of quotas. Women activists within the ANC have argued that the systematic and institutional bias against women as political actors has to be addressed through special interventions, such as a quota for women on electoral lists.[4] The 30 per cent quota that was adopted by the ANC for the 1994 and 1999 elections placed a substantial number of women MPs in Parliament, as appendices 1 and 2 demonstrate. By contrast, the Democratic Party (DP) has argued that the blockages to women's political participation will be removed over the longer term as women are economically and socially empowered. This gradualist argument is also supported, although rather weakly, by the New National Party (NNP) and the Inkatha Freedom Party (IFP). This approach assumes that as more women enter the workforce, as discriminatory practices such as job stereotyping are removed and educational opportunities are spread evenly between the sexes, women will move into the public political realm in greater numbers. The DP has been opposed to the use of quotas to increase women's representation, seeing these mechanisms as an unnecessary incursion into civil liberties. The DP has adopted a consistently liberal position on gender equality, whether in terms of representation or policy manifesto. Commenting at a round-table conference on 'Putting Women into Power' (Johannesburg, 23 February 1999) DP MP Kate Prinsloo argued that the quota system

> lets political parties off the hook with regard to women's empowerment. It creates the impression that the issue has been dealt with and leads to the view that those who are elected say everything's OK, we come from grassroots organisations and therefore we are equipped to speak for women.

By contrast, although officially rejecting quotas, the NNP has tended to be more reactive to the way in which gender issues are articulated by the ANC. This has allowed some room for gender activists within the party – some of whom support quotas – to make inroads into leadership despite the absence of a clear policy on gender equality. Tersia Wessels, an NNP member of the Gauteng provincial legislature, has acknowledged that the ANC's use of a quota had a positive impact on the NNP's party list, and the party has been making more active efforts to include women in leadership positions (Comments at Commission on Gender Equality – CGE – Gender Dialogue, 29 June 1998). Anna van Wyk, MP and executive member of the NNP's Women's Action Group, argues that 'gender should ultimately be eliminated as a criterion for choosing MPs, but in the meanwhile we need affirmative action'. She also argues for 'gender parity in party executives' (Comments at GAP/AWEPA Conference, 21 October 1998).

To the left of the ANC, the idea of quotas and the emphasis on women's representation on electoral lists is also criticised, albeit for different reasons. The black consciousness party AZAPO has argued that the key issue is the transformation of the structure of inequality in society and that focusing on electoral representation is a limited and reformist intervention. Rather, 'we need to empower women from the bottom up. We need to ensure that all categories of women are represented, not just professional women' (Kedibone Molema, Electoral Institute of South Africa – EISA – Roundtable, 23 February 1999). For similar reasons, the Pan Africanist Congress has also not supported the idea of a quota for women.

The DP's argument against quotas is that granting special status to groups reduces the choices of individual voters. However, party pre-selection exists in most electoral systems as candidates are selected before they are put to the public vote, and there is no particular reason why the criteria for pre-selection should not include gender. This is particularly true in a Proportional Representation with List (PR List) system, where the party leadership has significant power to set standards of representation. As Chapter 2 argues, there is no guarantee that equality will extend beyond the formal level despite the reduction of opportunity disparities between the sexes. The challenge for electoral politics in a democratic system is how to extend a general commitment to equality to the representative sphere. Even privileging women on party lists leaves unresolved issues such as the impact of poverty and rural marginality on women's effective participation. While quotas might assist in equalising formal participation through influencing electoral outcomes, they are not an effective mechanism for equalising representation of marginal interests (Phillips 1991: 63).

Representation: electoral outcomes

Women's electoral politics in South Africa has benefited from the creation of a range of mechanisms, including a constitutional provision, to advance gender equality in the democratic state. These mechanisms provide a legitimising framework as well as facilitating the advancement of gender claims. The constitutional clause on equality establishes gender equality as a core principle and value of South African democracy. This provision has had far-reaching formal impact, in that both political parties and the Independent Electoral Commission (IEC) have to ensure that women's participation is not prejudiced in any way by the nature of electoral campaigns or by the procedural aspects of the elections.[5] In addition, the presence of gender activists among IEC commissioners has facilitated attention to gender issues in the work of the Commission.

The increase in women MPs was due to the choice of an electoral system – PR List – that has been shown to significantly advance women's representation in a number of countries (Matland and Taylor 1997; Reynolds 1998). This choice was dictated in the first instance by non-gender considerations such as providing incentives to smaller parties to pursue political mobilisation within the formal political system and encouraging larger political parties to seek support outside of their traditional constituencies. At any rate, the outcome for women's representation was dramatic. A key reason is that PR List allows considerable latitude to party leaderships to determine the candidate lists and, from the perspective of women candidates, to use the list mechanism to override traditional sentiments against women in politics.

This advantage for the women's movement also has a number of inherent disadvantages that undermine other feminist concerns. First, proportional representation systems contain an in-built bias towards a centralist form of internal party politics that may be antithetical to women's movement emphases on democratic culture, thereby reinforcing the blockages to women's power within parties. A second, related consequence is the possibility that party leadership will choose women candidates that are 'token' representatives least likely to upset the political applecart, rather than those candidates with strong links to autonomous women's organisations. Third, the PR system favours accountability of representatives to political parties in the first instance, rather than to electoral constituencies. It places primary stress on intra-party lobbying, rather than constituency preference, as the route to electoral success. The power of party élites mitigates against building strong branch-level structures, and the ability to develop constituencies that can articulate interests from the bottom up against the official position of the party leadership, is undercut. Again, this runs counter to notions of accountability that were emphasised within the women's movement during the 1980s and early 1990s. I will return to these concerns below.

Increasing women's leverage within Parliament

Getting women into Parliament in large numbers was only one part of the task of representation. Another was ensuring that women MPs had some leverage in relation to policy decisions. In the South African parliamentary system, decisions are made at two crucial sites, Cabinet and the portfolio committees. Women's participation in these sites is crucial to exercising leverage. Yet, comparative research on women in the representational sphere suggests that entry does not usually translate into upward mobility within the hierarchy of Parliament. In a wide-ranging comparison of women parliamentarians in European democracies, Joni Lovenduski (1986: 241) found that women are kept at the bottom of legislative hierarchies and that there is an imbalance between the proportion of women in legislatures and their representation in executive bodies. This pattern was found to be true even for Scandinavian countries, which have a long history of the use of quotas in various forms. Vicky Randall reaches a similar conclusion, noting that 'at the apex of the representational hierarchy within national governments, women often virtually disappear' (Randall 1987: 109). When women do break into higher levels of Parliament, a distinct gender pattern in the allocation of ministerial portfolios emerges (Lovenduski 1986; Randall 1987). Women are generally allocated to the 'soft' ministries of family, welfare and culture, a pattern Lovenduski (1986) regards as a further aspect of gatekeeping, whereby the few women who are appointed to the ministerial level are relegated to less important posts.

Interestingly, South Africa does not easily fit this pattern. Following the 1994 election, the Cabinet had women at 15 per cent (4 out of 27) of ministers and 56 per cent (8 out of 14) of deputy ministers. This suggests that women were significantly represented at the highest levels compared to the proportion of women MPs. Although the 'social' portfolios (Health, Welfare, Housing) were assigned to women, these are key areas of social delivery which formed the cornerstone of the ANC's electoral manifestos in both elections. Moreover, the deputy ministers of the 'hard' portfolios of Finance and Trade and Industry in the 1994–8 Parliament were also women. A more significant gender pattern can be found in examining the membership of portfolio committees in Parliament during this period. Women's representation ranged from 0 per cent (Public Accounts) to 73 per cent (Health). Committees in which women dominated include Welfare (60 per cent), and Communications (66 per cent). Women are notably under-represented in Land Affairs (18 per cent), Mineral and Energy (12 per cent), Transport (12 per cent),

Foreign Affairs (12 per cent) and Labour (19 per cent) (Mtintso 1999: 64). Following the 1999 election, the new President, Thabo Mbeki, consolidated women's position in Cabinet. The new Cabinet has 8 women ministers (of 29) and 8 (of 13) deputy ministers. Notable new appointments are the head of the ANC Women's Parliamentary Caucus as Deputy Minister of Defence,[6] and the appointment of women as Minister and Deputy Minister of Mineral and Energy Affairs.[7] Both may be considered traditionally 'hard' portfolios.

The South African case therefore contrasts with the European pattern. Women are significantly represented at the highest levels compared to the proportion of women MPs. A similar situation exists in Australia, where Moon and Fountain have found that 'Australian women's political fortunes improve as they move from the party to the parliamentary arena' (Moon and Fountain 1997: 458). Their explanation for the counter-trend is twofold. First, they argue that in parties of the left, party 'gatekeepers' are responsive to the notion that selection of women is good for the party. They are therefore prepared to circumvent, through the use of the party list, traditional cultural and structural obstacles to women's political mobility. Second, they argue that once women are in Parliament, they are more likely to be judged on merit than on their gender. Given that women have to be 'twice as good' as men to overcome intra-party obstacles to their selection, those who are elected to Parliament are likely to be better qualified. There are important resonances on both counts in the South African case. The ANC, the majority party in both governments, was highly responsive to claims of gender representation and this has underpinned many party policies. Furthermore, the women's movement has made some inroads into public debate, contributing to a climate in which gender representation is part of the democratic discourse (although, as I note below, this is an élite discourse). This has given some leverage to the women's sections within political parties to win support for increased representation.

In South Africa, by contrast with Uganda, parties are diverse and relatively well institutionalised. The ANC had developed strong centralised structures in exile that facilitated the transition to an electoral party, although not necessarily to a deeply democratic one. White parties were highly institutionalised due to their participation in the apartheid electoral process. At both ends of the political spectrum, however, women's engagement with political parties has been as subordinate members. Political parties have not been comfortable homes for women activists. Political parties in South Africa, as elsewhere, have been male-dominated institutions, even while their ideological impetus has been provided by liberationist discourses and agendas. However, there was a relatively high level of internal debate about women's representation and about the political culture of the ANC compared to other political parties. It is important to recognise the positive impact of these struggles on those formations: without the kind of internal 'party' reforms of the 1980s (the focus women brought to bear on how decisions were made, by whom, and which issues were prioritised) it is unlikely that the ANC would have been so receptive to demands for representation and participation of women during the multi-party negotiations. The women's movement thus benefited enormously from the alliance with left political organisations. Concomitantly, the absence of such a history has affected the ability of women in the NNP and the DP to make room in the parties' highest structures, as the discussion in the next section shows.

The internal politics of constituency building

In 1994, Jenny Schreiner, ANC and SACP activist and subsequently ANC MP, suggested that women in the ANC should open 'bargaining' with their male colleagues to take up gender issues.

> We, women in the ANC, should consider approaching men and women nominees for our national and regional candidates lists on this basis: if you take up the issues of women such as job training, child care, access to permanent jobs for women, as part of what you campaign for in reconstruction during the election campaign, then we will vote for you and mobilise votes for you from branch to national level. This can be done to get women on the national list, as well as to make men on the list more sensitive to gender issues (Schreiner 1993: 101).

Although the idea was not pursued within the ANC (interview with Jenny Schreiner, November 2000), her concern about how to concretise the party's broad commitments to gender was shared within the women's movement. In 1994, the feminist journal *Agenda* published a set of questions for candidates, urging readers to 'measure the parties by their responses, and tell them we want action, not answers!' (*Agenda* 1994: 7).[8] Women's organisations campaigned to ensure that the majority of political parties expressed a commitment to gender equality in their electoral manifestos. For the most part, though, these were rhetorical commitments, thin on policy detail (Ballington 1999). By the 1999 elections, the response of women's organisations was to intensify demands on parties at public forums for greater policy specificity.[9] This was most evident with regard to the debate on offering HIV/Aids drugs

91

to pregnant women and to rape survivors, where women representatives from different parties were pushed into demarcating areas of difference on a key health policy issue. The CGE, together with the Women's Empowerment Unit, the Women's Development Foundation (WDF), the South African Local Government Association (SALGA) and the Women's National Coalition sent an open letter to all political parties challenging them to put women on their electoral lists. The CGE also visited all parties, but reported that the discussions were very general and that parties had little substantial policy responses to their questions (Interview with Mihloti Mathye, 5 May 2000). In addition, the CGE successfully lobbied media organisations on the importance of covering women candidates as well as gender issues.

Apart from the central role played by the CGE, a number of NGO initiatives tracked party positions on gender, including the Gender Advocacy Programme (GAP) in the Western Cape, EISA, the WDF and NISAA in Gauteng. The WDF and GAP launched a two-pronged national campaign aimed at increasing women's representation and at ensuring that women voters considered party positions on gender issues when voting. As Barbara Watson, Director of the WDF, pointed out, 'we have to challenge all parties to have a policy on women. At the moment we are too dependent on the will of the majority party' (Comment at GAP/AWEPA Conference, October 1998). A considerable media effort was launched. This included contributions to the mainstream media,[10] as well as the development of an *Election Bulletin* produced in both tabloid and electronic form by Women'sNet, on behalf of a range of women's organisations. These forums were used to debate how parties were taking up key issues such as violence against women, unemployment, housing and health care.

Not surprisingly, this shift to concerns about the quality of women's representation, and about accountability to women's interests, resulted in contestation between women in political parties over policy issues. Although women activists in all parties had been united about maintaining the pressure for greater political representation, within the domain of women's forums there has been a painstaking reiteration of the limits of common interests. Below the surface of collective action simmered discontent over the relative power of certain women's organisations over others, and mistrust about the extent to which particular political parties could be trusted to advance the agendas of the women's movement. Within Parliament, early attempts to create a multi-party forum for women MPs, such as the Parliamentary Women's Group (PWG), have foundered as a result of tensions between the DP, ANC and

NNP. The opposition parties constantly questioned ANC MPs' leadership position in the PWG, despite the track record in women's organisations of the particular ANC MPs concerned. Anna van Wyk, National Party MP, suggests that 'the small number of women in opposition parties militates against cooperation' (Comment at GAP/AWEPA Conference, October 1998). These tensions were exacerbated by the fact that the PWG lacked recognition in Parliament as an official structure. It operated without a budget, parliamentary rules were often used to undermine attempts to convene meetings, and, in some instances, male leaders of parties were critical of the existence of such a structure. Nozizwe Routledge Madlala, currently Deputy Minister of Defence, comments that

> An alliance between women MPs [from different parties] had to be built up outside of government. We agreed that we should agree on certain minimal things. Once inside parliament, it was not so much that there was no will to work together, but obstacles often came from women being dictated to by their caucuses. Some party caucuses were saying you can't belong to several caucuses. Even the ANC Women's Caucus survived only because of the party's moral and political obligations (Interview, 7 September 2000).

Women are not a homogeneous constituency. Even where women MPs are committed to broad principles of gender equality, their definitions of what this means, their strategies for achieving equality, and the constituencies of women they represent, may be vastly different. Former ANC MP Mavivi Manzini points out that attempts to build a common front of women in parliament would not succeed.

> We've tried that. It doesn't work. There are differences [between MPs of different parties] over what is to be transformed. There [are] only a limited number of areas in which women are able to speak in one voice. [Besides] party whips keep women MPs accountable to the party, not to women's issues (Comment at EISA Roundtable, February 1999).

It is not surprising that the driving force behind legislative reform to eliminate gender discrimination has been the ANC Women's Caucus, rather than the multi-party forum, reflecting the different weight given to gender equality by different political parties. Individual feminists in other parties have found it difficult to overcome the ideological resistance and lack of effective internal structures within their parties.

By the 1999 elections, women's organisations were much more sceptical of the extent to which women MPs represented women's interests rather than party or even personal political interests. The issue of accountability emerged very forcefully in various electoral forums.[11] Despite the deep concern with the idea of accountability in the women's movement, it remains an elusive notion, in part because the autonomy of women's organisations is not yet well established and in part because of the absence of an organisational centre in the women's movement that would field candidates and act as a source of political pressure. These factors have muddied understandings of accountability – accountability to parties? To women within parties? To all women?[12] Debates among gender activists have focused on both formal (to political parties) and moral (to the cause of gender equality) aspects of accountability. In both cases, however, ensuring accountability requires the consolidation of women – or even different groups of women – as a key constituency.

Ensuring formal accountability requires that women within political parties are relatively well-organised – both to enhance the effectiveness of women MPs within the legislative arena *and* to create internal party mechanisms for holding them accountable to women members and not just party leadership. There has been a tendency among women's organisations to conflate the tasks of building constituencies and representing constituencies. Women's sections of political parties (of which women MPs should ideally be active members) can play a significant role in articulating the interests of women supporters of their parties, and ensuring that these are addressed within the party's broad political platforms and electoral manifestos. In other words, such structures can be vital in the process of building a constituency of women in the party and of party supporters. If a representational strategy is to be pursued effectively, the ability of women's structures in parties to claim constituencies is crucial to their success within the party, as electoral politics centres on attracting votes. To the extent that women's wings of political parties can escape the role of 'catering committee', they would have to take on the tasks of grooming women leaders, and supporting them for internal party election. They would also have to function effectively as one among many conduits between women in Parliament and grassroots women. Without active women's sections within parties, women MPs can be left adrift, overburdened with the multiple tasks of committee work, party responsibilities and gender activism, and with no clear political direction (*vis-à-vis* gender) to their work. The primary task of women MPs should be to define areas of intervention in the legislature, and to support and report to women in the party: to *represent*, not to build, constituencies. The failure to separate these tasks has led to tensions between women in political parties and women's organisations in civil society (Comment by Barbara Watson at the GAP/AWEPA Conference, October 1998). There is also an expectation of moral accountability within the women's movement. The first cohort of women in Parliament was very aware of this responsibility, as it was argued that their election was the product of collective struggles. Mavivi Manzini, for example, argues strongly that 'women in parliament are not an élite; they take their lead from the ordinary mass of women' (Comment at EISA Roundtable, February 1999). Many women MPs made enormous efforts to consult with civil society, and to share information and build strategies collectively, despite the pressures of being pioneers. Joyce Kgoali, a trade unionist who became an MP in 1994, suggests that 'it is important that there are women's structures outside parliament. Without any support from outside it is pointless. Women parliamentarians must be part of these structures. During breaks in parliament women must go back and account to these structures' (*Speak* 1994).

However, the relative demobilisation of the women's movement since 1994 will result in fewer women on party lists who have long and deep connections to women's organisations. Without the moral and political pressure from outside Parliament, the danger exists that women MPs are unable (or increasingly unwilling) to represent the various interests of women adequately. Women's gains in and through parliamentary representation are an important facet of the long-term battle to recognise women as agents in political processes, and to provide voices for women in the various arenas of public decision making. It is important, however, to maintain a critical tension between MPs and government bureaucrats – male and female – who claim to be speaking on behalf of women and the constituencies in whose name these claims are made. Without strong mechanisms for upholding accountability, representation carries little power to advance the agenda of gender equality.

Representation and accountability: political parties post-1994

Women's entry into representative politics in large numbers opened questions of how electoral politics, institutional restructuring (of Parliament as well as party), and constituency/interest group mobilisation could be made to work in women's interests.

Women representatives were constrained by both external political conditions and internal cultural and institutional blockages to their effectiveness. Despite the many formal enabling conditions for gender equality, there is no social consensus in South Africa as to the political significance of women's interests relative to other issues of empowerment (most notably race). No significant differences between women and men on electoral issues or party preferences have been found by any of the electoral surveys, suggesting that the connections between gender inequalities and the position of women are either not recognised or are considered unimportant by women voters in South Africa (Gouws 1999). The attempt to mobilise the women's vote separately by the Women's Party during the 1994 election was singularly unsuccessful.[13] Many of the gains made at the formal level were won as a result of élite persuasion rather than by a mass movement of women. Commitments to the principles of gender equality were in effect negotiated by one sector of the women's movement with the leadership of a progressive party before it came to power (Hassim 2002). This 'negotiated revolution' from women's perspective has not yet developed deep social legitimacy for the values of gender equality and justice. The shallowness of support for gender equality has impacted on the process of building an electoral constituency, as the broad population of women voters did not appear to be convinced of the need to elect women into positions of power.

Stereotypes of women's (in)abilities as leaders persist, despite the greater visibility of women in politics. Anecdotal evidence of this abounds among women in political parties – women are regarded, even by other women, as incompetent, weak leaders (Comments by women MPs at CGE Gender Dialogue, June 1998). Where they do succeed, they are often held up for ridicule. As one newspaper article commented, strong women (and particularly black women) are regarded as a 'nuisance'.

> Their refusal to be cowed by disapproval has turned them into threatening objects of derision and even, it may be argued, icons of emasculation – a response that is in stark contrast to powerful black male role models who are seen as unthreatening and forgiving (*Sunday Times* 25 October 1998).[14]

Despite these constraints, the influx of women MPs impacted on Parliament as issues of washroom facilities, childcare and working hours had to be addressed to create a women-friendly institution. However, the 'critical mass' of *feminist* activists – rather than women as a group – also had a significant impact in ensuring that issues of gender equality would be raised. Although the *number* of women in Parliament was significant, re-shaping legislative priorities and reform measures was the work of feminists, MPs with a political commitment to gender equality. As Deputy Speaker Baleka Kgositsile pointed out, 'our achievement will be measured not just by getting to Parliament but what we do when we get there' (Comment at GAP/AWEPA Conference, October 1998).

The weakness of the multi-party Parliamentary Women's Group was a strong indication of the shallowness of common interest among women from different parties. Aside from the ANC, parties lacked a history of internal party struggle around equality. Gender work in the Democratic Party, for example, tended to be focused externally; inside the party the mainstreaming approach led to the effective invisibility of issues of gender equality. In the New National Party, the women's structure has not moved beyond its traditional role of tea parties and fundraising to raise issues of power inside the party. Neither the Democratic Party nor the New National Party have women's caucuses in parliament. As a result, women in the ANC take the lead on issues of gender equality in parliament, while other parties are reactive and sometimes resentful of the perceived dominance of the ANC MPs (Interview with Sheila Camerer, NNP MP, June 1999). Furthermore, it was difficult to maintain the façade of common interests when women in the National Party and the Democratic Party voted against legislation such as the Employment Equity Act, legislation that had been shaped by ANC women MPs to ensure greater protection for women workers.

But even within the ANC, the form of party institutionalisation has not always been conducive to the articulation of feminist claims. Centralist elements within the party have been strengthened as power within the party has increasingly come to be a stepping stone to power within the government. Increasingly, those in the party leadership who are associated with government positions are considered to be more powerful in agenda setting within the ANC. The Deputy Secretary-General of the ANC, Thenjiwe Mtintso, points out that even within the ANC, critics of government's failure to address inequalities are met with the response that they do not understand the exigencies of government.

> There is a tendency to want to close ranks on particular issues and say you don't have the broader picture. You're in Shell House (ANC Headquarters), you don't understand government responsibilities. These matters sometimes divert us.... They don't owe us anything, they are elected in their own right. So they are not accountable to 'these women' and 'these feminists'. Who are they, we've got our own political agenda (Comments at Wits Gender Seminar, 22 May 2001).

The ANC's Deployment Committee makes key decisions on which senior members of the party will be moved into key posts such as provincial premiers, mayors and heads of parastatal organisations. The leadership of the movement is able to use the PR electoral system to shift MPs around according to party leadership dictates.[15] A widely held view is that this power is sometimes used to sideline or silence critics within the party. An example often cited among feminist activists is the 'deployment' of Cheryl Carolus, a prominent United Women's Organisation (UWO) and United Democratic Front (UDF) leader. Carolus was one of only two women in the delegation that met with F. W. de Klerk to begin the negotiations process. In 1994 she was elected Deputy Secretary-General[16] and later Acting Secretary-General (reportedly only after other more favoured candidates had turned down the position). One columnist commented that 'she has stepped on too many toes. She attacked party positions, embarrassed ANC ministers and disagreed with influential members of the organisation' (cited in Stadler 1997: 7).

Carolus was later appointed High Commissioner to London, 'out of harm's way' according to a source within the Secretary-General's office.[17] Stadler comments that the deployment process suggests 'the declining importance of civic associations in relation to the ANC as well as the relatively lesser importance of the party in central administration compared with the party in office' (Stadler 1997: 7). In this more constrained party context, women MPs and ministers might find it difficult to articulate policy positions that differ sharply from those of the party leadership. The tendency of the PR system to favour accountability to the party rather than to particular constituencies may therefore hamper rather than facilitate the development of substantive representation over descriptive representation in the long term.

There are other reasons why an over-reliance on feminists within the party has many limitations. As IFP MP Suzanne Vos has pointed out, women MPs are hostage to hierarchical and male-dominated parties where the gender ticket is not the route to party power (Vos 1999). One ANC woman MP commented that 'we are there to represent women but at the same time one has to be careful because at the next election you could be pushed off the list. You have to take account of party loyalties' (Comment made on condition of anonymity, October 1998). In Cabinet women are bound by loyalty and are dependent on the leadership for their ministerial positions. Cabinet is

> structured in a hierarchical way, even if this is not openly talked of. There
> are unspoken rules, including how we sit, which allocates a certain role

to juniors. When I spoke at my first *lekgotla*, I had the feeling from some remarks that maybe I'd been out of turn, even though what I said had been acknowledged.... Maybe we need a caucus of women in Cabinet but there is the problem of space and time to sustain the caucus. But there is an attempt to support one another (Interview with Nozizwe Routledge Madlala, Deputy Minister of Defence, 7 September 2000).

These concerns are heightened by indications that the 'consolidation' phase of democratisation in South Africa is characterised by the increasing centralisation of power within the presidency (Marais 1998), and by a seeming attack on the role of Parliament and particularly the committee system which is the key forum through which executive accountability is measured. The degree of robust debate in Parliament and the public sphere suggests that there is no fundamental threat to democracy, but the tendency of the central party leadership to reassert control indicates a weakening of the ANC's internal democracy.

One avenue through which internal party accountability to its women supporters might be pursued is through its women's section, the ANC Women's League. The League has automatic representation on the ANC's highest decision-making body, and has the formal responsibility of representing women within the party. However, aside from the brief period of the WNC when the League articulated a strong feminist position, it has not managed to break free of its 'tea-making' role. Despite the fact that the League's president, Winnie Madikizela-Mandela, is an outspoken critic of the ANC's leadership (on issues other than gender), the League has not taken a consistent position on gender issues or assumed any leadership role in the women's movement. The League's long period of exile hindered the development of an organised con-stituency among women, and after 1994 it put very little energy into building branches and consolidating its membership base. In 1995, young feminists who were frustrated with the internal difficulties within the League resigned their membership of key positions and put their energies into the party as a whole. Within a very short space of time, the League returned to its more familiar role as auxiliary to the party, having little capacity to offer political leadership within the women's movement.

The failures of the League, as well as the women's sections within other parties, highlight the vacuum that can be created when institu-tional channels for representation of women's interests within political parties are weak. Without feminist-driven women's sections within parties, women representatives can be overburdened with the multiple tasks of committee work, party responsibilities and gender activism and may lack a sense of direct accountability to women supporters of the party. Even where women politicians might take seriously their representative roles – as the first cohort of women in the South African parliament did – the task of *building* constituencies cannot be done by individuals.

One long-term positive outcome of struggles for political representation is that political parties are being forced to consider women as an important voting constituency. Research conducted by the Commission on Gender Equality prior to the 1999 election showed that all parties had identified women as 'voting populations' (Seedat and Kimani 1999: 40). Parties emphasised the need to recruit women and to increase women's participation in party structures, not least because women form the majority of supporters of the two largest political parties in the country. The Democratic Party's audit of party membership indicates that 40 per cent of its branch chairpersons and 33 per cent of its local councillors are women (CGE/PWG 1999: 102), although only 18 per cent of its MPs are women. The party's leading feminist, Dene Smuts, argues that this shows that quotas are unnecessary: 'It's automatic. If there is a good candidate, she will be elected. People do not think twice about it now' (*ibid.*: 102).

Representation: an effective strategy?

The relative success of women in increasing their numerical representation begs the question of how they have used their electoral leverage to address the substantive issue of women's inequalities. Despite the numerical success, the difficulties of working in a male-dominated terrain,[18] the extra burdens of committee work on the relatively few women MPs, and a deepening rift between women MPs and women's organisations all worried many activists. In one of the first studies conducted on the experience of women MPs, Hannah Britton found high levels of stress and suggested that many women MPs might not stand for election again (Britton 1997).[19] As ANC MP Thenjiwe Mtintso points out, 'the quota was seen as a double-edged sword: providing opportunities but also adding burdens for women representatives' (Mtintso 1999: 53). Mtintso's own research, conducted in the latter part of the first Parliament, found that women MPs had overcome some of the cultural and institutional constraints on their participation. MPs she interviewed reported greater confidence, support and commitment as a result of experience with the technical processes (*ibid.*: 56). She reports that the women 'developed excitement and confidence when tracing what could be attributable to their own participation and contribution. The woman MP can proudly say at the end, 'this is mine. I did it for this country, for myself and for the women' (ibid.: 57).

The cultural and institutional difficulties described above had real impacts on the effectiveness of women MPs. As Nancy Fraser has pointed out, the removal of formal blockages on women's participation in the representative sphere is undercut continuously by patterns of deliberation that uphold particular power relations. Drawing on Mansbridge, she argues that 'deliberation can mask domination', as 'social inequalities can infect deliberation, even in the absence of any formal exclusions' (Fraser 1997: 79). While political parties, particularly the ANC, trumpeted the large number of women in Parliament, their underlying ethos was that party loyalty, rather than loyalty to con-stituencies such as women, was primary. Women MPs were in any case not all committed to feminist ideals, and, under party leadership pressure and belittling of the importance of gender,[20] many did not identify openly with feminist agendas. Suzanne Vos comments that male dominance and patronage inhibit the articulation of feminism. 'There is no doubt that the PR/List system ensures that all politicians must remain popular with (mostly male) party bosses to survive. Male leader-ship also invariably selects which women are promoted within party structures and within Parliament. They decide who sits on what committee and who gets speaking time in the House, on what and when.... Survival instincts triumph.... Men are the game, they control the game' (Vos 1999: 108–9).

The constraints described above made it difficult for feminist MPs to define strategies for legislative intervention. The Parliamentary Women's Group failed to provide either a support structure or a lobbying point for women MPs. The ANC Women's Caucus, by contrast, acted as the key pressure point within Parliament, even within the multi-party Joint Standing Committee on the Improvement of the Quality of Life and Status of Women.[21] This committee, under the experienced chair of Pregs Govender,[22] provided an important institu-tional forum within which to identify a set of legislative priorities and begin to lobby for policy changes. Three far-reaching pieces of legislation were passed in the first term. The Termination of Pregnancy Act of 1996 provides women with access to abortion under broader and more favourable conditions than previously. The Domestic Violence Act of 1998 provides protection against abuse for people who are in domestic relationships, regardless of the specific nature of the relationship (whether marital, homosexual or family relationships). The Maintenance Act of 1998 substantially improves the position of mothers dependent on maintenance from former partners. In addition, a number of policy programmes, such as free health care for pregnant women and children, are explicitly directed at improving women's position.

These gains were made because of the linkages that existed between gender activists in civil society and the ANC, in particular (note, not solely) ANC women MPs. In the first years of the new Parliament, women MPs struggled to establish a role and gender equality was not prioritised as an area for legislative change. The three pieces of legislation were only placed on the parliamentary calendar in 1999, the last year of the first Parliament, and only after high-level lobbying by the ANC Women's Caucus with the support of progressive men MPs, including, by some accounts, President Mbeki. The legislation then had to be fast-tracked through the National Assembly so that the first Parliament would be seen to be concerned with gender equality as a substantive issue. The key advocates for the legislation were women MPs who in all likelihood would have been on the ANC list regardless of the quota, and male MPs who had a commitment to gender equality. Pressure to push the legislation through before the end of the first term came from gender activists outside the state.

In the case of the Termination of Pregnancy Act, the proposed legislation was consistent with the ANC's health policy and with its electoral platform (the Reconstruction and Development Programme, RDP), which included reproductive rights. Nevertheless, the passage of legislation was extremely slow. The legislation might have languished on the parliamentary calendar had it not been for the momentum of activism outside of Parliament by organisations such as the Reproductive Rights Alliance, which had been formed in 1995 in part to advocate for progressive pro-choice abortion legislation (Albertyn 1999: 69). As part of the consultative policy process established by the ANC government, several women's health and legal advocacy groups also made submissions to the *ad hoc* Committee on Abortion and Sterilisation constituted by Parliament in September 1994. Indeed, rather than interventions of women MPs *per se*, both Albertyn's and Meintjes's (in Chapter 5 below) accounts of policy reform suggest that it was the historical relationship of trust between activists outside government and the ANC that facilitated the passage of legislation. As Albertyn points out, 'These relationships meant that civil society was able to access decision makers within the ANC, engage them directly on the issue and provide information and support' (Albertyn 1999: 79).

Despite these capacities and networks, women MPs made little impact on key areas of policy such as finance. Despite their numbers and their presence in the highest forums of Parliament, women Cabinet ministers were unable to question or even facilitate debate within the ruling party on macro-economic policy. During the first Parliament, the ANC shifted from the redistributive RDP (the party's election manifesto in 1994) to a policy of fiscal constraint (the Growth, Employment and Redistribution policy, GEAR). This shift removed the enabling discursive environment within which the policy demands of women's organisations could be articulated. The RDP had been drafted with extensive participation of women in the ANC, and provided detailed proposals for the integration of gender into most sectors of government policy. Unlike the final constitution, the RDP firmly argued that gender equality should override customary law. Key shifts away from the RDP thus represented in some measure both a less participatory approach to policy formulation and the narrowing of decision making in the policy arena to an élite within government. 'Cabinet loyalty' precluded open opposition to the new macro-economic policy which, arguably, dramatically constrained the government's ability to effectively implement policies outlined in the RDP, many of which required increasing expenditure. In part this was a consequence of the decision by the President and the Ministry of Finance to place the macro-economic framework outside party debate and make it a 'non-negotiable' aspect of ANC policy. The weak response of women MPs (and most male MPs) to this centralisation and hierarchisation reflects the extent to which a PR system can undermine both internal party accountability as well as accountability to voter constituencies.

This situation poses a number of dilemmas for women activists in South Africa – and in other African contexts. How can *feminists* gain access to influential positions within the party and within Parliament? How do feminists within political parties balance the often contesting aims of women's advancement and party loyalty? How can women's movements mitigate the perverse consequences of demands for greater representation of women in elected office: in particular, the emergence of élite women leaders with relations of dependency to parties rather than to constituencies of women?

In part, the answer lies in the extent to which party and state organisation can affect the capacity of the women's movement to sustain a relationship of solidarity with women politicians which at the same time includes demands for accountability to a female constituency. Equally important is the extent to which these moments of transition can be used by women to recruit support from *men* who support substantive equality within the party. The extent to which *feminists* find spaces within political parties, through demands for representation – even merely descriptive representation – is also central. From this point of view, the tendency in the literature to consider descriptive and substantive representation of women as different kinds of strategies is misleading;[23] rather, the 'minimal' demand for a numerical increase in women's representation can become the grounds upon which a deeper struggle may be fought.

The apparent paradox in South Africa between the demands of women as an identifiable constituency in electoral politics, and the internal debates about different interests within that constituency suggests that women's politics is conducted simultaneously at two levels. At an external level of politics, a narrow terrain of common purpose is mapped out, articulated and defended, while at an internal level there is vigorous contestation over specific policies and party political manifestos. This tendency in women's politics seems counterproductive: it may be argued that women might do better in terms of increasing their political leverage if their external (in this case electoral) politics was directed at articulating their interests within the framework of party-political contestation, rather than a non-partisan, 'common front' approach. However, this dual politics is the outcome of the need for women to simultaneously build a constituency that will have political leverage – to present the illusion of a united constituency, if you will – *and* articulate the diverse interests of women arising from the intersections of race, class and gender inequalities. However, without some form of autonomous women's movement located in civil society, or in other words, without a women's movement that is driven by women's organisations rather than women in parties, it is unlikely that the policy demands of different groups of women will be addressed.

Appendix 1 Women MPs in national legislature by party affiliation, 1994

Political party	No. of women MPs	Women MPs as % of total MPs of party
African National Congress	90	35.7
National Party	9	10.0
Inkatha Freedom Party	10	23.3
Freedom Front	0	0.0
Democratic Party	1	14.0
Pan Africanist Congress	1	20.0
African Christian Democratic Party	0	0.0
TOTAL	111	27.7

Source: Government of South Africa 1997

Appendix 2 Women MPs in national legislature by party affiliation, 1999[24]

Political party	No. of women MPs	Women MPs as % of total MPs of party
African National Congress	96	36.0
United Democratic Movement	2	14.3
United Christian Democratic Party	0	0
Minority Front	0	0
AZAPO	0	0
National Party	3	10.7
AEB	0	0
Inkatha Freedom Party	7	20.6
Freedom Front	0	0
Democratic Party	7	15.8
Pan Africanist Congress	1	33.3
African Christian Democratic Party	2	33.3
TOTAL	118	29.5

References

Agenda (1994) 'Key Questions for Election Candidates', *Agenda*, 20.

Albertyn, C. (ed.) (1999) *Engendering the Political Agenda: a South African Case Study*, Johannesburg: Centre for Applied Legal Studies (CALS).

Alvarez, S. (1990) *Engendering Democracy in Brazil: Women's Movements in Transition Politics*, Princeton: Princeton University Press.

Ballington, J. (1998) 'Women's Parliamentary Representation: the Effects of List PR', *Politikon*, 25, 2.

—— (1999) 'Political Parties and Gender Equality: What Do the Manifestos Say?' *Election Update*, 14.

Britton, H. (1997) 'Preliminary Report on Participation: Challenges and Strategies', unpublished report, Syracuse University.

CGE/PWG (1999) *Redefining Politics: South African Women and Democracy*, Braamfontein: Commission on Gender Equality/Parliamentary Women's Group.

Fraser, N. (1997) *Justice Interruptus: Reflections on the 'Postsocialist' Condition*, New York: Routledge.

Gouws, A. (1999) 'The Gender Dimension of the 1999 Election', in A. Reynolds (ed.), *Election '99 South Africa: from Mandela to Mbeki*, Cape Town: David Phillip.

Government of South Africa (1997) *CEDAW Report*, Pretoria: Government Printers.

Hassim, S. (2002) '"A Conspiracy of Women": the Women's Movement in South Africa's Transition to Democracy', *Social Research*, 69, 3.

Hirst, P. (1990) *Representative Democracy and Its Limits*, London: Polity Press.

Jacquette, J. S. and S. L. Wolchik (eds.) (1998) *Women and Democracy: Latin America and Central and Eastern Europe*, Baltimore: Johns Hopkins University Press.

Lovenduski, J. (1986) *Women and European Politics – Contemporary Feminism and Public Politics*, Brighton: Wheatsheaf Books.

Marais, H. (1998) *South Africa: Limits to Change*, London: Zed Books.

Matland, R. and M. Taylor (1997) 'Electoral Systems' Effect on Women's Representation: Theoretical Arguments and Evidence from Costa Rica', *Comparative Political Studies*, 30, 2: 186–210.

Moon, J. and I. Fountain (1997) 'Keeping the Gates? Women as Ministers in Australia, 1970–96', *Australian Journal of Political Science*, 32, 3.

Mtintso, T. E. (1999) 'The Contribution of Women Parliamentarians to Gender Equality', unpublished MA thesis, University of the Witwatersrand.

Phillips, A. (1991) *Engendering Democracy*, Pennsylvania: University of Pennsylvania Press.

—— (1995) *The Politics of Presence*, Oxford: Clarendon Press.

Randall, V. (1987) *Women and Politics: an International Perspective*, London: Macmillan.

Reynolds, A. (1998) 'Women in African Legislatures', unpublished EISA discussion paper.

Seedat, F. and L. Kimani (1999) 'Gender profile of parties', in CGE/PWG, *Redefining Politics: South African Women and Democracy*, Braamfontein: CGE/PWG.

Speak (1994) 'Women in Power', *Speak*, 62.

Stadler, A. (1997) 'The Rise and Decline of Party Activism in South Africa', paper presented to the African Studies Seminar Series, Wits University, October.

Vos, S. (1999) 'Women in Parliament: a Personal Perspective', in CGE/PWG, *Redefining Politics: South African Women and Democracy*, Braamfontein: CGE/PWG.

Williams, M. S. (1998) *Voice, Trust and Memory: Marginalized Groups and the Failings of Liberal Representation*, Princeton: Princeton University Press.

Young, I. M. (1990) *Justice and the Politics of Difference*, Princeton: Princeton University Press.

Zondo, Ntomb'futhi (1994) 'Women and the Vote', *Agenda*, 57.

Notes

1 This chapter is based on ten interviews conducted between 1999 and 2001 with women parliamentarians. In addition, I attended and/or chaired several workshops, seminars and discussions involving women parliamentarians and activists in civil society. These include the CGE Gender Dialogue, June 1998; the GAP/AWEPA Conference, 'Women at the Crossroads/Women in Governance', Cape Town, October 1998; EISA Roundtable, 'Putting Women in Power', Johannesburg, February 1999; NISAA Forum on 'Women and Politics', March 1999. I was part of the Gender and Elections Reference Group convened by the Electoral Institute of Southern Africa and a member of the editorial group of *Election Bulletin*.

2 The ANC Women's League took an especially strong stance over women's representation in constitutional negotiations, threatening to boycott the first non-racial elections with the slogan 'no women, no vote'. Although it is unlikely that it would have been able to organise a women's boycott of the elections successfully, the threat exposed the limitations of claims to democracy by progressive political organisations.

3 Although gender inequalities should be a matter of concern for both men and women, it has generally been women who have politicised gender issues and who, because of their subordinate position, are most likely to raise issues of unequal power.

4 However, they have not succeeded in winning a quota for elections to positions within the party's structures.

5 The Electoral Act requires that all registered political parties and candidates subscribe to an Electoral Code of Conduct designed to promote conditions that are conducive to free and fair elections. These include the tolerance of democratic political activity, and free political campaigning and open public debate. Item 6 of the Code specifically requires political parties to give effect to the rights of women.

6 The Deputy Minister of this 'hard' portfolio, Nozizwe Routledge Madlala, is both a feminist activist and a Quaker.

7 They are Phumzile Mlambo-Ngcuka, formerly Deputy Minster of Trade and Industry, and Susan Shabangu, who retains her post.

8 *Agenda*, 1994, "Key Questions for Election Candidates", *Agenda*, No. 20, p. 7.

The questions related to the valuing of women's unpaid labour, provision of childcare facilities and welfare support, greater representation of women in party structures, policies on violence against women and maternity leave, educational and literacy policies, support for women's human rights, women's access to land, housing and pension, pay equity, and differential taxation.

9 In a notable example, the Commission on Gender Equality expressed its discontent with the quality of party presentations at its Gender Dialogue on the Election in June 1998. Echoing this, the Deputy Speaker of the Gauteng Legislature, Lindiwe Zulu, commented that 'there was nothing earth shattering about the presentations…. This is not acceptable. It is an insult and disservice to women.' The report was sent to all political parties (CGE, 'Women Politics and Elections: a Gender Dialogue Report').

10 Culminating in a front-page lead in the Johannesburg daily, *The Star*, entitled 'One Woman, One Vote Is the Key to Power: Majority of Voters are Female – and They Mean Business' (5 May 1999).

11 These included the CGE Gender Dialogue in June 1998, the AWEPA/GAP conference, 'Women at the Crossroads: Women and Governance' in October 1998, and the EISA roundtable, "Putting Women into Power', in February 1999.

12 For example, the question of whether Congress of South African Trade Unions (COSATU) women MPs represented the union or working-class women was not clarified by candidates interviewed by Fiona Dove in 'Questions of Accountability', *Agenda*, 20 (1994): 53.

13 The Women's Party, led by feminist artist Nina Romm, was unable to secure a single seat in Parliament, despite the relatively low cut-off threshold.

14 Following her proposal of stringent anti-smoking legislation, Health Minister Nkosazana Zuma had been the subject of a *Hustler* magazine article that portrayed her as 'the underpaid domestic worker who sadly escaped degradation and became a medical doctor'. Readers were advised to cut out the picture of Zuma that accompanied the article and place it on their toilet seat.

15 In the most recent example, MP Andrew Feinstein, ANC representative on the parliamentary committee on public accounts, was removed from his position as head of the ANC's study group after pushing for an investigation into the government's R3 billion arms deal, against the wishes of the President. Justifying this 'redeployment', the ANC's parliamentary whip said the study group was being 'strengthened so that the ANC, from the President downwards, could exercise political control' (*Sunday Times* 4 February 2001. The *Sunday Times* journalist noted that 'nothing would go from the committee to the plenary of the National Assembly without first going through the caucus and any leaks would be investigated' (*ibid.*).

16 Several interviewees laughingly referred to the post of Deputy Secretary-General as the burial ground for militant feminist activists, citing the subsequent redeployment of Thenjiwe Mtintso from the CGE, where she was successfully establishing an independent and forceful organisation, to this post as evidence.

17 In July 2001 Carolus announced that she was taking up a position as head of Tourism South Africa, a non-political job.

18 Many male MPs, even within the ANC, saw women's presence as token gestures to equality. One male MP commented to Thenjiwe Mtintso: '[Men]

don't think that this woman comrade is there because in her own name and right she deserves to be there. What also happens is that because of the quotas even in delegations abroad some women comrades go ten times more even before some male comrades have ever had a single chance to go. Some of these women comrades are almost like flowers that must decorate every delegation.' (Mtintso 1999: 52.)

19 'Linda', a woman MP interviewed by Mtintso, commented in 1995 that 'this place gives me the creeps. It is unfriendly and unwelcoming. It was meant to make the people feel the power, even in the building itself. I feel overwhelmed and completely disempowered. I cannot see myself making any input never mind impact here. I feel lost. I do not think I will even finish my term of office.' (Mtintso 1999: 56).

20 Feminists who spoke up in the National Assembly were laughingly called 'that lot who went to Beijing' (Vos 1999: 108).

21 This committee was initially established as an *ad hoc* committee to oversee the implementation of the UN Convention on the Elimination of All Forms of Discrimination against Women (CEDAW). Skilful lobbying by feminists within the ANC resulted in its upgrading into a proper standing committee, able to command parliamentary resources (such as a researcher) and regular slots on the parliamentary timetable.

22 Govender was the project manager of the Women's National Coalition and a leading union and women's organiser. She has recently retired from Parliament.

23 Although I would agree with Anne Phillips (1995) that these strategies may be based on vastly different and contradictory assumptions about the nature of the political system, and the roles and capacities of women to impact on the underlying values and institutions of democracies.

24 These calculations were made by Julie Ballington at the Electoral Institute of Southern Africa, based on party lists and electoral results.

4

The Problem with Patronage: Constraints on Women's Political Effectiveness in Uganda

ANNE MARIE GOETZ[1]

One of the many achievements for which Yoweri Kaguta Museveni's government in Uganda has been applauded internationally is the increase in the numbers of women in representative politics from the national legislature (25 per cent of MPs are women as of the June 2001 parliamentary elections) down through all five tiers of local government (where women average 30 per cent of local councillors). High-profile appointments of women to senior civil service positions have also significantly enhanced women's presence in the administration. These increases in women's public presence have been accomplished through the creation and reservation of new seats in national and local government for women, and through a principle of affirmative action in administrative appointments. This chapter considers how the means of women's access to politics has affected their legitimacy and effectiveness in policy making. Particular attention is paid to the extent to which women have benefited or lost from the suspension of party competition in Uganda's 'no-party' democracy. The relatively non-democratic means of women's access to power through reservations and affirmative action has been effective in ensuring their rapid promotion through the 'benevolent autocracy' (Norris 1993: 329) that Museveni's government represents (at least as far as women are concerned). But this has been at the cost of politically internalised safeguards on these gains. Without institutionalised parties, and without a democratic decision-making structure within Museveni's 'Movement', women have no means of asserting their rights to be fronted as candidates in open elections, of bringing membership pressure to bear on party executives to introduce gender sensitivity in the staffing of party posts, or of using the dynamic of multi-party competition to develop political clout around a gendered voting gap. Instead, they have been recruited to the project of legitimising the

110

THE PROBLEM WITH PATRONAGE

Movement's no-party state, risking the discrediting of the entire project of representing women's interests in the political arena should the present system collapse.

The association of party competition with ethnic violence in Uganda,[1] and the historical lack of interest that parties showed in promoting women's interests, led many women and feminists inside and outside of Uganda to give a cautiously positive reception to the National Resistance Movement's 'temporary' suspension of party competition when it came to power in 1986. This freed women from the near-impossible task of getting party backing for their candidacies. New reserved seats for women in Parliament and local government freed some women politicians from competing with men, and Museveni's willingness to appoint women to important posts in the public administration and the judiciary seemed to make a major crack in the 'glass ceiling' which so often holds able professional women back. This chapter will begin by explaining the initial relative enthusiasm of women and other social groups for Museveni's 'no-party' democracy in the context of Uganda's history of ethnic conflict. I will then describe the 'no-party' political system in Uganda, and go on to detail the measures taken to bring greater numbers of women into politics. I will review the record of women politicians in promoting gender equity in important new legislation on property rights and domestic relations. And I will consider how women's presence and interests have been institutionalised in the National Resistance Movement (NRM) itself to consider the longer-term prospects for women's influence on policy making.

Antipathy to political parties in Uganda

As noted in chapters 1 and 2, there is a strong tradition in feminist political science and activism which has been sceptical about the capacity of liberal or bourgeois democracy either to include women amongst decision makers, or to admit of meaningful representation of their interests. This has led to an interest in alternatives to liberal representative democracy, particularly any measures which support the principle of group representation for women in politics – through, for instance, affirmative action measures to put some minimum number of women in political and bureaucratic positions, or to give representative groups of social and political minorities some powers of review in policy making which affects their interests (Young 1990). The dismal track record of mainstream political parties in representing women's interests

111

or fronting women candidates has produced a tradition of antipathy to political parties in women's movements the world over.

The association of party competition in Uganda with ghastly ethnic conflict has encouraged the antipathy to parties of many women and other social groups. No single party has been able to transcend limited constituencies based on religion, ethnicity, language or region. The two most significant parties, in terms of size of membership and role in post-colonial Ugandan politics, are the Democratic Party, founded in 1956, and the Uganda People's Congress, founded in 1958. The DP is a party of Catholics with its power base in the South. It has never been in office. The UPC is supported by the Protestant church and is strongest in the North, though it has been in and out of alliances with the people of Buganda – the largest and most powerful ethnic group, based in the centre of the country. The interests of the Baganda people, who still dominate the administration but have never come close to capturing power, have been represented variously by the Kabaka Yekka (Kabaka [King] Alone) party at the time of independence, and the Conservative Party now.

Uganda's first independent government was formed by the UPC in alliance with the Kabaka Yekka, in opposition to the Catholic DP. But the UPC clashed with Buganda, and in 1966 Obote suspended the constitution, declared a one-party state, and banished the political kingdoms, sending the Kabaka into exile. Amin's 1971 coup installed people of his Western Nile region in power. This paradigmatic homicidal military phallocrat did not, of course, bother with parties, vesting all executive and legislative powers in his own person. In the elections held after the 1980 Tanzanian invasion which put an end to Amin's regime, it is thought that victory was stolen from the DP by UPC election fraud (Human Rights Watch 1999: 34). Also failing badly in that election was a small new party, the Ugandan Patriotic Movement, formed by the Defence Minister in the transitional government: Yoweri Kaguta Museveni. He promptly turned to armed rebellion against the increasingly despotic Obote regime.

Neither the UPC nor the DP had a commitment to advance women's interests in politics, although the UPC did support a number of 'Women in Development' initiatives which were beginning to attract foreign funding in the first half of the 1980s. Neither party challenged conservative ethnic and religious conventions about women's social, economic, or political rights and roles. Both parties had women's wings through which women party members were expected to provide a hostessing service for leaders. There were some prominent women politicians prior to 1986, such as Cecilia Ogwal and Mary Okwa Okol in the UPC. After 1986 other women have made an impact outside of the NRM, such as Maria Mutagamba and Juliet Rainer Kafire in the DP. These are not 'token' representatives of women. They were hard-core party activists who had made it up through the ranks. While these women did not see themselves as representing women's interests in politics and have never taken a feminist stance in policy debates, it is perhaps not surprising that frustration with the sclerotic leaderships and slavish sycophancy of the middle ranks prompted women such as Ogwal in the UPC and Maria Mutagamba in the DP to struggle for internal party reform in the post-1986 period, and eventually either form breakaway factions, or leave their parties altogether and join the NRM.

The 'no-party' system

The very first official act of the NRM government after the military triumph of the National Resistance Army (NRA) was the suspension of party politics.[2] From the start, Museveni promoted an alternative and, he argues, particularly Uganda-appropriate version of democratic politics. It is based on the notion that all Ugandans can compete for office without party backing, but on the basis of their 'individual merit'. The democratic content of this 'no-party' system is grounded in the multiplication of opportunities for ordinary people to participate in decision making through the local government Resistance Council (RC) system. Museveni justifies the continued suppression of party competition on the grounds that parties exacerbate ethnic conflict in Uganda (Museveni 1997: 187; Kasfir 1998: 60).

The system has evolved through various self-imposed moments of reckoning, each of which has stiffened the executive's resistance to political competition, and provided occasions for winnowing out more democratically minded members of the NRM. These moments include the extended process of national consultation over a new constitution (1989–94), the Constituent Assembly debates to finalise the new constitution (1994–5), and the referendum on political systems of 29 June 2000. Since the passing of the Movement Act in 1997, the 'no-party' system has been known as the 'Movement' system. This Act gives the 'Movement' privileged constitutional status, where it is described as the country's political system, a system which prohibits parties from functioning through elections (though they are not formally banned), and will do so until a national majority recalls the system through a referendum. The 1997 Movement Act creates a new set of local council structures paralleling the existing system, and culminating in a National Movement Conference and a permanent secretariat. Membership in the local Movement Councils is mandatory for all Ugandans, and all members of Parliament are obliged to be members of the National Conference. The Movement Secretariat, located across the street from the national Parliament, has a budget vote, and indeed the entire Movement structure is directly funded by the Ugandan state, making it a bureaucracy supported by taxpayers, not by its own members' contributions.

Although the system is obviously inspired by other one-party states in Africa, Museveni has been at pains to distinguish the NRM's regime from them. However, there is tremendous ambiguity over what exactly the system is. As Schlichte notes, 'Even the description of that system is a matter of intense debate and this fact highlights the importance of the question [of] who is entitled to compete with whom about what' (2000: 18). David Apter describes the system as a 'consultative democracy' (1997: lxviii), in which various measures are used to share opportunities for the enjoyment of political office with excluded groups or with potential opposition groups. The NRM has another name for this consultative spirit: 'broad-based' governance – the notion of embracing as many different interests within the NRM as possible. However, the mechanics of achieving this 'broad-based' character have never been clearly spelled out, and it seems that it is left to the discretion of Museveni to decide who or what groups are included (Besigye 2000).

The first and highly successful demonstration of this consultative spirit was the way the Uganda Constitutional Commission (1988–93) conducted seminars in all of Uganda's 870 sub-counties, specifically consulting socially excluded groups such as women, and collected over 25,000 submissions. Another expression of this consultative mode was the introduction, after 1989, of a range of affirmative action measures to institutionalise a voice in politics for certain social groups: women, the disabled, youth, and workers. Women have been the most spectacular beneficiaries of these measures, which began in 1989 with the reservation of one seat for a secretary of women's affairs on each RC council, and the selection, through an electoral college composed of RC leaders, of one woman from each district to sit on the National Resistance Council (NRC).

Reconciliation of social differences and moderation of ethnic tensions have also been approached through the restoration of some of the traditional kingdoms, most notably the powerful Buganda kingdom in 1995. This was an important form of compensation to Buganda for the regime's failure to pass a constitutional amendment giving it federal status in the 1994–5 constitutional debates. The restoration of traditional leaders and the revived cultural rights enjoyed by tribes can conflict, however, with the equal rights granted to women in the constitution, since customary laws tend to subordinate women's property and personal rights to men's. Another strategy for the moderation of ethnic tensions has been the creation of ever more numerous new districts to channel development resources and political status to smaller ethnic sub-groups. Six new districts were created just before the 1996 presidential elections to satisfy disgruntled ethnic groups (Muhereza and Otim 1997:5), and eleven new districts, some absurdly tiny, were created in late 2000, just in time for the 2001 presidential elections.

Museveni's vision of consultative democracy does not rule out opposition. However, as Apter notes, it is opposition of a 'barometric' kind – one that helps the leadership identify unpopular government actions and public grievances and thereby acts as a signal to the executive to change direction. It 'is useful as a guide to what needs to be done, but is not in any way an instrument of state accountability, nor an electoral threat' (1997: lxxi). Reconciliation and the representation of social differences were initially approached through the formation of a highly inclusive coalition government in which important representatives of all active political parties were given significant Cabinet positions. This coalition has narrowed over time, both because of the disaffection of opposition members with official corruption and government complicity in human rights violations, and because of a narrowing and tightening of the army and southern-based clique around the President (Human Rights Watch 1999). Pains are still taken to assign political and administrative positions to people across the spectrum of sectarian and other affiliations, but the result is now not so much reconciliation as intrigue and clientelism as people compete for access to prebends and opportunities to dispense patronage. In other words, the representation of social differences is approached as a strategy for palliating the ambitions of other parties to have access to power and economic resources, not as a way of building accountability.

The 'Movement' continues to resist definition as a political party, because of course otherwise it would be in violation of Article 269 of the constitution which controls party activities. Critics, however, are at pains to advertise the many ways in which it does nevertheless act as a party: actively campaigning for its candidates during elections, with a distinct active membership composed of the 'historicals' involved in the guerrilla war and newer members, and with its caucus in Parliament

(Human Rights Watch 1999: 59). Its rural structures (the local Movement Councils paralleling the local government system) were used in the June 2000 referendum to mobilise support for the government's position, just as a political party's branch structures might have been employed to support a political campaign.

Women's engagement with the National Resistance Movement

Women's professional organisations, religious associations, non-governmental development organisations, rural self-help groups and feminist policy advocacy groups have thrived under the NRM, constituting, according to Aili Mari Tripp's detailed study of the Ugandan women's movement, 'one of the strongest mobilised societal forces in Uganda' (Tripp 2000: 23), and indeed, 'one of the strongest women's movements in Africa' (*ibid.*: 25). This was not the case at the moment of the NRA's victory in 1986, when what remained of autonomous women's associations had been driven underground by the efforts of Uganda's authoritarian rulers to coopt and control the country's female constituency. Amin, for instance, had banned independent women's organisations, while Obote had absorbed major women's associations into what was in effect a women's wing of the UPC (prior to 1971), and tried to transform the national umbrella body for women's associations, the Amin-era National Council of Women, into a party organ (after 1979).

Though the Ugandan women's movement had atrophied by the mid-1980s because of Obote's predatory efforts, it is testimony to the resilience and energy of women in civil society in Uganda that a small group of urban women's organisations mobilised to lobby Museveni soon after his takeover. They demanded that women be appointed to leadership positions, arguing that women's support for the NRA during the 1981–6 guerrilla war justified this. Later that year, one new urban feminist association, Action for Development (ACFODE), a small group of professional women, conferred with other women's organisations to generate a list of demands to present to the new government (*ibid.*: 70). This hastily compiled women's manifesto called for the creation of a Women's Ministry, for every ministry to have a women's desk, for women's representation in local government at all levels, and for the repeal of the 1978 law linking the National Council of Women to the government.

Museveni made quick political capital out of urban women. In response to their initial submission, he appointed women who were strong NRM supporters to very prominent positions: Gertrude Njuba, a high-level combatant in the NRA, was appointed Deputy Minister of Industry, Betty Bigombe was given the vital task of leading the project of pacification in the North, and Victoria Sekitoleko became Minister of Agriculture. Two years later, Museveni appointed two women lawyers to the Constitutional Commission (Miria Matembe and Mary Maitum), and also created a Ministry of Women in Development. He acceded to the demand to create a seat for a woman at all levels of the now five-tier (village to district level) Resistance Council system. This was put into practice in the 1989 local council elections. And, in a gesture which laid the foundation for the pattern of patronage appointments which was to follow, Museveni went one step beyond women's demands for political representation. They had asked for seats for women in local councils, but he added 34 dedicated seats for women in the national assembly (the National Resistance Council), one for each of the country's districts. Election to this position was to be determined not by popular suffrage, but by an electoral college composed of leaders (mostly male) of the five levels of the RC system.

A critical opportunity for the women's movement to embed its concerns in the institutions and politics of the country was presented by the extended period of preparing a new (the fourth) constitution for the country between 1989 and 1995. The two women lawyers on the Constitutional Commission (which prepared drafts between 1989 and 1993) introduced clauses on matters of importance to women, and the Women's Ministry organised a nation-wide consultation exercise to compile a memorandum for the Commission which set out women's interest in seeking the repeal of legislation which discriminates on the basis of sex, particularly in relation to marriage, divorce and property ownership.

Fifty-two women, or 18 per cent of delegates, participated in the Constituent Assembly (CA) constitutional debates of 1994–5. Most of them were occupying the seats reserved for women representatives from the districts, but nine had won in open contests, this time on the basis of universal adult suffrage, to be county representatives. The large number of women in the CA enabled women to act as a distinct negotiating and voting bloc. Most of them joined a non-partisan Women's Caucus, which was very strongly supported by the women's movement, particularly when it came to lobbying for gender equity clauses in the constitution. The Women's Caucus was instrumental in ensuring that a number of key provisions were included in the constitution: a principle of non-discrimination on the basis of sex; equal opportunities for women; preferential treatment or affirmative action to redress past inequalities; provision for the establishment of an Equal Opportunities Commission; as well as rights in relation to employment, property and the family.

One of the most contentious issues defended by the Women's Caucus at that time was the use of the principle of affirmative action to reserve one third of local government seats for women. Many male CA members objected to this on the grounds that it violated the principle of equal rights in the constitution. Women delegates countered that participatory democracy did not deliver equal participation of women without specific instruments to enable women to attain representative office, particularly at the local level (Ahikire 2001: 13). The measures proposed by the Women's Caucus and by women in civil society before 1994 to promote women's presence in policy-making arenas rely on the mechanism of affirmative action: giving women a special advantage in compensation for a history of disadvantage and a sexist culture that inhibited their capacity to compete on an equal footing with men. The practical methods of operationalising affirmative action in politics do not involve giving women advantages in political contests with men, but, rather, the creation of new public space reserved exclusively for women: new bureaucracies for women, new parliamentary and local government seats for women-only competition, new ministerial positions. This 'add-on' mechanism of incorporating women into public life has negative implications for the perceived legitimacy, and ultimately the political effectiveness, of women politicians, as is evident from a closer look at the impact of the 30 per cent reservation for women in local government.

Implications of reserved seats for women's legitimacy as politicians

The way the one-third reservation for women was implemented in the 1997 Local Government Act raises ambiguities about the constituencies they are supposed to represent. The one-third reservation has not been applied to existing seats in local government councils. Rather, the number of seats on all Local Councils (LCs – previously Resistance Councils) save at the village level have been expanded by a third to accommodate women. The 'women's seats' therefore do not disturb established competitions for ward seats. Instead, new 'women's seats' are cobbled together out of clusters of two to three wards, in effect at least doubling the constituency which women are meant to represent, compared to regular ward representatives. The 'afterthought' nature of these seats is emphasised by the fact that elections for the women's seats are held separately, a good two weeks after the ward elections. And the mechanics of voting are different: instead of a secret ballot, voters indicate their choice through the old bush war system of physically queuing up behind the candidate in question (this was changed to a secret ballot for district-level women's councillor seats in 2001, in time for the 2002 Local Council elections). In the 1998 local government elections, irritation with this unwieldy system, as well as voter fatigue, resulted in failure to achieve quorums for electing women to reserved seats all over the country. Eventually, after several attempts to re-run these ballots, the results from sub-optimal voter turn-outs were accepted, with obvious implications for the perceived legitimacy of the women who won the seats. Women now in these seats express confusion over who or what they are supposed to represent: women in their wards, or all of the population in their wards. Either way, they are very often sidelined by the 'real' ward representatives, to whom locals go first with their problems (Ahikire 2001).

Similar ambiguities and constraints afflict the women in the 53 reserved district-level parliamentary seats. As detailed by Sylvia Tamale in her book on women parliamentarians in Uganda, it has never been clear that these women district representatives are supposed to represent women's interests. The constitution makes a subtle distinction between these women representatives and other categories of special representatives (for whom there are simply a few national seats, not district seats), such as youth, workers and disabled people. Representatives of other special interest groups are elected directly by their national organisations, but women are elected primarily by district local government politicians. Affirmative action seats for youth, the disabled, the army and workers are described as being for people who will be 'representatives *of*' these special interests. Women district representatives, in contrast, are not described in the constitution as representatives *of women*, but as representatives *for* each district (Tamale 1999: 74). Women running for these seats must therefore appeal to a narrow electorate of mostly male district élites, not a broader electorate, and inevitably this favours élite and socially conservative candidates. The women MPs in affirmative action seats are not necessarily people who may appeal to a wider women's constituency. Indeed, in many districts, professing a commitment to women's rights might well constitute a disqualification in the eyes of the electoral college. However, it should not be assumed that affirmative action women MPs are necessarily diffident about the gender equity agenda. One of the most outspoken feminists in

Parliament is Miria Matembe, who has repeatedly run for and won the affirmative action seat for her district.

The 'add-on' mechanism of incorporating women into politics has been based on a principle of extending patronage to a new clientele, and indeed of 'extending the state' – creating new representative seats, new political offices, and where possible, new political resources. Women are not the only beneficiaries of this approach. It is the principle behind the reinstatement of traditional kingdoms in 1995, and behind the creation of new districts prior to each presidential election.[3] And in the capital city, one of the most visible examples of this has been the continuous creation of new ministries and 'Minister of State' positions which have bloated the Cabinet. One third of these new 'Minister of State' positions are held by women. Young parliamentarians are the other chief beneficiaries of Museveni's imagination in fabricating new positions. A sudden expansion in these positions in 1999 scotched an incipient rebellion by young parliamentarians and women MPs who were expressing concern about corruption in high places.[4]

The 'add-on' method influences the relationship between women in office and those in the women's movement. The reservations for women-only competition mean that women are treated as a social group whose disadvantage justifies protected access to the state. But this recognition is not accompanied by an acknowledgement that women as a group may have specific interests which need to be identified through a process of public debate involving women in civil society. Thus it is their gender, not their politics, that is their admission ticket. The implicit assumption is that gender acts as a proxy for the political and social values held by an individual (Tamale 1999: 77). Moreover, it is assumed that these values are shared by all women. There are no further screening processes beyond ascertaining the candidate's gender, no process of winnowing out likely candidates according to their effectiveness in promoting any particular party platform or social programme, and no process to enable the women's movement to review candidates. The efforts to include women do not threaten the position of incumbent politicians or entrenched interests. They do not challenge these interests by suggesting that women as a group may have a set of interests to represent which may change the orientation and beneficiaries of these institutions.

Women's resistance to patronage

The pay-off for the NRM of this patronage of women is a large vote bank. Moreover, the NRM has made efforts to construct women as a non-sectarian political constituency, a model of the non-ethnic vision of citizenship and political participation promoted in the 'no-party' political system, and therefore key to Museveni's legitimation project. In the view of one opposition candidate for the presidential elections of 2001, one of Museveni's greatest successes has been to capture the female voting constituency:

> Museveni has tremendous hold, especially in rural areas. Women have been exposed to change possibilities. Out of 10 rural women, 7 will be favourable. He reached them by demonstrating that he could put women in the leadership. (Interview conducted in February 2000, name withheld on request.)

This notion of women as a vote bank reserved for Museveni was invoked in a series of advertisements appearing in the newspapers in January 2001 before the presidential elections. Entitled 'Message from the Women's Movement for the Return of Yoweri K. Museveni (WORK)' – the mysterious organisation 'WORK' speaking for the entire women's movement – the advertisements enjoined women to vote for Museveni on the grounds of 'what he has done for them'. His gift was elaborated thus: 'Museveni's administration has made women visible, given them hope for themselves and their children together with power to: participate in nation building and decision making; access education and microfinance; express themselves at all levels' (*New Vision*, 9 January 2001).[5]

This vision of grateful sycophancy is highly unrepresentative of the women's movement's position on the NRM and Museveni – it has not been uncritical of the NRM's instrumental interest in women as a constituency. But it has often been in a reactive rather than proactive position in the competition to establish the authoritative discourse on the purpose and means of women's inclusion in politics. Up to the June 2001 elections, the domestic women's movement had not put pressure on the NRM to institutionalise women's political gains and secure them from a future loss of patronage. Such institutionalisation would involve revising the electoral system to enable women to compete more effectively against men for 'mainstream' seats. This would require a review of means of articulating and promoting women's interests in politics, which would include a review of the regulations on political parties, starting with the NRM itself, and with the perpetually stalled Political Organisations Bill that is intended to establish just how limited the freedoms of association will be until the next referendum on political systems.

There were a number of occasions on which it would have been possible for the women's movement to reflect upon the implications of the country's political system for women's political effectiveness. During the 1994–5 Constituent Assembly debates, the Women's Caucus did not take a stand on the debate over the country's political system. As the Women's Caucus was deliberately non-partisan, it did not enter into a relationship with the multi-party caucus, the National Caucus for Democracy, made up of most of the 66 delegates known to be associated with opposition parties. Article 69 of the new constitution provided for the continued suppression of both political party activity and freedom of association in order to entrench the no-party 'Movement' system of government, subject to review after five years by a nation-wide referendum. A motion moved in the Constituent Assembly by the multi-partyist delegates to repeal this article was defeated by 199 to 68 votes, and this resulted in a dramatic walk-out by 64 multi-partyists and sympathisers. The six women who joined were those who were already associated with a pre-1986 political party.

The Women's Caucus's positions on key debates in the CA were in part informed by the nation-wide consultation process which the Women's Ministry had conducted in the preceding years in order to collect women's perspectives on important areas for legal change. The training materials for this consultation and the final recommendations to the Constitutional Commission contain little reflection on the implications of different party and electoral systems, or different ways of controlling executive power, for democratic freedoms or for women's electoral prospects. The concern at the time was with the (admittedly important) issues of extending all basic human rights to women, entrenching the principle of affirmative action to compensate for historical discrimination, and the repeal of legislation which discriminates against women. In the Women's Ministry summary of the advantages of the new constitution for women, no mention is made of the constraints on political parties. A passing reference is made to the fact that gender equity provisions in the constitution mean that no women- or men-only party can be formed, and that the national executive of any political party must have representation of women. However, what this might mean in a 'no-party' context is not discussed (Ministry of Gender and Community Development 1995: 8–9).

There was a similar lack of discussion of the implications of a lack of pluralism for women's policy ambitions, and for their prospects as politicians, on the occasion of the June 2000 referendum. The engagement of political parties in the referendum was highly controlled by the

Movement, which appointed a Movement-sympathetic 'multi-partyist' to head the campaign for pluralism. The use of government resources by Movement organs throughout the country to support the government's position also undermined the capacity of opposition parties to participate, and in consequence they observed a boycott, hoping to challenge the legitimacy of the results by discouraging participation in the vote. Women's organisations did not step in to protest the suppression of engagement by opposition parties, or to review whether the NRM's achievements merited a vote for an indefinite continuation of no-party rule.

The restraint shown by the women's movement in engaging in debates on pluralism should not be taken as collusion with the deepening authoritarianism of the Movement. It is testimony, instead, to the growing risks associated with opposing the Movement, the lack of credible alternative arenas for political activism in the malingering old parties, and scepticism about the value of engaging with the state. Just before the 2000 referendum, the feminist lawyer Sylvia Tamale explained women's neutral stance on the 'Movement versus multi-party' debate:

> Yes, one state machinery may offer a better opportunity for women to advance their cause than the next. But women understand that at the end of the day, they have to fend for themselves. The state, by its patriarchal nature, is not a promising or consistent ally of women (*Sunday Monitor* 9 April 2000).[6]

This statement invokes the importance of autonomy for the women's movement, and contains a reminder about the reasons why women in Uganda have for so long avoided engaging with the state. But the failure to keep a critical eye on the undermining of democracy in the country – risky as it is to challenge the NRM – has contributed not only to a deepening stagnation and paralysis in the old political parties, but also to an erosion of democracy within the NRM itself. By neglecting questions of party development, the women's movement has failed to scrutinise the position of women within the NRM, and, as will be shown below, has done little to promote the institutionalisation of gender equity concerns within the party – in its recruitment, candidate promotion, policies, or leadership.

There is an exception to this. In the run-up to the 2001 parliamentary elections one umbrella women's organisation, the Uganda Women's Network (UWONET), spearheaded an initiative which took public steps towards challenging the lack of internal democracy in the Movement. UWONET's 'People's Manifesto', backed by like-minded

NGOs, broached the issue of internal reform in the Movement, raising the need to bring gender-equity concerns to the attention of the National Executive Committee and the Movement Secretariat.[7] Although a UWONET representative admitted that there had been little uptake of this manifesto amongst women's organisations or electoral candidates at the time,[8] there is evidence of a sea-change in the relationship of the women's movement to the NRM since the 2001 elections. For a start, more women than ever before were elected to the open seats, making up nearly one quarter of the women in Parliament (17 out of 75). The new sense of female assertiveness this represents is underwritten by current efforts to revitalise the Women's Caucus in Parliament. Meanwhile, many women's associations, badly bruised by losing important legislative battles over the Land Act in 1998 and the much-postponed Domestic Relations Bill (both discussed in the next section), are reassessing the value of the NRM's patronage, considering that it has not been willing to follow its constitutional commitments to gender equity through to legislative change. A new association, the Coalition for Political Accountability to Women, was formed in March 2001 to act as a lobby to support women politicians in taking a more independent stance in advancing gender equity issues in Parliament.

One area in which women's resistance to the NRM's patronage has been most marked and successful, though least coordinated and overt, is in relation to the NRM's admittedly muddled efforts to create a female party organ along the lines of an 'old-style' women's wing. Early in the NRM's tenure, when Museveni responded quickly to many of the women's movement's initial demands for the representation of women, he held back on one key demand: the repeal of legislation linking the National Council of Women to the state. This body maintained a register of women's associations, and its formal connection to the government was a reminder of the tradition of ruling parties controlling women's associations in Uganda. In 1993 Museveni abolished the link between the NCW and the state, but instead established a much more comprehensive and complex system of supervision of women's association activities in the country, confusingly titled 'National Women's Councils'. Designed by the Directorate of Women's Affairs in the NRM Secretariat, the National Women's Councils parallel the country's five-tier local government councils. They are designed to mobilise rural women into political and development work, and to channel development resources to rural women. In effect, they impose a double duty of political participation on women, as women are also enjoined to engage with the local government system.

The government's behaviour on the issue of a state-controlled umbrella body for women's associational activity is perhaps the strongest indicator of its ambivalent attitude to women's freedom of association in the country. Symptomatic of this has been the uncomfortable relationship, from the start, between the Directorate of Women's Affairs in the NRM's Secretariat (the Secretariat being the only institutional expression of the NRM which approximated a party headquarters between 1986 and 1997) and the Ministry of Women's Affairs.[9] The former, in charge of mobilising women to engage in local politics and development processes, clashed frequently with the Ministry, which has had excellent relations with women's associations in the country, and with international aid donors supporting gender equity in government policy making. In the 1993 repeal of the NCW decree, coordination and management of the new National Women's Councils system was assigned to the Ministry of Women in Development. One of the objectives was to push the Ministry for Women into a controlling and supervisory role in relation to the country's women's movement, rather than the role of catalysing and monitoring policy development which its staff and its women's organisation supporters preferred (Tripp 2000: 90).

In the end, however, the new National Women's Council system failed to pose the expected threat to the autonomy of women's civil society activism. There are several reasons for this. One is because of a desperate shortage of resources for the National Women's Council system. The late 1990s public sector reform programme included the shrinking and progressive starving of funds of the Ministry of Gender, Labour and Community Development, making it ill-equipped to manage the National Women's Council system. Another reason is the lack of enthusiasm of women in the country for these parallel councils, and for the political control of women's activism which they portend. Urban women's associations are highly suspicious of the potential of the NCWs to function as a women's wing of the NRM. Some rural women have taken advantage of the NCW system as an arena of political apprenticeship, with the chairwoman of district-level Women's Councils often going on to run for a woman's seat in the regular District Council. However, the fact that few development resources are accessible through the NCWs discourages the majority of rural women from taking them seriously. But though the NCW system is in many places near-moribund, it represents an institutional structure which could be revived to constitute a women's wing of the NRM if necessary.

Women in politics and gender-friendly legislation

One measure of the institutional security of women politicians, and of their relative autonomy from male or party interests which are hostile to a gender equity agenda, is their capacity to promote gender equity legislation. Women in Parliament started out well on this score, passing an amendment to the penal code in 1990 that made rape a capital offence. A few years later, women Constituent Assembly delegates were effective in writing gender equity provisions into the new constitution. But between the CA debates and the run-up to the 2001 parliamentary elections there was a notable flagging of energy around a gender equity agenda, or around efforts to act in concert on other issues. The Women's Caucus in Parliament was largely inactive between 1996 and 2001. Women politicians did not use their valuable positions on parliamentary committees to support each other or to push a united policy agenda, and, as will be shown in the discussion of the 1998 Land Act, there is considerable disagreement between them on key pieces of legislation which have related to women's rights in the past few years. A major stumbling block is that it is impossible to pass new legislation without the endorsement of the top leadership of the Movement, yet, as will be shown in the next section, there are no means of debating new legislation within the Movement, even if women politicians within the Movement were to coordinate efforts. At least two important recent efforts to promote women's rights have quite clearly lacked this essential Movement endorsement.

The most dramatic example of Movement hostility to women's concerns, and indeed, direct presidential sabotage, was the undermining of efforts to include a clause in the 1998 Land Bill to give women equal rights with men over joint property, such as the homestead. Women in civil society first took up this issue in 1997, joining the Uganda Land Alliance (a civil society coalition), and conducting research nation-wide into women's land ownership patterns. They demonstrated the prevalence of the tragedy of widows being forced off of their homesteads by their husband's families. They also argued, in favour of what became known as the 'spousal co-ownership' amendment, that without wives' right to homestead land, husbands could sell family land without their wives either consenting or gaining any financial benefit from the transaction.[10]

Assiduous lobbying by women's groups generated support from many women MPs (but not three of the then five women in Cabinet, who remained strongly opposed). Particularly important was the fact that Miria Matembe championed the amendment on spousal co-ownership of the marital home, and land used for daily sustenance of the family, tabling and passing it in Parliament on 25 June 1998.[11] But when the Land Act was published a week later, there was no trace of this amendment. It took months for women MPs and women in civil society to trace this 'lost amendment'. They were told that there had been procedural irregularities in the way they had tabled the amendment which then disqualified it. In the end, the President admitted that he had intervened personally to delete the amendment (Tripp 2002). He had already made known his opposition to the notion of women having rights in their husbands' property, partly through allegations that women would make a capital accumulation strategy out of serial marriage and divorce. His justification for the move was that the amendment belonged more appropriately to the pending Domestic Relations Bill.

The President's suggestion of appending the co-ownership amendment to the Domestic Relations Bill (DRB) has as good as extinguished the amendment altogether, because of the political near-impossibility of passing the DRB. Various drafts of the DRB have been debated since 1964. Since 1995 the need for legislation to bring family laws in Uganda into conformity with the guarantee of sexual equality in the constitution has become urgent, but the DRB has not even been tabled in Parliament. The Bill aims to protect women's rights in relation to polygamy, bridewealth, child custody, divorce, inheritance, consent in sexual relations, and property ownership. This kind of legislation, which challenges men's rights to control women and children in the family, is inevitably deeply controversial in a sexually conservative society. The item in the Bill which has aroused the most ferocious objections from many men relates to criminalising marital rape. In addition, the Muslim community has objected to the restrictions on polygamous unions in the Bill. Already burdened with these 'unpassable' clauses, the DRB can hardly act as a vehicle for pushing through the spousal co-ownership clause.

The Bill has no champion amongst women MPs. Rebecca Kadaga, whose background as a women's rights lawyer makes her a likely supporter of the DRB, and whose position as a Cabinet Minister in charge of Parliamentary Affairs would enable her to smooth the passage of the Bill, has not offered any support. Other prominent women MPs who are vocal on women's rights, notably Winnie Byanyima, Miria Matembe, Winnie Babihuga, or Proscovia Salaamu Musumba (who extended, then withdrew, an offer to table the DRB as a private member's bill), have

127

also not wanted to risk their political careers on such unpopular legislation. The objections of the Muslim community made the last Minister of Gender, Labour and Community Development, Janat Mukwaya, herself a Muslim, deeply ambivalent about the Bill. She has refused to be associated with it. The criminalisation of marital rape has made the Bill hard for the Minister of Justice to stomach. A politician from the old Buganda party, he has exhibited marked indifference to gender equity legislation, and has admitted to members of the women's movement that he has had trouble in presenting this Bill to Cabinet because he simply cannot understand the concept of marital rape.

The Minister of Justice has done more than footdragging to hobble another important piece of legislation: the Sexual Offences Bill. This draft legislation, which raises the age of consent to 18, is very popular among Ugandan women because of the deep outrage about what is called 'defilement' of young girls, particularly in the context of the rapid spread of HIV/Aids. However, when the Minister of Justice presented it to Cabinet in 1999, it was referred back to the Law Reform Commission because of the poorly prepared principles and missing background documentation justifying the law. The Commission was mystified, given that the principles and documentation had been prepared in full. It transpired that the Minister of Justice, personally objecting to setting the age of consent at 18, had taken it upon himself to revise the draft legislation and lowered the age to 16, redrafting the legislation in great haste.[12] This cavalier disregard for the views of the women's movement as expressed in the Commission's work shows contempt for the expression and pursuit of women's interests through political processes.

Another sign of a lack of a women's rights agenda in politics is the non-appearance of the Equal Opportunities Commission. All of the other government commissions foreseen in the constitution have been created (commissions, for example, on human rights, law reform, elections and judicial service). It is the responsibility of the Ministry of Gender to ensure that the Equal Opportunities Commission is set up. But after an initial costing exercise in 1998, no further effort was made by the Ministry. The issue has no particular champions in Parliament.

There is, however, one noticeable contribution which women MPs have made: some of them are beginning to constitute an anti-corruption lobby. Winnie Byanyima is the most outspoken critic of government corruption, spearheading the first censure motion in Parliament against the MP Brigadier-General Muhwezi, and subsequently Sam Kutesa. Other MPs such as Proscovia Salaamu Musumba have joined in with efforts to pass a Budget Bill which would impose much greater transparency and disaggregation in the presentation of budgets for ministries and also for districts. In the Ministry for Ethics and Integrity, which is the focal point for all anti-corruption bureaucracies and campaigns, the Minister is the important woman's rights activist Miria Matembe. Opposition MPs such as Cecilia Ogwal (UPC) and Juliet Rainer Kafire (DP) have been much more eager to join in efforts to challenge corruption than in women's rights legislation, for the obvious reason that this gives them a means of exposing the Movement government.

For women within the Movement, it may be that raising issues of corruption is the only way in which to make an implicit critique of the lack of internal democracy in the Movement. Figures who have been targeted in Byanyima's censure motions are in fact key members of the privileged clique around Museveni. Women MPs have concentrated more closely on corruption than any other group in Parliament, save for the group of new/young parliamentarians between 1996 and 1999, after which key leaders amongst them were neutralised by being absorbed into the Cabinet as Ministers of State. There is some evidence that Byanyima's crusade is beginning to bite, in the sense that she herself has come under increasingly personal attack from the President himself. Her relationship with him worsened dramatically following her husband Colonel Kiiza Besigye's outspoken statements on corruption in the government and the army in early 2000, and his campaign running against Museveni for President in early 2001. Amazingly, Besigye's presidential aspirations, combined with Byanyima's unpopularity within the Movement, did not prevent her from being re-elected in 2001, when her Mbarara constituency rallied behind her. However, ostracism by the Movement now profoundly undermines her capacity to continue to work for internal democracy in the Movement.

The non-party movement – problems of institutionalisation and consequences for women

The preceding discussions about the means of promoting women in politics, and their effectiveness as representatives of women's interests while there, beg questions about how women have been incorporated into decision making within the Movement itself. Is Museveni's promotion of women a personal project, or does it stem from a decision taken by the Movement, perhaps as a result of pressure from women within the Movement? Does the Movement have a vision of gender equity and women's rights which it hopes to promote politically? Does it have measures to support women Movement supporters who stand for open seats? Answers to these questions reveal the extremely limited extent to which the Movement is institutionalised as a political organisation, and reveal, therefore, the severity of the obstacles which women face to institutionalising gender equity in political competition in Uganda.

Though the government insists the Movement is not a party, there is little doubt that today the Movement system does function as a ruling party in the sense that it promotes the electoral prospects of its own members. It will therefore be considered as a party here. This section will look at the engagement of prominent women with the NRM, and it will discuss the consequences for women – and indeed any Movement member unconnected to significant patronage systems – of the following features of Movement organisation (or lack of organisation): structure of the local Movement Councils, selection and role of the National Executive, role of the Movement Secretariat, support to candidates for local and national elections, and the lack of a Movement policy statement.

In the first half of the 1980s, no efforts were put into constituting the NRM into a political party – it was merely the public negotiator for the National Resistance Army (NRA). At the time of its coming to power in 1986, the NRM/A was primarily a guerrilla army, given coherence by its overwhelming loyalty to the person of Museveni and its one priority of getting rid of Obote and seizing power. Aside from presiding over the Resistance Council system in liberated areas, the NRM/A had no formal internal structures for electing leaders or debating policies. It was also not a 'movement' in any sensible use of the term. It had started out as a fighting force of a little over thirty men, and by the 1986 victory, controlled just 20,000 soldiers, with no real branch structure, and no political base beyond the army and the ethnic group of the Banyankore in the South, and the allies it had gained among the Baganda people in the Luwero triangle. Between 1986 and 1997 the NRM set up shop in an office block in Kampala and established directorates to perform some functions associated with a party: political mobilisation, organising Resistance Council elections, supporting the NRM representatives in the districts, supporting a caucus of NRM MPs in government, and organising political education and self-defence for villagers (*chaka muchaka*). Since 1997 the Movement Act, as shown earlier, has generalised the NRM's idea of no-party democracy into a national political system.

The women's movement, like most other sectors of civil society, was not centrally engaged in Museveni's liberation struggle. However women in combat areas in the centre and South of the country did give marked support to the bush war by acting as couriers, providing nursing skills and caring for orphans. A few women were prominent as fighters in the NRA and activists in the NRM, but they had not formed themselves as a distinct constituency. There was no women's wing, and senior women such as Gertrude Njuba did not identify themselves with women's issues. The NRM thus differed from liberation movements in other African countries such as South Africa, Ethiopia or Eritrea in the sense that it was not a broad-based social movement. Women supporters and combatants had not had a chance to articulate a position on internal representation of women, or on gender equity in party policy. In the post-1986 period, senior women within the NRM have diverged according to their interest in gender equity in politics. Some, such as Gertrude Njuba, Betty Bigombe, Vice-President Specioza Kazibwe and Janat Mukwaya, have not taken a feminist stance on policy debates. Others, such as Miria Matembe, Winnie Byanyima and Rebecca Kadaga, have been much more critical in relation to government footdragging on gender equity. Some of these women appear to have been neutralised by inclusion in the Cabinet (Matembe, Kadaga), and an attempt was made to bring Byanyima into the solidarity of the 'High Command' by making her Director for Information in the Movement Secretariat in 1997 (she was forced to resign shortly afterwards because of her continued outspokenness on corruption).

There has been no structured approach to encourage women's engagement in setting policy priorities within the NRM. Senior women in the Movement appear to have focused upon the politics of national reconstruction in the post-1986 period, rather than upon internal democratisation. The Movement has one official system for articulating and aggregating interests, and that is through the Movement Councils parallel to all Local Councils — in effect a rural party branch system, intended to act as a caucus for Movement members in the Local Councils. The chairperson of every Local Council automatically chairs the parallel Movement Council. There are no measures to ensure parity in the participation of women in these Movement Councils, nor to ensure their representation in the leadership of these councils. In any case, the automatic leadership of these councils by the LC chairperson ensures almost completely male leadership, since most elected LC chairpersons at all levels are men.

One possible reason that little attention was paid to women's engagement in the Movement Councils is because a parallel structure exclusively for women was set up earlier: the National Women's Council system. No provision for a structured input of policy concerns from the Women's Councils to the Movement Councils (or even the Local

Councils) exists. This underlines women's separateness, and strengthens the notion that women's participation in politics is constructed around notions of their difference from men, rather than equality.

There are other organs for policy making in the Movement: the National Executive Committee of the Movement, elected at the Movement's National Conference, and the Movement's Parliamentary Caucus. More important still are the decision-making arenas in government: the Cabinet, and the informal and shifting collection of friends and advisers around the President. Elections for the first Movement National Executive Committee took place in July 1998 at the first National Movement Conference composed of 1,600 delegates, almost all of whom, with the exception of the directly elected local government representatives, were from a range of NRM-created political positions – such as representatives from the National Councils for Women, and councils for youth, workers, the disabled, and so on. Elections to the top three posts – chairperson, vice-chairperson, and national political commissar – were unopposed, going to Museveni, Al-hajji Moses Kigongo (vice-chairperson of the NRM since the days of the bush war), and James Wapakhabulo (the parliamentary Speaker). There was no discussion of whether a woman ought to take one of these positions, and indeed, Vice-President Kazibwe had to suffer the indignity of not being awarded a sinecure parallel position in the NEC in the way that Museveni and Wapakhabulo had been (in her case, she could have been the Movement vice-chairperson). There are 150 people on the NEC. This includes a few seats for representatives of special interest groups (five are for women), while the rest are filled by the 45 district chairpersons (all men), and one MP chosen from each district (most of whom are men). According to one of the few women MPs on the NEC, there has been no discussion since 1998 about gender issues, no mention of any need for the Movement to offer women special support in elections, or to create a quota to ensure that a certain proportion of Movement candidates are women. The NEC has never functioned as an effective policy-setting body. Prior to 1997 it was supposed to meet at least once every three months, but it had not met for three years prior to the promulgation of the 1995 constitution (Besigye 2000), and has met rarely since 1998. Obviously, important policy positions are established elsewhere.

The Movement Secretariat is legally charged with ensuring that legislative activity is in line with the Movement's policy. Its directorates for legal affairs, development, information, mobilisation and so on monitor and occasionally review legislation before it is seen by Parliament.[13] The NEC is supposed to appoint these directors but, in practice, it is the

President who personally nominates them, and expects the NEC to approve them. There are 16 directors in the Secretariat, three of whom are women. The head of the sub-directorate for Gender, Labour and Development, Beatrice Lagada, is not connected to the women's movement, and her directorate has made few efforts to ensure that the government is enacting the legislation previewed in the constitution to protect women's rights – such as the Equal Opportunities Commission, the Domestic Relations Bill, or protection of married women's rights to property, particularly land.

There is no comprehensive statement of Movement policy, and it would be difficult to put a single label on the Movement's ideology. Its values are summarised in a thin 1999 document that updates the NRM's 1986 ten-point programme into a 15-point programme. Gender is mentioned at point 14, which endorses affirmative action as a means to encourage political, social and economic participation of marginalised groups (Movement Secretariat 1999: 46). The justification for this is instrumental: 'the policy of fending for the oppressed and marginalised has clearly shown that there is a lot of potential which can be tapped if gender and marginalised group-responsive programmes are emphasised' (*ibid.*: 46). The terms 'gender equity' or 'equality' are never used, nor are any measurable goals mentioned, in terms of aiming for parity in women's and men's political or economic engagement. According to a member of the four-person committee in the directorate that wrote the 15-point programme, this 'gender' point was not raised by the one woman on the committee, nor was it promoted or supported by the Secretariat's gender sub-directorate. Instead, it was put there by other directors conscious of the importance of consolidating the Movement's success with the female constituency.

The Cabinet is an important forum for debating policy. But although there were six women ministers in the 1996–2001 Cabinet, none of them was close to real decision making. Research by the Forum for Women in Democracy (FOWODE) has shown that these women control small budgets in low-visibility ministries with few staff (FOWODE 2000: 10). The Vice-President has been sidelined, described by one woman MP as 'just an errand girl for the President'.[14] She used to be the leader of government business in Parliament, but was forced to surrender this power to the new Prime Minister when the President made the important patronage appointment of Apollo Nsibambi, a prominent Muganda, to this position. The Vice-President is ostensibly the chairperson of Cabinet but this function is usually usurped by the President. In any case, the Cabinet is not the true locus of decision making for the

Movement. Insiders say that most decisions are debated by a very tight circle of close army comrades of the President's: friends on the Army Council, the President's brother Salim Saleh, and a few senior Movement stalwarts in the Cabinet. This is popularly known as the 'Movement Political High Command'. There are no women in this inner circle.

Because membership in the Movement is mandatory and universal, it does not have policies on recruitment, and hence women have not had the opportunity to push for focused recruitment of women members. There has been no structured approach to improving women's chances as Movement candidates in open contests. The no-party principle of electoral competition on the grounds of 'individual merit' means that the Movement has always claimed that it neither cultivates nor promotes particular candidates in local and national elections. It does not put a limit on the numbers of people who can compete on the basis of 'individual merit'. There is no official system for deciding between the many people who may put themselves forward as 'Movementists'.[15] This means that there is no way for women to insist that the Movement provide backing to a quota of women candidates in the way that their South African sisters so successfully did in the African National Congress (ANC).

However, the absence of a formal candidate selection system does not mean that there is not in fact one in place. Ever since the CA elections of 1994, the NRM Secretariat has unofficially sponsored district-level committees to recommend 'NRM candidates' for support. At the time, the objective was mainly to eliminate candidates supportive of pluralism (Besigye 2000: 32). Nevertheless, most of the women politicians interviewed for this study who had come to Parliament through competition for an open county seat (as opposed to an affirmative action seat) claimed they had received no support from the NRM in the 1996 parliamentary elections. By keeping the candidate selection system unofficial and informal, personal preferences can be muscled through by local strongmen. This muscling is substantial: women candidates who are out of favour with the NRM can expect physical harassment and intimidation – two women critics of the government, Byanyima and Babihuga, suffered intense harassment during the 2001 elections. Women politicians who wish to receive Movement backing must buy into these local power structures. Since the informal district election committees are not acknowledged to exist, there is no internal Movement directive to oblige these committees to encourage women to stand for open contests with men, to receive priority support from the local election committees, or to get priority access to campaign resources.

There have occasionally been efforts to democratise the movement from within, but all the individuals who have dared to challenge abuses of power have lost their positions within the Movement.[16] For instance, Winnie Byanyima, a prominent feminist politician, lost her post as Director of Information at the Movement Secretariat in early 1998 when it became clear that this appointment had failed to silence her protests at official corruption. Two years later she was roundly booed at the Movement's National Conference when she pointed out that the endorsement of Museveni as the Movement's sole presidential candidate was in contravention of the policy of allowing anyone to stand for any position on the grounds of individual merit (*Sunday Vision*, 'Movt Delegates Boo Byanyima', 26 November 2000).

The no-party system allows the Movement to resist defining itself as a party, while its constitutional status as the country's political system allows it to enjoy the privileges of a monopoly on state power – in effect a one-party state without the party. The absence of a party structure condemns women's engagement in politics to remain at the level of special pleading and success in gaining patronage appointments, not at a more institutionally secure level of sustainable change in party structures, candidate support systems and party policy.

Conclusion

Feminist political scientists are increasingly sensitive to the fact that choices made in the design of political institutions – the powers of the executive in relation to the legislature, the design of the electoral system, the nature and degree of party institutionalisation – determine women's prospects in electoral competitions, and their capacity to influence policy once in office. As Georgina Waylen argues, '[t]he focus of analysis then becomes the nature of the institutional measures proposed by women activists and the ways in which variations in political systems, for example in terms of party structures and electoral systems, affect both the goals and strategies of those activists' (Waylen 2000: 791). Ugandan women's arguments and strategies for admission to representative politics and to policy making are all framed by one key feature of the current institutional framework: the suppression of parties. By ruling out pluralism, Museveni has emasculated the development of accountability mechanisms, and by extending an ever-widening net of patronage, he has neutralised oppositional energies, including those of women pushing for a legislative agenda which would challenge male rights within gender relations. As summarised by a Ugandan feminist lawyer:

If there was pluralism here, there would be space for women to influence political structures. Right now, no political organisation has affirmative action internally. That would give women leverage. Women are captive to the Movement now.[17]

The problem, however, is not just the absence of pluralism, but also the way affirmative action has worked as a tool for accommodation and control of women in politics. While it is true that Ugandan women have not been able to use the competitive dynamic of a pluralist system in order to build leverage around their political demands, and nor can they use the rules and representative systems within well-institutionalised parties to press for equitable inclusion at all levels, it is important to remember that liberal multi-party systems in Africa and elsewhere do not automatically promote women's rights. Women have made gains in terms of their numerical presence in political arenas, and their feminist influence on policy, only where the women's movement is strong and autonomous, and where political parties are sympathetic to feminist goals, and electoral systems and other political institutions can give voice to socially excluded groups.

Arguably, many words could have been saved in this chapter by simply stating that authoritarianism is as bad for women's electoral prospects, and for their chances of promoting their interests once in office, as it is for any other socially marginalised group. But to put it this baldly misses the point. The NRM regime is not – or at least was not at the start – a stereotypical authoritarian tyranny. Museveni's experiment with popular and no-party democracy has benefited from a great deal of good faith domestically and internationally, and, for feminist observers, the suspension of socially destructive party competition offered an important window of opportunity for women to enter politics. The no-party system held many attractions as an approach to 'neutralising ethnicity' (Muhereza and Otim 1997: 5). But the current compromised status of women in politics in Uganda offers an important lesson: though women can benefit enormously from direct presidential patronage, their effectiveness in promoting a gender equity agenda is low if they have not institutionalised a presence for themselves as legitimate competitors for the popular vote, and for their policies as legitimate matters for public debate. It is hard to see how this institutionalisation can be accomplished outside of regularising women's participation as decision makers and candidates in political parties. This cannot be accomplished if parties are overly personalised, secretive in decision making, and lacking clear rules for supporting electoral candidates and debating policy. And substantial party reform is only really possible in a pluralist political system.

References

Ahikire, J. (2001) 'Gender Equity and Local Democracy in Contemporary Uganda: Addressing the Challenge of Women's Political Effectiveness in Local Government', Working Paper 58, Centre for Basic Research, Kampala.

Apter, D. (1997) *The Political Kingdom in Uganda: a Study in Bureaucratic Nationalism*, Third Edition, London: Frank Cass.

Babihuga, W. (2000) 'Women's Paths to Political Participation and Decision-Making', paper presented during ACFODE Week Public Dialogue, 17 November, Uganda.

Basu, A. (ed.) (1995) *The Challenge of Local Feminisms: Women's Movements in Global Perspective*, Boulder: Westview Press.

Besigye, K. (2000) 'An Insider's View of How NRM Lost the 'Broad-base', *Sunday Monitor*, 5 November.

FOWODE (2000) *From Strength to Strength: Ugandan Women in Public Office*, Forum for Women in Democracy publication, Kampala, May.

Human Rights Watch (1999) *Hostile to Democracy: the Movement System and Political Repression in Uganda*, Human Rights Watch, London.

Kasfir, N. (1998) '"No-Party Democracy" in Uganda', *Journal of Democracy*, 9, 2: 49–63.

Lovenduski, J. and P. Norris (eds.) (1993) *Gender and Party Politics*, London: Sage Publications.

Ministry of Gender and Community Development (1995) *Women and the 1995 Constitution of Uganda*, a WID–DANIDA Constituent Assembly Project, Kampala.

Movement Secretariat (1999) *Movement Fifteen Point Programme*, pamphlet, Movement Secretariat, Kampala.

Muhereza, F. E. and P. Omurangi Otim (1997) 'Neutralising Ethnicity under the NRM Government in Uganda', mimeo, Centre for Basic Research, Kampala, November.

Museveni, Y. K. (1997) *Sowing the Mustard Seed*, London: Macmillan.

Norris, P. (1993) 'Conclusion: Comparing Legislative Recruitment', in J. Lovenduski and P. Norris (eds.), *Gender and Party Politics*, London: Sage.

Onyango, Odongo (2000) *A Political History of Uganda: the Origin of Yoweri Museveni's Referendum 2000*, Kampala: The Monitor Publications.

Schlichte, K. (2000) 'The President's Dilemmata: Contradictions of State-building in Uganda', mimeo, presented to the Congress of the International Political Science Association, Quebec City, August.

Sunday Vision (2000) 'Movt Delegates Boo Byanyima', 26 November.

Tamale, S. (1999) *When Hens Begin to Crow: Gender and Parliamentary Politics in Uganda*, Kampala: Fountain Publishers.

Tripp, A. M. (1994) 'Gender, Political Participation, and the Transformation of Association Life in Uganda and Tanzania', *African Studies Review*, 37, 1.

—— (2000) *Women and Politics in Uganda*, Oxford: James Currey.

—— (2002) 'Conflicting Visions of Community and Citizenship: Women's Rights and Cultural Diversity in Uganda', in M. Molyneux and S. Razavi (eds.), *Gender, Justice, Democracy and Rights*, Oxford: Oxford University Press.

UWONET (2000) 'The People's Manifesto', mimeo, UWONET, Kampala.

Waylen, G. (2000) 'Gender and Democratic Politics: a Comparative Analysis of

Consolidation in Argentina and Chile', *Journal of Latin American Studies*, 32: 761–93.

Young, I. M. (1990) *Justice and the Politics of Difference*, Princeton: Princeton University Press.

Notes

1 A shorter version of this chapter was published in the *Journal of Modern African Studies*. This chapter is based on in-depth interviews conducted between 1998 and 2000 with ten MPs, ten local government councillors (both MPs and councillors were a mix of women and men from across the political spectrum), six activists from political parties, six women's rights activists, and six representatives of development organisations, as well as a number of academics. This chapter also draws on group discussions held with women local government councillors in December 2000 and organised by the Centre for Basic Research in Kampala.

2 Through Legal Notice No. 1 of 1986.

3 The creation of ever more numerous new districts channels development resources and political status to smaller ethnic sub-groups, and is seen as a strategy of responding to the demands for recognition and resources made by ethnic groups. Six new districts were created just before the 1996 presidential elections (Muhereza and Otim 1997: 5), and eleven, some absurdly tiny, were created in late 2000, just in time for the 2001 presidential elections.

4 In the 1997–2001 Parliament, 97 MPs were either young or new to national politics or both. They formed a 'Young Parliamentarians' group and worked closely with the more active and critical women MPs. They registered their concerns about corruption through their activities on key parliamentary committees, particularly the Select Committee on Railways, which was dominated by new MPs, the Privatisation Committee, which investigated a corruption scandal involving Uganda Commercial Bank (illegally purchased through Malaysian brokers by the President's brother, Salim Saleh), and the Legal Committee, through which a young parliamentarian, Nathan Byanyima, mobilised support for a censure motion for corruption against MP Sam Kutesa. In 1999 ten young parliamentarians, many of them women, were made Ministers of State for newly created 'ministries' (of sports, disability, children). As one member of this group says: 'the flood of new ministries was an effort to break up our group. It has worked. Others have been promised ministries, and are on the waiting list.' She felt that this had divided people critical of the Movement by coopting some to the Movement 'High Command', where they were expected to inform on critics (interview with woman MP, 25 February 2000, name withheld on request).

5 I am grateful to Josephine Akihire of the Centre for Basic Research for bringing this to my attention.

6 I am grateful to Sylvia Tamale for drawing my attention to this article and this passage.

7 UWONET (2000), 'The People's Manifesto', mimeo, Kampala.

8 Interview, Sheila Kawamara Mishambi, Coordinator, UWONET, 6 December 2000.

9 The 'Women's Ministry' has been through a number of changes in title,

function, and above all staffing and budget levels (always revised downwards). It started as the Ministry of Women in Development in 1988, based in the Office of the President as a Ministry of State. In 1991 it became a full Ministry, merged with Youth and Culture. In 1994 it was downsized to the Ministry of Gender and Community Development, and its current manifestation is as the Ministry of Gender, Labour and Social Development, a change which has held since 1998, but in which the gender section of the Ministry has been reduced to a handful of staff.

10 UWONET, *Women and Land Rights in Uganda* (Kampala: Friedrich Ebert Stiftung, October, 1997); UWONET and the Association of Women Parliamentarians (AWOPA), *Proposed Amendments on the Land Bill 1998* (Kampala, UWONET, April 1998).

11 The government newspaper reported on the passing of the amendment the next day: *New Vision*, 'Spouses to Co-own Land', 26 June 1998.

12 Interview with an ex-member of the Uganda Law Reform Commission (21 February 2000).

13 Interview with a Movement director (February 2000).

14 Interview with a woman MP (23 February 2000).

15 Increasing opposition to Movement candidates has, however, prompted the beginnings of a concern to set in place candidate selection procedures. The most spectacular challenge to the policy of not screening and selecting candidates came when, during the late 2000 National Conference, Colonel Kiiza Besigye, a veteran of the bush struggle, announced his candidature for presidency alongside the predictably unanimous call for Museveni to stand for a second time as presidential candidate. The National Executive Committee promptly declared that Museveni was the sole Movement candidate, making policy on the spot about formal endorsement of a sole candidate: 'Where a constituency is under threat from multi-partyism, full support should be given to one Movement candidate that would have to be identified' (*The Monitor*, 'NEC Resolves on Candidates', 25 November 2000).

16 They include Sam Njuba, a government minister who objected to the NRM's pressure on the constitutional commission to write the no-party system into the draft constitution, Onyango Odongo, an early Director of Information and Mass Mobilisation in the NRM Secretariat, who proposed procedures for electing the NRM's top leaders and limiting their terms of office (Onyango Odongo, 2000: 77–8), and Dr Kiiza Besigye, who was threatened with courtmartial for an open letter he published in the opposition paper in November 1999 discussing the Movement's lack of internal democracy and the corruption of high officials.

17 Interview, December 2000, name cannot be cited due to promised anonymity.

5

The Politics of Engagement:
Women Transforming the Policy Process –
Domestic Violence Legislation in South Africa

SHEILA MEINTJES

The context of the transition to democracy in South Africa during the first half of the 1990s opened new spaces for civil society, and especially formerly marginalised groups, to make political gains, and to influence the shape and nature of the state and social policy. Engaging the state had been, under apartheid, highly adversarial for opposition groups. Of particular significance, and often neglected in mainstream discussions of the transition to democracy in South Africa, was how the politics of gender entered the policy arena. The discourse of gender equality found its way into mainstream politics through strategic political mobilisation during the negotiations process, and after many years of women's involvement in the struggle against apartheid in South Africa.

This chapter focuses on how gender-based violence in particular became a policy issue.[1] It provides a brief history of the context within which the violence against women movement in South Africa became integrated into the broader politics of engagement of the women's movement. It explores, too, how the law reform process unfolded in the 1990s, in a new context of democratisation following thirty years of apartheid repression. During the negotiations process of the early 1990s gender and women activists engaged in coalitions that shaped the gendered discourse of rights to equality and full citizenship (Albertyn 1994; Meintjes 1998). The forces of change that intersected to influence the policy agenda included non-governmental organisations working against violence against women, international organisations and United Nations instruments such as the Convention on the Elimination of All Forms of Discrimination against Women (CEDAW), and key institutions and individuals in the state itself.

The argument put forward in the chapter is that the successful integration of gender policies in the state requires necessary and sufficient conditions. The first necessity is that women in civil society are mobilised politically. A second prerequisite, is that there exist key support networks amongst women politicians, and within the bureaucracy, to take up gender issues within the state. Third, a substantive normative or democratic discourse and framework that integrates gender is necessary for key alliances to work effectively in promoting change. But none of these is sufficient. General mobilisation around specific issues will not succeed unless there are people in civil society with the knowledge and skills to engage in highly complex processes of intervention and negotiation with appropriate state apparatuses. Moreover, within the state apparatuses, both in the political sphere of the legislature and in ministries, key individuals in leadership positions have to be committed to and champion the issue on a constant basis. These key women leaders have to be in a position to develop alliances with key male politicians in order for the policy and legislation to succeed.

Promoting gender institutions in the state

Academic arguments about the nature of the state had percolated through civil society during the 1970s and 1980s, and highly abstract debates had found meaningful expression in the ways different sectors of the opposition to apartheid acted to break the stranglehold of the apartheid system. In the post-apartheid period of the 1990s new strategic relationships between civil society and different sectoral elements in the state together developed policies that met the needs of different interests. The political activism and participation of these elements – civic movements, the trade union movement, youth, rural movements – had laid claim to strategic policy areas in the post-liberation settlement. Women's organisations and activism had also asserted claims to participation in national politics on an equal basis with men. The poor representation of women in the negotiations for a constitutional settlement in the early 1990s led to the formation of a broad coalition to ensure that women's claims to gender equality and full political participation were honoured in the new democratic era.

The Women's National Coalition was launched in 1992, comprising political and non-political organisations. The WNC provided a forum for the interaction of women politicians and women's organisations in civil society in the period before the first democratic elections in 1994. Large numbers of women who had been involved in the WNC were encouraged to participate in the first election as candidates for different political parties. This laid the basis for the politics of engagement between

141

women in civil society, women in politics, and women in the bureaucracy. The case of domestic violence shows how this interaction enabled a social problem to become a policy and legal question. The case study provides a useful mechanism to evaluate both the relationships and the institutional mechanisms introduced by the first democratic government to ensure the promotion of gender equality.

During the negotiations period in South Africa, there was much debate among gender and women activists about the kind of state machinery necessary to ensure that women's needs and interests were integrated into mainstream public policy. In the early 1990s, the WNC played a pivotal role in its national campaign around gender equality and, with other organisations such as the Institute for Democratic Alternatives (IDASA), in promoting an expanded understanding of equality and a democratic culture that included gender. The WNC held an international conference in May 1993 to discuss what might work best for South Africa. It drew on democratic examples and comparisons of structures in Australia, Scandinavia, Canada, Bangladesh and Uganda to suggest a 'package' of institutional mechanisms to realise gender equality in state and society. The outcome was an agreement between women activists in civil society and politicians that what would work best for South Africa would be a combination of structures rather than a single mechanism as argued for by the United Nations.

This 'package' included a multi-party Standing Committee in Parliament that would ensure that all legislation would be gender-sensitive, and meet women's needs and interests specifically. An Office on the Status of Women in the presidency would ensure that government departments would mainstream gender policies and develop equity policies in the state. An independent body that would monitor the progress of gender equality in state and civil society was also envisaged. Finally, activists recognised that for this package to be successful, civil society itself had to be vigilant, mobilised in a gender and women's movement to ensure that the state fulfilled its mandate on gender equality.

These mechanisms were not formally agreed upon by the different parties to the negotiations until the eleventh hour, after a crisis about the Bill of Rights saw women's rights to full equality challenged by traditional leaders. Women in the negotiation teams of all the parties, but particularly the African National Congress, realised that without at the very least a strong constitutional mechanism to protect gender equality the gains made for gender equality during negotiations might be challenged and undermined in the final constituent assembly (Albertyn 1994). Thus there was a somewhat forced and quick resolution about what kind of gender machinery should be put in place to ensure gender equality in state and society. The Commission on Gender Equality was conceived during this crisis, and was realised in Chapter Nine of the constitution, along with other devices to promote and protect different elements of democracy, such as the Human Rights Commission, the Public Protector and the Electoral Commission.

In this phase of debate and activism, a significant feature of participation was the shift from grassroots participation to that of professionals with specific political and legal expertise. The process of engaging the state on matters of constitution making, of policy and legislative reform, required levels of professional and technical expertise around how governments worked and how laws should be framed. Constitutional issues were the domain of constitutional lawyers, and feminist constitutional lawyers were particularly important in the interventions that finally saw substantive equality accepted as a foundational principle in the constitution.

As engagement with the state around particular issues occurred, and they became the subject of state policy, so professionalism developed within issue-based movements in civil society. In the violence against women movement, grassroots activists did not always have the legal and technical expertise required to address the complexities of policy and law making in the realm of policing, safety and security, or in terms of service provision in the realm of welfare and psychological counselling. Professional expertise became a prerequisite during the post-apartheid era. Professionalism was a contested terrain as grassroots activists resisted losing control. Control by professionals tended to blunt the political edge of organisations.

How successful have the new institutional mechanisms set in place by the activism of civil society been in achieving their objectives? Who were the key actors in ensuring that the 'women's agenda' remained an issue of public policy? What alliances were significant in promoting gender equity and equality policy? The rest of the chapter traces the progress of a single issue, that of violence against women, in order to evaluate the effectiveness of the new institutions and to assess which relationships made a difference to gender equity policy.

How violence against women became a public policy issue, 1970–90

The first legislation to deal specifically with violence against women was passed as the Prevention of Family Violence Act, No. 133 of 1993, after many years of pressure from civil society organisations working with abused women. Success in getting the issue onto the policy agenda was the result of almost twenty years of organising around violence against women. The Act was passed in the context of the impending constitutional and political change in the country, and extremely high levels of violence against women in South Africa.

Researchers in South Africa blamed high rape statistics, both during apartheid and in the transition, on the gender and racial inequalities spawned by the social and political apartheid system and its aftermath. The particular ways in which patriarchal traditions intersected with cultural and religious customs tended to create patterns of male control that subordinated women from all class and ethnic groups in South Africa. Violence or the threat of violence was and remains deeply embedded within sexual relationships. In research conducted for a submission to the Truth and Reconciliation Commission in 1996, Goldblatt and Meintjes argued that the increasing militarisation of South African society, combined with patriarchal traditions of control and possession of women, needed to be taken into account (Goldblatt and Meintjes 1996). Johanna Kistner, a clinical psychologist working in Katlehong, a township south-east of Johannesburg, argued that 'People have become used to employing violence as a means of resolving conflict or asserting power over others. It will take generations to recover our psychological and social balance' (Newsday 1994: A4). The same may be said for the 'patchwork quilt' of patriarchies that exist all over rural and urban South Africa (Bozzoli 1983: 139).

Rape was hardly a new phenomenon when organisations formed in the late 1970s to provide support for women survivors of domestic abuse and rape. The context of their formation was the emergence of a range of social movements opposed to the apartheid state and demanding civil rights. A burgeoning trade union movement after strikes in 1973 coincided with a growing youth movement based upon black consciousness that challenged subordination. Children took to the streets in 1976 in a revolt against the Bantu Education system. Civic movements opposed apartheid local government and spawned rent and consumer boycotts throughout the late 1970s and 1980s. Alternate repression and reform did not appease opposition. In the 1980s, separate women's organisations joined the broad struggle against apartheid, but infused their demands with a new discourse of women's liberation.

The anti-rape movement was the most vociferous, basing itself around demands for an end to violence against women. Rape support

144

groups in the late 1970s grew from the initiative of white women, who often propounded explicit feminist, often radical feminist, agendas. In the 1980s groups formed in black townships too. They raised awareness of the role of the police and the courts in exacerbating the trauma of women rape survivors. The first organisation, Rape Crisis, was formed in Cape Town. Its focus was on training women counsellors, and researching policing and legislative procedures. In 1979, People Opposing Woman Abuse (POWA) was formed in Johannesburg. Although it attempted to recruit its members and support from a broader constituency, it remained a largely white organisation during the 1980s, focused on counsellor training in particular. National conferences of regional groupings met during the 1980s to share experiences and training initiatives. It was the specific engagement of these organisations with the justice system that led to an engagement with the state bureaucracy.

One of the main reasons that so few women came forward to report rape and sexual abuse was their experience of the police and the courts. First, police were reluctant to intervene in what they deemed were 'domestic concerns'. This view derived from the conventional wisdom that men had rights over their intimate partners. Once a domestic violence case got to court, women faced not only the social prejudices and patriarchal norms of judges, but also particular legal constraints. Rape support organisations counselled survivors on how to deal with these problems but they also challenged the perceptions and understandings of judges and the law.

Organisations challenged the conventional wisdom about rape. They exposed the context of fear and the power asserted by perpetrators. The criminal justice system viewed rape as a crime worthy of the death sentence under the Criminal Procedure Act (51 of 1977). Yet convicting judges in many cases of rape seldom gave perpetrators more than three- to six-year sentences. Part of the reason was that, in law, women were viewed as 'suspect witnesses', whilst the view of rape as a sex act and not a case of assault prevailed. A central aspect of rape trials was to prove that the survivor had not given 'consent', that sexual intercourse had in fact occurred and was forced upon the victim. Both the reporting procedures and the subsequent court case were difficult and humiliating for survivors. The adversarial nature of criminal procedures opened survivors to cross-examination by hostile defence advocates – in effect, a form of 'secondary victimisation'.

The legislative framework within which sexual violence was mediated consisted mainly of two acts: the Sexual Offences Act of 1957 and the Child Care Act 74 of 1983. These largely dealt with what were considered unlawful sexual acts between same-sex partners and children. Neither dealt with the question of domestic violence against women. This lacuna was the object of considerable lobbying in the 1980s by organisations which were generally concerned with the condition of women, including NGOs not necessarily opposed to the government, such as the National Council of Women and the Women's Bureau. This general interest provided opportunities for dedicated rape crisis organisations to find a platform to engage the state. The process of ensuring a policy and legislative response was carefully orchestrated, with strategic alliances between particular champions in civil society and influential actors, decision makers and legislators in the state.

From lobby to policy – the significance of strategic alliances and individual champions

Conservative women's organisations concerned with growing levels of violence, and the awareness raised by more radical groups, led to a general acceptance of the need for law reform. The Women's Bureau, a national network of consumer groups, under the leadership of Margaret Lessing, put its weight behind attempts at law reform in the late 1970s and early 1980s. Amongst its members was Dr Frances Bosman, an academic from the University of South Africa, who spent some time in the Department of Justice in the 1970s. Dr Bosman had considerable influence both as a law professor and as the editor of *De Rebus*, a respected and leading South African legal journal.

Her particular concern was the issue of violence and its effects on juvenile offenders and she presented evidence to a Commission of Enquiry into Juvenile Offenders, the Hoexter Commission, in 1979 on these questions. Her intervention brought her to the attention of the Minister of Justice, Kobie Coetzee. She then became his adviser on family matters (Bosman interview 1999). Kobie Coetzee became pivotal in ensuring that the woman's agenda, such as it was in the late 1970s and 1980s, became a policy issue.

Although much criticism has been levelled at the limits of legal reform before the 1990s, it is well to recall the highly conservative and patriarchal nature of the former state. Many of the reforms were wrung out of the regime as compromises. The Minister of Justice was comparatively enlightened compared to his predecessors. It was he who led the secret discussions with Mandela and other imprisoned ANC leaders during the late 1980s. In the early 1980s, Coetzee was open to suggestions for change from Frances Bosman and Margaret Lessing. In the late

1980s a partnership between Bosman and Lessing and the Justice Ministry occurred. In 1986 the issue of violence against women was taken up with serious intent by the South African Law Commission (SALC), prompted by Minister of Justice Kobie Coetzee.

The SALC conducts research into issues that require legislation. Its practices and procedures have not changed markedly since the 1980s. The process involves setting up a committee comprised of legal researchers employed by the Commission, as well as drawing in experts from civil society. The task of the committee is then to draw up issue papers and discussion documents that are circulated for public comment. The SALC uses the media to publicise its work. Once public discussion has occurred, the draft legislation is then drawn up and sent to the parliamentary Justice Portfolio Committee for debate. The Justice Portfolio Committee in turn draws in other relevant portfolio committees to discuss the new legislation. Before 1994, the process of public participation was confined largely to 'expert' opinion.

The relationship between Bosman and the rape crisis organisations was of particular importance, for she was persuaded by their arguments about secondary victimisation,[2] and pushed for their inclusion in the project report. She pushed too for the establishment of a Family Advocate's Office that could deal with intimate family violence. But this brought her into conflict with the rape crisis organisations, as we shall see. The Office was set up in 1989 through the Justice Department, and Bosman was appointed to the position. The establishment of the Family Advocate was a path-breaking move on the part of the inherently conservative legal establishment. But the real test came with the reform of laws relating to violence against women.

Law reform under apartheid – The Prevention of Family Violence Act (133 of 1993)

In the late 1980s a new set of strategic relationships developed, this time between the Attorney-General in the Cape, Frank Kahn, Rape Crisis and other service providers in the field. Kahn responded to protest about secondary victimisation by setting up the Cape Attorney-General's Task Group on Rape. This led to a more sensitive approach to domestic violence and rape cases, including a specialised pilot rape court to handle rape cases (Hanssen 1992: 17). Whilst considerable advances were made in the Western Cape, this was not true elsewhere in the country. Conservative attitudes prevailed everywhere. Moreover, there was little national coordination amongst rape groups of these initiatives.

147

It was not until 1994 that regional organisational networks and a national violence network were established.

The new strategic alliances materialised in the emergence of new policy concerns within the Justice Ministry and in the SALC in 1989. In 1990 vigorous debate on how the issue of violence against women should be taken forward in the new constitutional arena ushered in a new discourse and gave impetus to the pressure from rape crisis organisations. In a critique of the existing framework and especially of the Family Advocate, Rape Crisis, represented by Desiree Hanssen, a criminologist from the University of Cape Town, argued strongly for a critical appraisal of the rights of the family in the context of women's oppression and experience of physical violation. Hanssen suggested that protecting the family would entrench women's subordination (Hanssen 1990). The Rape Crisis intervention was important in establishing a new understanding and discourse around the relationship between gender advocacy and the state. This led to a coordinated plan for dealing with battered women in the Western Cape.

In the early 1990s, in the context of the looming political contest with new opposition groups like the ANC, the apartheid state sought to repeal all discriminatory legislation. Kobie Coetzee appointed Sheila Camerer, a former lawyer and local government politician, as his Deputy Minister in 1992, and gave her the task of overseeing the changes in legislation. Together with the Cape Attorney-General, Frank Kahn, Coetzee pushed for an increase in the number of women magistrates in the face of considerable opposition from the Justice Department (Camerer interview, 1999).

But new political actors were on the scene after 1990. In the early 1990s there emerged a small caucus of women activists which included a strong feminist presence within the recently unbanned ANC and ANC Women's League (ANCWL). This group included amongst others members of the ANC's Emancipation Commission, Frene Ginwala, the Deputy Head, and Baleka Kgotsitsile, who was also the Secretary-General of the ANCWL. A think tank was set up which drew in sympathetic internal ANC supporters, academics and activists to debate a 'woman's agenda', and ensure that women's needs were catered for in the negotiations process.[3] The group prepared a number of submissions to the technical committees of the constitutional negotiations. Amongst these was a brief report and advocacy submission by the ANC on violence against women. This document drew on the 1993 Vienna Protocols with respect to violence against women. It also pointed to the nature of endemic violence against women in South Africa, and argued for a gun-free South Africa and gender training in the police, and those in the justice system in general, including magistrates and justices (ANC Emancipation Commission 1993)

International protocols contributed also to setting the key priorities for gender activists and women politicians. The 1993 Vienna Protocols were a landmark in the development of new international institutional mechanisms for monitoring violence against women nationally. The scope of discrimination in CEDAW was extended to include the issue of violence against women in the United Nations Declaration on the Elimination of Violence against Women (United Nations 1993). Included in its definition of violence was not simply physical and sexual violence, but also psychological violence, and the threat of such violence. In 1994, the appointment of the UN Special Rapporteur on Violence against Women became strategically significant during the South African NGO campaign to make the issue of violence a priority in the policing and legal reform process, as we shall see below.

The WNC campaign and research to identify the needs of women corroborated much of the work undertaken by violence support organisations, and brought to the fore the endemic nature of domestic violence in South African society. Women across race, class and cultural groups experienced domestic violence. The demands which women made during the campaign were reflected in Article 10 of the Women's Charter for Effective Equality. The demands included legal protection against sexual and racial harassment, abuse and assault; the call for facilities staffed by trained personnel where women could report cases of violence; and the provision of shelters and counselling services for survivors and appropriate education and training for all service providers, including the police, prosecutors, magistrates, judges and district surgeons (*Women's Charter For Effective Equality* 1994).

In 1993, the National Party government published the Prevention of Family Violence Bill. This caused a furore, for the publication of the Bill was undertaken without consultation or discussion with the WNC, even though the National Party was a member of the Coalition. The first public forum in which the process was discussed was an international conference in May 1993 held by the WNC. Violence against women organisations criticised the Bill for not reflecting the real needs of women. They argued that the Bill was introduced with undue haste and lack of adequate consultation with organisations working with abused women. However, powerful voices, including that of Helen Suzman, argued that the gender lobby should be wary of rejecting either the process or the Bill; instead women should 'take what they could get', even if that were crumbs from the reform table.[4] These cautionary voices drew upon long years of experience of lobbying within the old order for a change in attitudes towards violence against women. However, the process was divisive, and revealed the thin veil of consensus that existed at that time even within the WNC. None of this prevented the Bill from becoming law.

The 1993 Act in practice

The Act did make a difference. First, it introduced an interdict system, which enabled battered women to seek protection from a judge or magistrate against abuse by a partner. This was accompanied by a suspensive warrant of arrest should the abuser break the terms of the interdict. The Act also simplified the court process, by allowing interdicts to be issued through the magistrates' courts rather than the Supreme Court. The procedure was certainly less costly than the previous route via the Supreme Court. Moreover, as Joanne Fedler, a lecturer in law at the University of the Witwatersrand and member of People Opposing Woman Abuse, noted in her critique of the operation of the 1993 Act, it served an 'ideological function in its recognition of the problem of abuse and the condemnation of its practice' (Fedler 1995: 233).

From the beginning, however, the Act had limitations. First, abused women were reluctant to avail themselves of the law. Moreover, many women could not access the courts even if they had wanted to, as many were prevented by violent husbands from leaving their homes, or lived in areas remote from any magistrates' court. Magistrates were often ignorant of the Act, and the regulations were not accompanied by clear directions to magistrates. Many magistrates continued to issue peace orders and not interdicts. (Peace orders 'bound abusers to keep the peace', but did not have the same force and authority as the interdicts, which restrained perpetrators from continuing their abuse on pain of facing arrest.) Most significantly of all, few women were aware of the existence of the new remedies available under the Act. Other criticisms were raised of a more legal and technical nature, including the fact that domestic violence was not properly defined, and needed to be understood in the context of unequal power relationships, and of psychological abuse as well. Further, a broader definition of domestic abuse in family and intimate relationships was needed, and problems of economic dependence, custody and maintenance needed to be addressed (ibid.). These were strong arguments in favour of reform and the new democratic government came to power in 1994 with a strong commitment to reform the law that had been so strongly resisted by it own women members.

Lobbying for change in the law: partnerships between the state and civil society

Pressure for changes in the law came from different sectors, both nationally and internationally: NGOs dealing with violence against women on a daily basis; the legal profession; the political parties. After a year of testing the Act in operation, many service organisations and legal experts in the area of battery and violence against women began to press the Ministry of Justice and to write in law journals about the limitations of the Act. Government commitment to addressing the issue of violence against women had crystallised after the Beijing World Conference in 1995. But even before this, important initiatives and commitments had been made on this issue by the new ANC-led government (*Beijing Conference Report* 1994). This took the form of partnerships with organisations in civil society working on violence against women.

During 1994 NGOs and the Department of Welfare came together after a conference held at the University of South Africa to devise strategies to eradicate violence against women. Their approach was essentially multi-disciplinary, with law reform forming only one aspect of policy discussions. They formed an interim committee, the Desk on Domestic Violence, whose task was to form local and regional networks. The Desk also organised a national conference in Cape Town in November 1995. The Minister of Welfare and Population Development, Geraldine Fraser-Moleketi, and the Deputy Minister of Justice, Dr Manto Tshabalala-Msimang, provided significant support for the domestic violence lobby. The latter in particular put her weight behind the national campaign which culminated in the International Day of No Violence Against Women, 25 November 1995.

Following the 1995 conference in Cape Town, the government entered a partnership with civil society organisations to combat violence against women. This was the origin of the National Network on Violence against Women, which brought together relevant government departments – Health, Welfare and Population Development, Justice – as well as NGOs. The Network was organised at provincial level as well. Funding for this initiative came from the United Nations Development Programme (UNDP) and from government. The Network functioned at different levels of efficiency and effectiveness. Coordination was, and remains, a problem. But the Network was important in ensuring the circulation of information about policy initiatives. This meant that organisations were able to input into the policy and legislative process at different times.

At the same time that UN initiatives were advancing in South Africa, Human Rights Watch had conducted research under the auspices of its Women's Rights Project entitled 'Violence Against Women in South Africa: the State Response to Domestic Violence and Rape' (1995). The report found that despite the political changes in the country after 1994, the state's response to violence against women was woefully inadequate. Human Rights Watch was particularly critical of the responses of the police. Police were 'hostile and unsympathetic to women who had been battered by their partners or sexually assaulted ... ignorant of the legal remedies open to women, and incompetence or indifference meant that many perpetrators were not arrested or that changes against them were dropped'. The report also suggested that prosecutors were poorly trained and paid and 'were likely to treat cases of violence against women with less seriousness than other assault cases'. Judges and magistrates were adjudged to have the same prejudices as the police and prosecutors. Moreover, the report suggested, state doctors, too, had little understanding of the needs either of the victim or of the requirements of the legal system in cases of rape and abuse.

Pressure on the government to deal with intimate family violence in the criminal justice system did not abate in the wake of its stated commitments. In October 1996, the Special Rapporteur appointed by the United Nations, Radhika Coomaraswamy, visited South Africa. She reported that the criminal justice system needed to be overhauled in order for crime, in particular crime against women, to be appropriately and adequately dealt with (Coomaraswamy 1997). A regional conference on the issue of prevention of violence against women in the Southern African Development Community region was held during 5–8 March 1998. Translating legislative commitment into policy discussions and the promotion of inter-regional cooperation, the conference culminated in the signature of a draft SADC Declaration on the Prevention and Eradication of Violence Against Women and Children (Combrinck 1998: 1). The declaration 'recognises that violence against women constitutes a serious violation of fundamental human rights and reflects the unequal relations of power and value between men and women'.

In terms of proposing practical measures to eliminate violence against women, the conference made a number of proposals. Legislative measures on sexual offences and domestic violence, accessible and effective policing, prosecution services, health and social services as well as gender training of judicial service providers were all seen as important. A key aspect of the recommendations was that the SADC Mauritius Summit in September 1998 adopted the SADC draft

Declaration. This provided a framework within which SADC states would accept responsibility for developing effective policies and practical measures to end violence against women. The Declaration initiated an important process of bringing violence into the regional discussions about human rights.

Changing the law under a democratic government, 1994–8: collaboration of service providers in state and society

In 1995 the SALC received a number of complaints about the unconstitutionality of the Prevention of Family Violence Act from attorneys representing a number of men who believed that their right to a fair hearing had been violated by the Act (Dicker 1994: 213). Countering arguments suggested that the harm experienced by the victim, and the urgent need for relief, justified the departure from the rule about both sides being heard. The SALC then set about canvassing the views of the Department of Justice and the Family Advocate's Office, and in February 1996 set up a Project Committee, Project 100, to review the issue of domestic violence. This Committee comprised a representative grouping of legal experts and members of support organisations working on domestic violence. Submissions were called for after the publication of an issue paper on domestic violence. The issue paper identified problems raised earlier by critics of the act. The Project Committee worked on a detailed discussion paper, produced in February 1998, and drew up draft legislation. Both were widely distributed, with a three-month period given for comment.

NGOs and service organisations were well prepared to respond to the issue paper. The collaboration between organisations in the National Network on Violence Against Women had given service providers considerable access to planning the changes which they saw as necessary to the policy and legal framework. In the Western Cape an informal lobby comprised of the Human Rights Committee (an NGO), the Black Sash, the Women and Human Rights Project at the University of the Western Cape, Rape Crisis (Western Cape) and the ANC Parliamentary Women's Caucus met in a consultative forum to compile a submission to the Law Commission. It focused on international and constitutional human rights jurisprudence. A further workshop was then held with the Law, Race and Gender Unit at the University of Cape Town to discuss, and comment on, the submission to be made to the Law Commission. Participants included the Gender Policy Unit of the Department of Justice, magistrates, and service organisations. The final draft of the submission was endorsed by the Western Cape Regional Network on Violence against Women.

Concurrently with the Law Commission's process, a high-level campaign spearheaded by Deputy Minister of Justice Dr Manto Tshabalala-Msimang was undertaken from November 1996 to 21 March 1997. This included workshops within the Department of Justice to train staff in the justice system to create a sensitive environment in cases involving violence against women. At the same time, the Department undertook a public education campaign, widely distributing leaflets and posters. Finally, in July 1997, an inter-departmental task team, with members of the National Network on Violence against Women, drew up a manual for the use of all role players in the justice system and counselling services in cases involving sexual violence against women. State and society appeared to be working in a coordinated partnership.

The parliamentary process: strategic partnerships of women and men

In Parliament, meanwhile, Pregs Govender, chairperson of the Parliamentary Committee, took the issue up quite specifically in a review of progress in areas established as priorities by the Committee in 1997. In February 1998 the Parliamentary Committee for the first time acquired the services of a full-time researcher, Corianne de Villiers, a trained lawyer. She assumed part of the responsibility for the process of monitoring the progress of policy and legislation affecting women and establishing priorities. But Govender was the driving force, providing both insight and supervision (Corianne de Villiers interview, 1999).

The review considered three areas: budgetary considerations, policy priorities and legislative reform. Amongst the priorities identified by the Parliamentary Committee had been that of domestic violence legislation. In the process of drawing up the review, de Villiers consulted widely with various sectors, including the SALC, women's organisations and research groups. The Parliamentary Committee, in establishing priorities in 1997, had identified domestic violence as an 'urgent' issue, and had argued in its annual report that a Bill had to be tabled in 1998. By early 1998 this had not yet occurred. According to the timetabling of the parliamentary process, in order for the Bill to be considered during the 1998 session, the tabling of the Bill would need to be made by June 1998 at the latest. In discussions with the SALC, it became clear that the Project Committee of the SALC, awaiting representations on its dis-cussion paper, would not be ready by then.

The Parliamentary Committee was intent on ensuring that its priori-ties should be met, and that the Bill should be rushed through Parliament, regardless of the status of the Draft Bill and the lack of comment from civil society and lawyers working in the field. Govender devised a strategy to ensure that the Bill was pushed through Parlia-ment before the end of the session. The ANC Women's Caucus was gal-vanised. The matter was also discussed at the highest level in the ANC. At this point the Minister of Justice, Dullah Omar, and the chairperson of the Justice Portfolio Committee, advocate Johnny de Lange, inter-vened to expedite the production of the Draft Bill for discussion in Parliament. Their intervention was crucial in ensuring that the SALC delivered to Parliament the report of the Project Committee findings and a Bill that reflected their findings.

The Project Committee was informed that it had to produce the Bill urgently, and that public hearings on the proposed Bill would have to by-pass the SALC process. The public would be given an opportunity to comment on the Draft Bill at the parliamentary public hearings. The Project Committee then sent its report and Draft Bill to the commis-sioners of the SALC for sanction. The report reflected the detailed discus-sions it had been having in its review of the 1993 Act.

However, the report and the Bill were rejected by the chairperson of the Commission, Judge Olivier, and one of the commissioners, who then drew up a minority report, and sent this to Parliament. A major area of contention between the Project Committee and the two commissioners resided in the view held by the latter that the SALC should use gender-neutral language in its proposals. The Project Committee argued that a more gender-sensitive and more specific approach should be adopted. 'Domestic relationships', as a phrase attempting to capture the notion of a live-in partnership, obscured the fact that the majority of survivors of violence were women. Instead of taking these arguments seriously, the commissioners had written a dismissive one-page report on the work of the Project Committee. The researcher on the Project Committee at the SALC, Michael Palumbo, then flew to Cape Town from Pretoria to present the second, revised, Bill from the Law Commission (Corianne de Villiers interview, 1999).

Members of the Project Committee, most of whom were experts in the counselling of domestic violence survivors, or else were legal experts in this field, including legal academics and practising lawyers, were incensed at the attitude of the SALC commissioners. There was intense

155

lobbying behind the scenes. De Lange, Justice Committee chairperson, was briefed by Govender and de Villiers. He read the minority report and objected to its dismissive tone. He demanded to see the full report of the Project Committee. He also demanded to see the original Bill drawn up by the Project Committee. In this way, although there were considerable problems with the Draft Bill as it was first presented to the Justice Portfolio Committee in Parliament, it was the Project Committee's Bill that became the substantive Bill ultimately presented to Parliament. Members of the Justice Committee and the Parliamentary Joint Monitoring Committee on the Quality of Life and Status of Women then jointly sat with drafters from the Justice Ministry to process a Bill which could be presented to joint public hearings. The Domestic Violence Bill (B75–98) was tabled before Parliament during the mid-year recess in 1998.

Prior to the public hearings, a workshop of interested parties, including members of the Commission on Gender Equality, the Human Rights Committee, Rape Crisis and the Community Law Centre of the University of the Western Cape, was held. Corianne de Villiers, the Parliamentary Committee researcher, was key in facilitating the presentation of submissions to Parliament. The next stage was the Joint Public Hearings on 18 and 19 August 1998. De Villiers ensured that the Justice Committee was provided with all the relevant arguments and information emanating from the thirty submissions that were presented. She made sure that all the summaries (written by Michael Palumbo of the SALC) reflected the substantive points made in the submissions.

The Bill that was eventually debated in Parliament was accompanied by an important innovation: a carefully worded memorandum on the objectives of the Bill. This memorandum reiterated the commitment of the South African government to the eradication of violence against women: it intended 'to comply with the provisions of the Beijing Platform and has ratified the Convention on the Elimination of All Forms of Discrimination Against Women (CEDAW) during 1995'. The memorandum noted the limitations in the Prevention of Family Violence Act, 1993 (Act No. 133 of 1993). It noted, too, that the Domestic Violence Bill broadened the scope of the 1993 Act: 'The Bill recognises that domestic violence is a serious crime against society', and presented 'an obstacle to achieving gender equality'. Specifically, the new Bill broadened the definition of a domestic relationship and of the meaning of violence. The definition was widened to include psychological and economic deprivation. The Bill also made it incumbent on the police to inform victims of their rights at the scene of any incident of domestic violence. Perhaps most important of all, the Bill provided for the arrest of suspected violent abusers by a peace officer without a warrant of arrest.

The debate in Parliament with respect to domestic violence was uncontroversial. It was passed as part of a trilogy that also featured the Maintenance Bill and the Customary Marriages Bill. The National Party tried to score points about being the first, politically, to recognise domestic violence as an issue. Suzanne Vos of the Inkatha Freedom Party asked perhaps the most pertinent question in relation to the passing of the new Act: 'Show me the money that the Justice Department can use to really make a difference to the lives of millions of women and their children in this country' (Hansard 2 November 1998: 7224). This proved a prescient question. It was certainly not answered in the debate, and the question of resources has proved to be a major stumbling block to the adequate implementation of the new Act.

The passing of the Act was simply the first step along a much longer road. Regulations to implement it took more than a year to be drawn up and ratified by Parliament. The fast-tracking process had itself created considerable difficulties, not the least of which was the fact that the funding for the implementation of the Act had not been included in the state's budget for different departments. Departments themselves were not adequately prepared for the procedures required. The Act itself had flaws that were subsequently identified by service providers. The first of these was that too much onus was placed upon the police in providing support for victims of abuse. The second was that inadequate thought was given to the need for regulations to coordinate the activities of the departments called upon to provide services from the time of the rape through to the court case itself. NGOs involved in providing support found that, after the second election in 1999 and the appointment of new and different political leaders to head up ministries, some of the champions who drove the policy and legislative development were removed. Increasing bureaucratisation of the relationship between civil society and the state has also asserted itself, making the possibility of deepening relations between civil society and the state more difficult.

Conclusions

The detailed narrative analysis of the process of policy development in the area of violence against women highlights a number of significant factors that are of more general relevance in characterising and under-standing women's engagement with the state around a woman's agenda. One prerequisite for the successful mobilisation of women around the issue of violence was the existence of a broader political women's movement. This provided the basis for specific aspects of women's needs and interests to became public policy issues. The success hinged on civil society's relationships with key champions of women's issues in Parliament and in the bureaucracy. These champions are politicians and officials with close connections to women's organisations and the women's movement. In the case of the Domestic Violence Act in South Africa, there was a long history of activism that forced the matter onto the political agenda more than twenty years before the transition to democracy. The issue would never have come to the attention of decision makers, however, had it not been for the role of particular women, champions committed to ensuring that the issue became a matter of policy: Frances Bosman during the 1970s and 1980s, Sheila Camerer in the late 1980s and early 1990s, Geraldine Fraser-Moleketi, Manto Tshabalala and Pregs Govender after 1994. They drove the policy and legislative processes. Throughout the different periods, these committed individuals turned to male supporters, all decision makers, who were able to ensure that the legislation was steered through to legislative finality. Finally, though, the context of democracy and new institution building were crucial. But whilst the new institution-building process, including the negotiations for a new constitution, gave opportunities for women activists to ensure that a new set of political interests were inserted into the state's political and policy agenda, the earlier activism and organisation of the 1970s and 1980s had made the gains possible.

References

African National Congress Emancipation Commission (1993) *Submission to the Violence Technical Committee on Violence against Women*, Multi-Party Talks.

Albertyn, C. (1994) 'Women and the Transition to Democracy in South Africa', in C. Murray (ed.), *Gender and the New South African Legal Order*, Johannesburg: Juta.

Bozzoli, B. (1983) 'Marxism, Feminism and South African Studies', *Journal of Southern African Studies* 9, 2: 139–71.

Combrinck, H. (1998) 'Preventing Violence against Women in Southern Africa', *Women and Human Rights Documentation Centre Newsletter*, 2, 2.

Coomaraswamy, R. (1997) 'Report of the Special Rapporteur on Violence Against Women: Its Causes and Consequences', UN Document E/CN.4/1997/47.

Dicker, L. (1994) 'The Prevention of Family Violence Act: Innovation or Violation?' *De Rebus*, 213.

Fastold, M. and A. Hellum (1985) 'Money and Work in Marriage: Women's Perspectives on Family Law', Working Paper 3, Oslo University.

Fedler, J. (1995) 'Lawyering Domestic Violence through the Prevention of Family Violence Act 1993 – an Evaluation after a Year of Operation', *South African Law Journal*, 112: 231–51.

Goldblatt, B. and S. Meintjes (1996) *Gender and the Truth and Reconciliation Commission. A Submission to the Truth and Reconciliation Commission*, Johannesburg: Centre for Applied Legal Studies, University of the Witwatersrand (CALS).

Hansard, Monday 2 November 1998, 7224

Hanssen, D. (1990) 'Working against Violence against Women: Concrete Recommendations from Rape Crisis', Workshop: Violence Against Women, unpublished manuscript.

—— (1992) 'A Shock to the System: the First Rape Court and the Legal Recognition of Rape Trauma Syndrome', *Agenda*, 10.

Meintjes, S. (1998) 'Gender, Nationalism and Transformation: Difference and Commonality in South Africa's Past and Present', in R. Wilford and R. L. Miller (eds.), *Women, Ethnicity and Nationalism: the Politics of Transition*, London: Routledge.

Pretoria Women's Charter, Women's National Coalition (1994) *Beijing Conference Report: 1994 Country Report on the Status of South African Women*, Johannesburg: Government Printer.

South African Law Commission, (1997) 'Discussion Document 70: Project 100'

United Nations (1993) *Declaration on the Elimination of Violence against Women*, Resolution 48/104 of 20 December 1993.

Women's Charter for Effective Equality, 1994, Article 10.

Interviews: Sheila Camerer interview, 20 April 1999.
Corianne de Villiers, telephonic interview, 13 April 1999 .
Joanne Fedler, telephonic interew, 13 April 1999
Francis Bosman, telephonic interview, 8 July 1999.

Notes

1 This chapter draws upon research undertaken for a report by Cathi Albertyn, Beth Goldblatt, Shireen Hassim, Likhapa Mbatha and Sheila Meintjes (1999), *Engendering the Political Agenda: a South African Case Study*, prepared for United Nations International Institute for Research and Training for the Advancement of Women, Centre for Applied Legal Studies, University of the Witwatersrand.

2 This term refers to the possible discrimination experienced by survivors of violence from the police and the courts in the course of investigation of the complaints. Indeed, often the police are themselves dismissive and abusive of women who lay charges, reflecting the strength of the myth that 'women ask for it'.

3 The author was a member of this group.

4 The debate occurred at the WNC International Conference on Women's Machinery, May 1993.

6

The 'Lost Clause': The Campaign to Advance Women's Property Rights in the Uganda 1998 Land Act

SHEILA KAWAMARA-MISHAMBI
and IRENE OVONJI-ODIDA [1]

This chapter analyses women's efforts in Uganda to bring gender equity into land law reform. An ongoing campaign that started in 1995 and was spearheaded by two advocacy coalitions, the Uganda Land Alliance (ULA)[2] and the Uganda Women's Network (UWONET)[3] has aimed to establish married women's rights to co-own part of their husband's land.[4] In spite of substantial resistance to this proposition from across the social spectrum, from the ministry in charge of preparing the Land Bill, and from many politicians, the women's movement and its political allies succeeded in passing its 'co-ownership clause' in Parliament just before the Bill was to become law in July 1998. But this clause failed to appear in the published Land Act, dropping out through a combination of procedural error and high-level hostility to what was seen as an erosion of men's property rights. This chapter traces the efforts by women in civil society and politics to define and promote women's land rights in the campaign to promote the 'co-ownership clause'. It describes the resistance they faced and the extraordinary exercise of executive *diktat* in quashing the clause. In discussing the way the clause was 'lost' it poses questions about the political effectiveness of women in civil society and in government in Uganda.

In 1998, the government of Uganda introduced a Land Bill in Parliament. Many social groups, interested in land reform for various reasons, had monitored the land law reform process since 1995 and had proposals of their own. The women's movement had participated in the civil society organisation around the issue under the Uganda Land Alliance. However, by 1997 women's NGOs had moved away from the ULA because they felt gender concerns were being sidelined. Led by UWONET, these women's NGOs highlighted many sections in the draft 1998 Land Bill that they found unsatisfactory, proposing alternatives that they felt would more genuinely resolve gendered asymmetries in land rights. One particular and controversial amendment which was championed by the women's movement has come to be known as the co-ownership clause, and proposed spousal co-ownership of family (or 'homestead') land. In Uganda most subsistence farmers are women: this clause was seen as a means of protecting their access to land.

This co-ownership clause became a public issue in Uganda during the debates surrounding land law reform in 1998. Although proposed by the women's lobby earlier than 1998, it came to the fore during a workshop organised by the Forum for Women in Democracy (FOWODE)[5] for members of Parliament in April 1998, in which the President expressed reservations about the clause. His concern was that women, if given rights over their husband's land, might engage in serial monogamy in order to build up personal landholdings. He proposed limiting 'conditions' including a 'probationary period' of marriage before land could be co-owned by a spouse.

The proposal was included in a memorandum to the Parliamentary Sessional Committee on Land, Works, Transport and Communication in charge of drafting the Bill, but the committee did not include it among the amendments it proposed to Parliament in its report. The co-owner-ship clause was therefore moved as an amendment by the Woman Member of Parliament for Mbarara District, and now Minister of Ethics and Integrity, the Hon. Miria Matembe. The amendment proposed was:

> where land is held or acquired for the joint occupation and use of the spouses, the spouses will hold the land as joint owners and the recorder shall register the spouses accordingly.
>
> In the case of polygamous union, each wife shall jointly own with her husband a piece of land on which she resides and works. Where there are many wives occupying and working on the same piece of land, they shall hold the land jointly with their husband.

The intention was that family land – homestead land on which a family resided or from which it derived its sustenance – should be vested jointly in both husband and wife/wives, and be owned as such. The amendment was designed to compensate for the fact that, although the Land Bill would give women equal rights to purchase land, in practice their lack of resources to purchase land would mean that few would be able to do so. The Land Bill would therefore produce little change in men's virtual monopoly on land ownership in the country.

The women's movement carried out extensive lobbying and publicity during the parliamentary debate, and working with the Women's Caucus

161

in Parliament, was able to convince a majority of MPs to accept certain principles relating to spousal co-ownership of land. As summarised by the Speaker James Wapakhabulo, who was chairing the debate in June 1998 during the second reading, the principles on which consensus had been reached were:

> Where land is occupied as a home, where land is used, it should belong to the husband and wife. In a polygamous situation they should be the wives and the husband where they work and reside should belong both to the husband and each of the wives [sic]. Where they (wives) work on the same piece of land they shall hold the land jointly with the husband (Hansard 25 June 1998: 117–18).

At the end of the debate, based on the consensus evident in the discussion, the Speaker referred the matter for drafting. He said:

> Now as far as this one is concerned [the proposed clause] we have made a decision. It will be referred to the drafting committee of experts and then it will come back here for us to baptise it with a section and adopt it. Otherwise these are drafting instructions to what appears to be a popular position subject to clarification and drafting (Hansard 25 June 1998: 119).

The clause was unanimously accepted during the parliamentary debate and its supporters looked forward to its appearance in the Act which was approved by Parliament. However, on publication it was found that the co-ownership clause was missing. Astounded members of the ULA and UWONET tried to find out how it had been omitted. From the reading of the parliamentary record in Hansard, it appears that there was a procedural failure: the House Speaker, who had previously declared the clause as accepted, had not re-introduced the clause to Parliament once it had gone through the drafting committee to have it formally adopted (Tripp 2002).

Thereafter, the women's lobby group and sympathetic women parliamentarians challenged the omission, and held several meetings with the Sessional Parliamentary Committee and various high-level government officials to seek clarification. The government position was that the Act could only be amended if the clause was introduced afresh – as an amendment to what was now law. However, the NRM government is reluctant to re-open debate on the Land Act, and with it the many other unresolved tensions over competing land claims of different ethnic groups that had dominated debates over land law reform.

Land tenure reform in Uganda

Uganda's new land law is intended to regulate land ownership, management and use, to simplify ownership and tenancy systems, and to liberalise the land market. The Land Act has been heralded by its chief architects as providing 'fundamental reforms' and entailing 'revolutionary' aspects related to land ownership, tenure and management. In particular, the law enables people to transform usufruct into ownership rights, thus enabling many land users to have more secure tenure.

Since Uganda's independence in 1962 there had been no significant land ownership or tenure reform, besides the 1975 Land Reform Decree. Prior to the decree there existed four tenure systems in the country: customary, *mailo*,[6] freehold and leasehold. The last three had been introduced during colonial rule. The 1975 decree abolished all forms of tenure greater than leasehold – that is, *mailo* and freehold – eroded the rights of customary landholders, and declared all land public land. However, this decree was never fully implemented due to the protracted civil war and political instability endured by Uganda between 1979 and 1986.

The NRM government which took power in January 1986 began a number of reform programmes, including a constitutional review process initiated in 1988. A constitutional commission (the Odoki Commission) of twenty eminent Ugandans, including two women and headed by a senior judge, Justice Benjamin Odoki, was given the mandate to consult Ugandans at home and abroad on various issues considered crucial to the constitutional order. Two issues that generated particularly intense debate were the land question and women's human rights.

Although the Odoki Commission made efforts to consult widely and address concerns of less influential groups such as women and the poor, women, especially in rural areas, had fewer opportunities than men to present their proposals. This was largely due to their lower social status and inability to voice their concerns in public gatherings. Consequently, women's organisations, individual women in and outside politics, and the Ministry of Women in Development organised a parallel process of collecting views from women. Regarding land, it was highlighted that, for cultural and economic reasons, very few women in Uganda owned land. This led to a proposal that women's land ownership in their own right be promoted in the constitution.

The draft constitution was debated by a Constituent Assembly (CA) set up for that purpose. During the debates on land reform the CA became extremely fractious, with several competing interests advanced.

163

The main controversy has to do with efforts by the central Uganda kingdom of Buganda to regain its cultural and economic prominence. During the colonial period, the power of the collaborationist kingdoms of Buganda, Toro and Ankole had been inflated by altering traditional land tenure arrangements to reward supporters of the colonial regime. The 1900–1 agreements with these kingdoms gave chiefs and collaborators ownership rights over significant tracts of land in an arrangement referred to in the vernacular as *mailo*. Through this a new land-owning class was created, *mailo* land holders, and the customary users of land became tenants, *bibanja* holders.

These and the 1975 policy changes produced insecurity of access to and control over land for many. The specific issues which raised tensions in the CA debates included:

- The split in ownership and occupancy rights between *mailo* owners and *bibanja* holders,[7] resulting in lack of secure tenure for *bibanja* holders and lack of user rights and ability to transact in land under occupation by *bibanja*. This has produced what is essentially a class conflict between rich and poor peasants.

- The phenomenon of alien absentee landlords in a part of Bunyoro kingdom (which had resisted British colonialism). The British granted *mailo* tenure to chiefs from Buganda kingdom over a significant amount of land of this neighbouring group, in effect alienating two whole counties from this area. Much of the debate over the Land Bill in 1998 concerned whether these two 'lost counties' would be returned.

- Ownership of 9,000 square miles of land granted to the King of Buganda by the 1900 agreement and taken over by central government in 1966 following the crisis that led to the abolition of kingdoms in Uganda. Southerners associated with the President's ethnic group were seen to be making use of this land, raising anxieties about the ever-deepening entrenchment of this group in the centre of the country.

These historical and ethnicity-based conflicts dominated the CA debates. Other tensions were over the rights of non-citizens to land use and control. The government's liberalisation agenda has driven an interest in easing the access of investors to land, but this has raised concerns that poor land users will be squeezed out of land markets.

The issue that took centre stage was the conflicting interests of *mailo* landlords and tenants in Buganda. The question of the competing rights of users of land and of registered owners (under *mailo* tenure) was highly politically charged. The CA delegates recognised that positions adopted in the CA would influence elections to the first Parliament following the enactment of the constitution, and hence they were reluctant to take a clear stand on this and other contentious issues prior to the first elections. Therefore, with a view to supporting their prospects in the upcoming 1996 parliamentary elections, the CA delegates deferred land law reform to the first Parliament to handle within two years of its first sitting. Article 237(9) of the constitution required Parliament to enact a law by 2 July 1998 that would regulate the relationship between users and registered owners and enable the former to acquire a legal interest in land.

In this charged atmosphere, issues affecting politically weaker groups became harder to advance. The need for reform in relation to land tenure relations as they affect the differential rights of family members and the historical gender imbalances in land holding were never considered seriously. However, an attempt was made by one woman delegate to introduce a clause for joint sharing of property in marriage. The motion read:

> On dissolution of marriage, men and women shall have the right to equitably share all property acquired during the marriage (Hansard 8 September 1994).

The motion was thrown out. Of the 231 delegates present during the vote, 103 delegates voted in favour of the motion, 127 against it and there was a single abstention. On the whole the Assembly did not see the need to extend the new principles on gender equity in civil and political rights to other areas such as land ownership rights, partly because the land debate in the CA centred around mediating historical ethnic conflicts and competing interests in land.

Women's land rights and the 1997 Draft Land Bill

In the pre-colonial era, land in Uganda was by and large communally owned and its use and control were guided by custom, which protected women's land use rights (Kharono 1998). Elders, usually male, were the custodians of the land; they had no powers of sale but held land in trust for the next generation. Individual men, women and adult children had equal access and user rights. The power of disposal of land was only exercisable by elders as a group, and transfers could be made only after consideration of the interests of the whole community.

Elders ensured social harmony and the protection of everybody's user rights.

The effect of colonial rule and Western influence ('modernisation') has been to transform the custodial role of male elders into an ownership power of male adults. Colonial rule introduced individual *ownership* by males and transformed the relationship between the various groups who live on land, including between men and women within the family (Ovonji-Odida 1999). Thus, individual men have assumed the role of elders and started disposing of family land originally controlled by customary practices. This change in culture has affected the patterns of access rights and led to the intensifying commercialisation of land, and the loss of women's (and other vulnerable groups') user rights to land. In the new urban land market the majority of women are left without any land to sell, exchange or transfer. Today, with their powerlessness to prevent the sale of land by individual men, women are caught between cultural restrictions that do not allow them to own land, and the new laws that encourage land registration and a liberal land market to which they have rights of access, but nothing to trade with once there.

In order to draft the Land Bill a Technical Committee was formed by the Ministry of Lands, Housing and Physical Planning. The Committee was composed mainly of male technocrats from the ministry with only one woman out of ten members. The draft Land Bill addressed land tenure systems, acquisition of land by government and individuals, acquisition and restriction of land transfer to non-citizens, land administration and management, and rights under different forms of tenure (*mailo*, freehold, customary and leasehold).

Despite the glaring gender imbalances in land ownership in Uganda, the Technical Committee did not regard the issue of improving female control of land as of primary importance. According to it, the land user rights customarily accorded to women were enough of a guarantee to protect family land from abuse by male relatives. However, existing research[8] and experiences of organisations such as the Uganda Women Lawyers' Association – FIDA(U) – in legal aid contradicted this position. Nonetheless, members of the Technical Committee expressed the view that the position advanced by the women's lobby groups regarding the co-ownership rights of spouses would interfere with the land market and amount to an abuse of property rights enshrined in the constitution. Their position was that a registered proprietor enjoyed unfettered rights so that the requirements of consent from a spouse to a sale of land would infringe those rights. The women's lobby group, however, pointed out to them that the provisions for the protection of the family not only formed a national objective and directive principle of state policy but were also contained in various articles of the constitution. The concern of the Ministry of Lands to broaden and liberalise the land market should therefore not trump these national obligations.

Hence in drafting the Land Bill some provisions aimed at increasing the legal protection of women's interests in land were included by the Technical Committee. A specific clause imposed restrictions on the sale, mortgage or transfer of land by family members: any such transfer would now require the written consent of the resident spouse(s) and dependent children (Clause 15, Draft Land Bill, 1997). Another clause voided any decisions affecting customary land that disregarded the rights of women and children, specifically where those decisions denied them access to ownership and use of land (Clause 7, Draft Land Bill, 1997). At the same time, this clause stated that any decision regarding customarily held land would be made in accordance with custom – creating a potential conflict when it comes to the rights of women and children. There were also various clauses that provided for a woman representative on all of the different land management bodies.[9]

Evolution of the women's coalition

The Uganda Land Alliance, which had been in existence since May 1995, was well prepared to react to the appearance of the 1997 Draft Land Bill. The ULA saw the process of developing comprehensive legislation to govern land use in Uganda as an important opportunity to protect the interests of the poor, and the main thrust of their reactions to the Draft Bill were in relation to its implications for poverty reduction. It argued that government should enact a fair land law that would effectively address social concerns to do with economically marginalised groups and thus promote poverty eradication. Thus, for instance, the ULA wanted the Draft Bill amended to address issues like the lack of restrictions on land holding size, which it feared would promote land-lessness as prospectors bought out small landholders. The alliance proposed that clauses be introduced with conditions and limitations on land acquisition so as to promote development and use of land and prevent the holding of land for speculative purposes.

The ULA queried the sincerity of the government's commitment to decentralisation in the implementation of the new land law, showing that in most respects land administration would still be centralised under the new law. The proposed Parish Land Committees, for example, had limited functions, powers and control over land matters. More powers were vested in District Land Boards, yet these entities would be less accessible to local communities. The ULA thus called for the Land Bill to incorporate mechanisms to ensure transparency and accountability of land administration bodies to the local communities. It was pointed out that the clauses on appointment and selection of members of these institutions, as provided in the Draft Bill, made the land management bodies accountable to the centre and not the local community. ULA also wanted the Bill modified to address gaps that it had identified, specifically relating to rights of various groups on customary land, including communal rights, and rights of landless groups in urban and rural areas (ULA 1997: 12).

The ULA also raised a number of process-related concerns, challenging the credibility of the information upon which land reform proposals were based, objecting to the lack of civil society consultation and government transparency in the process of drafting the Bill, and to the lack of connection between the Bill and other important policy reforms. The Technical Committee used very little new research to inform or justify its proposals for change in land tenure systems, relying heavily on a survey it had carried out. Though the survey apparently involved 1,509 people, the details of the characteristics of this sample and of the survey results were never released. Similar secrecy surrounded each new version of the Land Bill. Between 1996 and June 1998 when the Bill was debated in Parliament, the Technical Committee came up with eight different drafts, each trying to respond to the concerns raised by diverse lobby groups. But very often the ULA, which advocated for the Bill be made a public document and circulated widely before going to Parliament, had to resort to unofficial sources using personal contacts to access drafts. Throughout this process the ULA urged the Technical Committee to engage in wide consultation throughout the country on the proposed law, but this never took place.

The ULA also strongly felt that the preparation of such important legislation should have been preceded by a comprehensive land policy, which would guide the principles of the law. There was an apparent conflict between the proposed land law and various government development policies, such as the Poverty Eradication Action Plan (PEAP), the investment policy and the Plan for Modernisation of Agriculture (PMA). The PEAP is the core government development policy and is intended to form the basis of planning for all sectors. Its priority is agricultural modernisation. Among its goals is improving the ability of the poor to raise their incomes through, among other things, enhancing the ability of men and women to control productive resources. Failure to secure women's control over family land in the Land Act undermined this objective. The modernisation at the heart of the policy thrust of the PMA and investment policy is premised upon large commercial holdings. The PMA, for example, advocates a shift from predominantly subsistence to commercial agriculture responsive to market opportunities; this would dislodge many peasant families that derive their livelihood from subsistence agriculture.

The ULA was not insensitive to gender inequities in land ownership, and raised a number of concerns about the impact of the proposed Bill on women. For instance, in relation to land management institutions, the ULA observed that the Land Bill made insufficient provision for women's representation on land management committees. Whereas the 1996 Draft had a provision that one third of all land management committees should be women, the 1997 Draft that went to Parliament reduced women's representation to only one person on a body of four or five persons.[10] The ULA also made the crucial observation that clauses meant to restrict transfer of family land were inadequate, insofar as men as husbands or heirs had in the past, and no doubt would still, sell family land without the knowledge of other family members, particularly during family conflict or crises such as death or divorce, or when cash-strapped. But women's organisations within the alliance felt that the ULA could go further with a critique of the likely impact of the Bill on gender equity in land ownership. They disagreed with the mainstream stand within the Alliance that women's land interests could be effectively catered for within the context of generally protecting the poor. Women's organisations argued that the proposed measures were insufficient to improve women's situation on land, and that positive measures were needed to counteract cultural restrictions on women's land ownership rights, and practical constraints on their capacity to purchase land. Consequently a separate campaign focusing on women's land rights was begun under UWONET around July 1997. This, however, did not affect the ongoing participation of women's organisations in the ULA. Both lobby groups supported each other on the various campaign issues and avoided contradicting each other's positions publicly.

Changes the Uganda Land Alliance wanted in the Bill

Specific sections in the Bill affecting women's land rights were considered problematic by UWONET and the women's organisations in the ULA, and these became the focus of their lobbying efforts.

169

A major concern was with the so-called 'consent clause' that was intended to reduce insecurity of family members by limiting the land-holder's ability to alienate the family homestead. This was supposed to be achieved by obliging the landowner to elicit the consent of the family members to any transaction on family holdings. UWONET felt this section did not deal with the underlying reason why women and (especially) children lacked security, which was their lack of power to be part of decision making in the family about selling land. The view was that the proposed change did not adequately deal with the *de facto* unequal situation of women with respect to security of tenure, as their consent could be coerced due to the same lack of power. Women's 'consent' to a land transaction where they do not actually own the land was seen as relatively meaningless. Automatic and legally sanctioned spousal co-ownership of family land was thus felt to be the appropriate legal means of effecting security for women on family land. There were detailed proposals for dealing with co-ownership in various polygamous situations (UWONET 1998). Regarding consent, UWONET suggested improving the section by replacing written consent, which ignored high illiteracy rates (especially among women), with public verbal consent made before the land committee to approve land transactions. It suggested that a duty be placed upon the committee to satisfy itself beyond reasonable doubt that consent was freely given.

UWONET raised concerns about the potential conflict inherent in the Section 7 provision that retained customary rules in decision making on customary land, as it was often precisely these customary rules that discriminated against women and other groups like children and persons with disability. Proposals were made by UWONET to strengthen the proviso voiding discriminatory *decisions* based on custom by specifically prohibiting the customs or traditions themselves that undermined the status of women and other marginalised groups.

UWONET found that the representation of women on land management and adjudicative institutions was token. It proposed at least 30 per cent representation and also suggested removing the educational requirements for women serving on those bodies. High educational requirements would act as a barrier to the access of most women to these bodies. It also suggested that the land tribunals – which were to replace courts in handling land disputes – should explicitly be required to take into account rights of women and children to land security in the law.

Similarly, it recommended that the Act should make it mandatory that any regulations made under it be gender-responsive and that special consideration be given to women and persons with disability to access at least half the funds under the Land Fund to be set up.

Generating research on women's needs – arguments in support of women's land rights

UWONET, like the ULA, also raised concerns about the non-inclusive process of preparing the Draft Bill, and the poor background research that informed it. They noted that much as there was inadequate consultation of the population prior to producing the initial drafts of the Bill, this limited consultation was even more staggering when one took into consideration the interests and views of women. There was no indication of how many of the 1,509 people surveyed by the Ministry of Lands were women, how many of those might be rural farmers, and no indication of gender differences in concerns raised by respondents.

Women activists held the view that existing research that provided the basis for developing the Draft Land Bill appeared to have restricted its focus to land ownership within existing land tenure systems, with inadequate attention to informal land use arrangements. This focus ignored the situation of women who are the major stakeholders in land, constituting 80 per cent of land users in Uganda. Concerned about the overwhelming information gap with regard to the views and suggestions of women in the process of drafting the Land Bill, UWONET decided to carry out research, disseminate the findings and make women's voices audible and their contribution to Uganda's economy more visible. This would in effect put women at the centre of analysis and discussion of land issues in Uganda, given the fact that little attention is given to women farmers in most development projects and policy, including the Draft Land Bill.

Research on women's land rights

In October 1997, UWONET embarked on a study of women's land rights in six districts of Uganda,[11] to consult and document women's views and suggestions on the proposed Land Bill, and other land issues under the different land tenure systems in Uganda. They faced difficulty at first in financing this work. Powerful donors like the UK's Department for International Development (DFID) declined to fund the UWONET study and demanded an official authorisation letter from the Ministry of Lands to clear it. The Ministry refused to provide this, on the grounds that this was not government policy or practice. After approaching

171

other donors,[12] UWONET was eventually funded by the German-based foundation Friedrich Ebert Stiftung, which followed the entire land campaign through to Parliament. The funded activities included public sensitisation seminars; publicity on women's land rights both in the print and electronic media, and field consultations. The research covered 687 respondents, targeting both men and women. In order to come up with credible information, the researchers used a combination of methods like interviews, personal testimonies and various participatory appraisal methods.[13] The information generated was used to enrich public awareness and the lobby and advocacy activities UWONET was undertaking in order to influence the reform process. The study also provided baseline information for future monitoring of the impact of the enacted land legislation on women peasant farmers.

From its findings, UWONET highlighted the direct linkage between women's lack of, or limited control over, land and their reluctance to venture into long-term investment like building and the growing of crops for commercial purposes. Men, as the owners of the land in most parts of Uganda, determine land use patterns and control the proceeds. The discrimination against women in the various land tenure systems was further emphasised by the fact that women in most societies were still regarded as dependants and could not own land in their own right, but could gain access to it through their male relations. Even where women had the capacity to purchase their own land, in most instances they registered it in a man's name. Thus since the right of use is not complemented by ownership rights, women have no or limited control over the produce. Given the patriarchal systems of inheritance and property ownership in most societies of Uganda, it was pointed out that girls and women had ownership rights over clan land neither at their places of birth nor in their marital homes. There was ample evidence that in some societies in Uganda widows were kicked off their land by their husband's relatives, and at times by their own sons. At the dissolution of a marriage, women in most societies walked away empty-handed despite the years of work they had put in on the land. The study also revealed that, in all cases, cultural arguments were invoked to support the decisions made in relation to alienating land from women.

The campaign

On the basis of its findings, UWONET put its energies behind advocating the inclusion of the spousal co-ownership clause as a positive measure to overcome some of the constraints women faced in land markets. This decision pitted UWONET and its allies in the ULA against deeply entrenched conservative attitudes about men's prerogatives in relation to land ownership, and also against strongly held positions linking clan, tribal and ethnic identities to traditional patterns of land ownership and use. Another major constraint faced by UWONET was a restrictive time frame. The UWONET study was completed in late 1997, and, because of the constitutional provision that the land law had to be passed by July 1998, it had just half a year to generate support for its position. This part of the chapter analyses the ways in which the campaign framed its arguments, the strategies used to publicise its views and reach the ear of senior policy makers and parliamentarians, and the nature of the resistance it faced.

Justifying gender equity in land law reform – a range of discourses

During the debates that led to the enactment of the land law, a tremendous effort was made by women's and development organisations to clearly articulate interests and concerns in the land law as they affected women. However, these suggestions were often trivialised or completely ignored by the technical, Cabinet and parliamentary committees considering the Land Bill. These committees were heavily male-dominated, and often legalistic in their thinking. Because of this, arguments rooted in social development or gender analysis were not particularly convincing to them. UWONET therefore tried a range of justifications for positive measures to build women's land ownership rights in the Bill.

First, it pointed out that the government had made commitments to gender equity in the constitution and in various national policy documents like the National Gender Policy 1996, and in international legal instruments such as the Convention on the Elimination of Discrimination Against Women (CEDAW), which Uganda has ratified. The need to ensure a gender-sensitive reform of the land law was therefore justified in terms of a legal obligation; thus, the case for reform was presented as a means of giving effect to the human rights provisions in Uganda's 1995 constitution. The constitution specifically created an obligation on the state to take affirmative action measures to improve the status of groups historically marginalised, such as women (Article 32, 1995 Constitution of Uganda).

Second, UWONET argued that without a proactive change such as affirmative action to oblige men to cede some ownership rights to women, the mere legislative declaration of women's equal rights of access to land markets would neither alter community expectations about women's lack of land ownership rights, nor empower women to purchase land. The women's lobby group insisted that women's profound lack of secure land tenure required that conscious effort be made to introduce change, taking into account that women faced a range of discriminatory factors that constrained their access to and ownership of land. These factors included among others discriminatory cultural beliefs and practices; religious constraints; economic constraints; and socio-legal constraints (UWONET 1997). It was argued that the new law should directly and consciously address the structural factors that combined to produce gender inequality and blocked women's access to resources of production. It was further argued that any measure that did not address these extra-legal factors would not positively transform the situation of women's land ownership.

Third, the women's land campaign was also defined as a development concern, always a powerful argument in a country which has enjoyed international attention for its rapid growth since 1986. Because of their lack of control over resources of production like land, women's decision-making ability at the household level is inhibited. This limits their productivity and makes it next to impossible for them to access credit or to consider investing in land development or commercial crops. A right to co-own family land with their spouses was thus seen as a vehicle through which women's productive capacity and decision-making powers could be enhanced. The campaign drew on information from studies (some government-commissioned) related to macro-economic policies, such as the Poverty Eradication Action Plan and the Plan for the Modernisation of Agriculture that had shown the linkage between national economic goals and women's rights or gender equality.

Finally, women invoked a starkly political argument. They suggested that women deserved co-ownership rights in exchange for the well-known fact that, around the country, women had given the Movement government so much support. In effect, they suggested that they were calling in a debt, what Tripp calls the 'implicit *quid pro quo*' between Ugandan women and Museveni's government, in which women's votes have been given in exchange for an expansion of women's rights (Tripp 2002). For example, when moving the spousal co-ownership amendment in Parliament, Miria Matembe reminded the President and NRM parliamentarians of the political support given to the NRM by women during the 1996 elections. She invoked the potentially great electoral leverage which a disgruntled female vote bank might represent. This strategy was often attacked by the opponents of the women's lobby, who portrayed the campaigners as élite figures with views that were not representative of grassroots women. However, it appeared to be one of the more effective ways of eliciting a response from politicians.

Strategies used to amend the Draft Bill

As the two lobby groups intensified their campaign to amend the Bill, the level of animosity increased between them, on one side, and the members of the Technical Committee at the Ministry of Lands on the other. The committee viewed ULA and UWONET as attacking government policy and derailing or delaying the enactment of the Bill. Much as the Technical Committee appreciated the fact that the customary laws and unwritten practices governing property ownership rights, and women's economically disadvantaged position, grossly disqualified them from profiting from land tenure reform, it was adamantly against legislating in this area. In his speech to the UWONET workshop on 7 October 1997, the then Minister of Lands Francis Ayume said:

> it is true that most of the current family and inheritance laws are archaic and prejudiced against women, but these inequities cannot be corrected wholly by a land law. They will have to be tackled under the family law.

In suggesting that women's property rights ought best to be considered under family law – in other words, the much-postponed Domestic Relations Bill – Ayume relabelled the issue of women's property rights from an economic and survival matter to an intra-household matter. As it happens, this suggestion was eventually to become the official response to women's demands, with the President, once the co-ownership clause had been omitted from the Act, recommending that co-ownership be considered at a future date as part of the Domestic Relations Bill.

The articulation of women's concerns was achieved through the media, in strategic meetings and workshops organised with key decision makers, including legislators and policy makers. Among the strategic meetings were those held with the Technical Committee drafting the Land Bill, the Cabinet Committee on Land, and the Uganda Women Parliamentarians' Association (UWOPA). Workshops were held for various civil society organisations, policy makers and the legislators.

It was at one such workshop in April 1998, organised by UWONET and the ULA and hosted by the Forum for Women in Democracy (FOWODE), that the proposal for co-ownership of land by spouses was first clearly articulated and taken up more seriously by policy makers.

Significantly, the Forum brought together a large number of Members of Parliament, NGOs and donor agency representatives. The co-ownership proposal was made in a session on women and land rights, in which the key speaker was President Yoweri Museveni. He introduced a new dimension to the campaign, giving explicit voice to the objections harboured by many. He argued that in order for women to have entitlement to family land with their spouses they had to 'prove' themselves as being truly committed to the relationship (and not exploiting it for access to men's property). A woman could do this by being on a 'marriage probation' for a number of years. The woman's right to a share of family land would increase in accordance with the number of years she had 'served' in the marriage. In the President's opinion, if such safety nets were not provided, women would marry and divorce as many husbands as possible in order to accumulate land from different husbands. This argument was enthusiastically picked up by the detractors of the campaign and is still used to fight the co-ownership amendment.

Resistance in the Ministry of Lands

UWONET was faced with stiff resistance from government and some donors who viewed the women's campaign as an obstacle to the quick enacting of the land law. In 1997, when the women's land rights campaign began, the Ministry of Lands was very uncomfortable with the issues UWONET was raising because these required further research, while the Ministry wanted to table the Bill in Cabinet before the end of the year. In order to influence public opinion, the UWONET research findings were disseminated in two public workshops targeting Members of Parliament, government officials from relevant departments such as Justice, Lands and Law Reform, civil society and the media.

The Ministry of Lands rejected UWONET's research, claiming that it was 'driven by emotions' and poorly timed, in that the Technical Committee had finalised its consultation and was ready to present its Draft Bill to Cabinet. However, other groups like the Tenants' Association and the Buganda kingdom did much later on, as late as 1998, bring up issues that *were* addressed by the Technical Committee. UWONET published its findings anyway in a widely disseminated booklet, *Women's Land Rights in Uganda: a Document of Women's Views and Suggestions on Land Issues in Uganda and the Proposed Land Bill*, in October 1997. It kept a public debate going in the media about women's land rights, generating public interest and shaping public opinion. The research carried out by UWONET raised sufficient questions about gaps in information to persuade the Ministry to carry out further consultation specifically targeting women.[14]

The Ministry's consultations illustrated that women and children were central to effective land management and food and cash crop production in Uganda, but that they were inhibited from realising their full potential by customs premised upon a patriarchal approach to ownership. The concern of the Ministry and the Parliamentary Committee on Land was how to address the constitutional rights of women and children without upsetting the customary practices and norms: a contradiction in terms.

Resistance in Parliament

Following the Ministry consultations, the Cabinet Committee that was set up to consult on aspects of the Draft Land Bill did not include one woman MP. The male MPs were not only gender-insensitive but openly referred to most of UWONET's proposals as ridiculous and unrealistic in Uganda's context. UWONET met the Cabinet Committee on 9 February 1998. The Cabinet preferred to use an *aide-mémoire* prepared by the Ministry of Lands to guide the meeting, rather than allow UWONET to present its own findings and proposals. The Cabinet's main concern was how the Land Bill should provide for women to co-own land with their husbands without compelling the husbands to part with their interests in the land they owned. Their position was that spousal co-ownership of land should not be legislated but instead should be left to individuals to negotiate, and therefore that UWONET should focus on sensitising women to encourage their husbands to share their property voluntarily. For UWONET, legislation was essential in the light of the power distribution between men and women in Uganda, which prevents most women from negotiating with their husbands for equivalent ownership rights.

On 1 and 2 April 1998 UWONET linked up with UWOPA and met the Parliamentary Committee on Lands. A booklet on the proposed recommendations was compiled jointly by UWOPA and UWONET and presented to the Parliamentary Committee on 29 April 1998. Although a good foundation had previously been laid, the meeting with the Parliamentary Committee did not yield much for UWONET. Unfortunately, some representatives of a women lawyers' organisation, FIDA(U), disagreed with some of the recommendations made at the meeting, arguing that more research was needed to analyse the legal implications of co-owning property which belonged to another person (the spouse)

177

and the practicability of enforcing such a law. Their arguments that no law in Uganda prevented women from owning land in their own right were more acceptable to the Parliamentary Committee because they conformed to mainstream views. In addition, the Committee was happy to exploit apparent differences within the women's coalition to suggest that the UWONET position on co-ownership did not represent the views of a majority of the country's women.

Another source of resistance was a significant number of women MPs who were uncomfortable about pushing for land co-ownership. While some MPs held this position because they had neither read nor internalised the proposals by women, others who themselves owned land did not relish the implications that spousal co-ownership rights might have for their own property rights. There was a conflict of interest between propertied and unpropertied women, and this emerged subsequently in a Law Reform Commission workshop on women's property rights.

Victory, then failure

Realising that women's concerns would be left out in the eventual Land Act, several individual women and NGOs opted for an aggressive media campaign to highlight women's demands and expose the policy makers, in particular parliamentarians, who were standing in their way. In early 1998 the campaign focused on producing features on women's land rights in the print and broadcast media in a bid to shape public opinion.

In the last two weeks of June 1998, during the debate on the Land Bill, this media campaign intensified. The campaigners approached *The Monitor*, a daily newspaper known for its independent and critical stance on the NRM government, and got free space to articulate issues relating to women and land daily. In addition, UWONET hired a journalist to sit in Parliament and monitor, record and report positions of the different parliamentarians, particularly those contrary to the women's lobby. Daily debriefing sessions were held by the members of the women's lobby to analyse the debate and prepare responses. Positive and negative positions on women's land rights were highlighted in a spot in each issue of the newspaper, identifying the speakers and dubbing them winners or losers according to the statement made. When the amendment providing for spousal co-ownership was moved by Miria Matembe, on Monday, 22 June, and debated for the next few days, very few MPs were courageous enough to publicly express their anti-woman views. This strategy played a vital role in limiting aggressive challenges and negative remarks against the co-ownership clause, at least in Parliament.

The rest is not exactly history, as what happened to the clause is yet to be clearly established. On 25 June the amendment was adopted by Parliament, and newspaper reports the next day trumpeted: 'Spouses to Co-own Land' (Ofwono-Opondo *et al.* 1998). A week later the Act was published, minus the offending clause. For some time the reasons why the clause had been 'lost' remained a mystery, fuelling, of course, the impression of a top-level conspiracy against it. The Minister of Lands claimed not to recall any discussion of the clause on the day it was adopted. UWONET made repeated efforts to scrutinise Hansard, and asked for a tape recording of the proceedings on 25 June, but for a time was not given access to those records. Finally it was explained that a procedural error – the failure to re-introduce the clause at a third reading – meant that it had not received the proper parliamentary imprimatur. That this was something of a technical smokescreen for the high-level lack of enthusiasm for the clause was finally made clear nearly a year later, when the President admitted that he had intervened to pull the clause out and passed it over to the Domestic Relations Bill (Tripp 2002).

There is little doubt that the unpopularity of the 'women's amendment' is responsible for its disappearance, although generally poor record keeping, reporting and publishing systems in Parliament play a part. UWONET and the ULA were discouraged from pursuing the lost amendment on the grounds that this might revive the dangerous ethnicisation of the debate over land reform which dogged the passage of the Land Bill. This subordination of women's property ownership rights to the politics of ethnic compromise degrades the quality of women's citizenship.

In spite of this setback, the effect of the co-ownership campaign was to generate public discussion of women's land ownership rights as a national issue and provoke policy makers to confront their prejudices. As noted in a study on co-ownership commissioned by the government, 'The issue has firmly entered the public arena and caught the interest of citizens of various backgrounds, policy and law makers, interest groups and civil society' (Ministry of Water, Lands and Environment 2000). It also helped the women's movement to mature, grow more independent of government, and begin to analyse critically where it stands and who are its allies within civil society, the bureaucracy and the government. The last part of this chapter reviews the lessons learned about the experience of the women's lobby for women's land rights in Uganda – lessons which point to conditions for increasing women's effectiveness in advancing counter-cultural legislation to promote their rights.

179

Depth of resistance – challenging male prerogatives

The co-ownership proposal directly threatened the exclusive property rights of individual men, and also challenged deeply vested clan-based interests in preserving traditional patterns of land ownership. The resistance the proposal aroused took some women activists by surprise. The women's movement's successes since 1986 in advancing gender equity in policy making led to an underestimation of the ferocity of the resistance the clause would generate. Campaigns which had been successes include those that resulted in the enactment of the Children's Statute, 1996, and in the incorporation of important principles on gender equality, third generation rights and democracy in the 1995 constitution.[15] But legislative reform efforts in areas which directly and concretely improve women's rights in the family context (domestic relations, land) have had much less success. This can be attributed to the predominance of patriarchy and entrenched societal hostility to women's empowerment. The co-ownership approach was seen as a direct infringement of men's ownership rights, indeed as an almost a theft of men's land. It raised the spectre of profiteering women exploiting marriage for money and destroying the clan heritage.

Opposition came from many powerful policy makers and technocrats, especially in the line ministry, legislators and key members of the executive, including, most importantly, the President. Opposition to the proposals of the women's lobby was expressed through attacks on the credibility of their research, and on their right to represent poor rural women. Their proposals were ridiculed as impractical and they were accused of being 'élitist'. The women's lobby quickly learnt to tailor its messages in terms of achievement of macro-economic development goals, and political imperatives, rather than focus exclusively on issues of equity, which had limited appeal to policy makers and legislators.

Opponents were not consistent in their criticisms. When the women's lobby produced incontrovertible data on women's lack of land rights and the consequences of this for economic growth and food security, other arguments were used to discredit the campaigners. For example, when the women's lobby held a public hearing with testimony from rural women thrown out of their homes on divorce or widowhood as evidence of the need for law reform, opponents who previously had labelled the lobbyists 'élitists who do not speak for rural women' changed tack and accused them of being 'emotional'. Eventually, the research carried out by UWONET provided such disturbing information that the government felt obliged to carry out an independent study, which, ironically, came to similar conclusions on several key points.

The narrow social base of the women's lobby

Though the campaigners rejected the charge of élitism, they had to acknowledge that many advocates of the co-ownership clause were young, educated working women activists, and most of the women's organisations involved in the lobby were urban-based. The land campaign triggered the formation of a coalition amongst women's organisations early on, unlike other advocacy efforts which had tended to be championed by just one organisation, as was the case with the FIDA(U) on the domestic relations law reform.[16] However, this coalition lacked effective connections to rural women, and failed to build alliances with other civil society organisations like development and human rights NGOs, faith-based organisations, or farmers' and trade unions.

This narrow social base fuelled opponents' arguments that the women's lobby did not represent the majority of the country's women. The selection of the co-ownership clause as the main focus of the campaign may also have been a reflection of a class and even marital status bias amongst the campaigners. The campaigners assumed that women had a common understanding or views on the land issue, on the grounds that there is a general bias against women owning land, a bias arising from socialisation and patriarchy. But women are not a homogeneous group and on the issue of co-ownership they had conflicting interests and positions according to their class, clan, and marital status. The women who felt threatened by the co-ownership clause, and felt it would do nothing for them, included some propertied women, some rural women using customary land who feared that their user rights could be threatened, second wives who felt that the clause would give an advantage to the first wives, and above all, women in informal unions (cohabitation). Informal unions represent a great number of rural household relationships, and the co-ownership clause would not have had much of an effect on women in this position in the absence of a widespread marriage registration campaign.

UWONET's reflection on the fate of the co-ownership campaign produced the conclusion that the Ugandan women's movement needs to develop stronger links to other socio-economic issues such as poverty eradication, health, religion and environmental conservation, as a bridge for coalition building. In the past both women and men in Uganda have narrowly interpreted gender issues as women's concerns, limiting the appeal of these issues to non-feminists. Even 'mainstream' human rights organisations and activists often fail to relate to gender and women's human rights. It is also important to build links with powerful groups like donors and religious or faith-based institutions so as to increase the political power of the group. Most importantly, women activists need to create linkages with the grassroots communities whose interests they represent, and mobilise them and bring them on board.

Few allies in positions of power

The campaign gained enormously from the support of several strong, committed champions in decision-making positions ready to support co-ownership, particularly after clear opposition at the highest levels of government had been expressed. However, these politically prominent MPs, namely Matembe and Byanyima, were not able to build a sustainable support base for the co-ownership clause in government. In order for the women's movement to succeed in advancing a legislative agenda based on gender equity, it needs more influence in decision-making bodies. In spite of the NRM government's efforts to bring more women into politics and the bureaucracy, it was striking how few women had an official role in the land law development process. Only one woman sat on the Ministry of Lands Technical Committee to draft the Bill. Only one woman (out of twenty members) sat on the sessional committee of Parliament discussing land. She was the woman representative for Kibaale district, which had historical land problems involving absentee *mailo* landlords and tenants, and she was co-opted onto the committee to represent Kibaale issues, not women's issues.

During the Land Bill debate, women MPs formed a core group to back the Matembe amendment in Parliament. In the face of fierce government opposition, however, this group disintegrated. The presence of more women in Parliament proved less supportive than the women's lobby had hoped. They found that women leaders still required education on gender equity issues, and were not sympathetic to the co-ownership position simply by virtue of being women. Indeed, some women MPs and ministers largely disassociated themselves from the co-ownership clause as if it was the concern of a select group within civil society. Some of them have cautioned the lobby group against attacking government: for the moment, they say, land is not as important as education for women. Not only have women politicians not rallied to this cause, but key women in Cabinet have been used to oppose it – though some women MPs have continued their public support of co-ownership.

Matembe herself has been prevented from moving the matter forward because by the time Cabinet considered the problem of the omission of the co-ownership clause from the new law, she had been appointed a Minister. Bound by Cabinet collective responsibility, she was no longer in a position to speak out strongly against the government in defence of the co-ownership clause. There was, therefore, a fracturing of the pro-amendment base within decision-making structures.

In the end, the most effective alliance made by the women's lobby was with the media. The co-ownership campaign was greatly facilitated by *The Monitor* newspaper. Given the personal contact and good relations with media organisations established over time, the women's lobby group has been able to sustain the campaign and public interest in the issue. There were also allies within government (technocrats) who provided crucial information (for instance, Draft Bills) at key moments.

Building capacity to conduct advocacy professionally

Within the NGO community in Uganda, advocacy is relatively new com-pared to development work. In this, the NGO community differs from that in South Africa, where virtually the opposite is true, given the extended schooling in activism which civil society leaders received in the anti-apartheid struggle. In Uganda, many NGOs do not relate their devel-opment work to strategic, policy-making issues but prefer to focus on the fulfilment of practical needs. Just a few individuals within women's NGOs have acquired skills in gender analysis, lobbying and advocacy. Again, those who are most comfortable with advocacy are lawyers and gender analysis experts – and these, inevitably, are urban élite figures.

Overall, the advocacy strategy needed refinement. As noted above, arguably a mistake was made in terms of electing to focus the campaign on the co-ownership clause, which alienated a number of potential allies within civil society and did not appeal to as wide a spectrum of women as would have been desirable. Mistakes were made in terms of timing at various points in the process like when to go public (for example, not maintaining a large visible presence of supporters in Parliament during debates). There were difficulties in sustaining pressure at key points in the process, especially after Cabinet decided to move the co-ownership clause into the Domestic Relations Bill. And the key messages and mes-sengers might have been identified more strategically, in order to avoid giving the impression that the main advocates of the co-ownership clause were young, urban professionals unqualified to speak about the problems affecting rural women.

There were also errors made in terms of handling the law-making process within Parliament. It should be noted that at times the campaign received wrong information from Parliament – for example, on when an issue would be debated – which affected planning of the interventions. More worryingly, when the co-ownership amendment was not presented to Parliament for the third reading, which is the proximate reason for its ultimate omission, the women's lobby should have detected this procedural slip before it was too late. To do so, however, requires a level of awareness about parliamentary procedure that does not come automatically to people unaccustomed to engaging at this level. The failure of the Speaker to give a third reading to the clause cannot be blamed on the women's lobby – it suggests instead a breakdown in parliamentary reporting and scheduling procedures, and more broadly of accountability systems.

Conclusions: political accountability to women

From the advocacy campaign for the attainment of women's land rights in Uganda, there have been several lessons for UWONET and the broad women's movement. It can count as a success that with constant pressure on decision makers, the issue of women's land ownership rights has stayed on the public agenda for many years now and various studies have been done on it by both government and civil society organisations. Across the board, women exhibited their professionalism in lobbying and advocacy, legal literacy, policy and gender analysis, the ability to utilise the media and capacity to carry out research. These diverse skills enabled the women's lobby group to respond to different circumstances within a short time and at a negligible cost. There was a commitment among the women to achieve their set goals, hence many volunteered to work long hours on the amendment, participating in radio and television discussions and physically going out to lobby their parliamentarians.

A major lesson for the women's movement has been the realisation of the need to devise strategies for ensuring accountability of political leaders to those they represent, so that equity and social development concerns affecting the majority also factor into public policy formulation. Much as the NRM government has developed commendable gender policies and has undertaken the mainstreaming of gender in most government programmes, in practice the attitudes of most leaders have not changed. Many of them, including Museveni and some women leaders, broadly espouse commitment to women's empowerment but question the relevance of gender when it comes to specific sectors like the co-ownership of land and domestic relations. Criticism by the women's movement and the offering of an alternative position is often interpreted as attacking government and lack of appreciation for what Ugandan women have achieved under the Movement.

Given this, the women's lobby has realised that in addition to legal advocacy, there is a need for political advocacy. In March 2001 a Coalition for Political Accountability to Women (COPAW)[17] was formed to focus on political advocacy to put gender on the political agenda. It is to be hoped that this coalition can build effective electoral leverage from the women's vote and use it to promote greater responsiveness from decision makers to women's needs.

UWONET, the ULA and other NGOs continue to fight for an amendment to the Land Law, even though the Uganda Law Reform Commission is drafting clauses in the Domestic Relations Bill on women's property rights. These clauses, however, follow the President's suggestion that women should have rights in their natal family's land, not in the land of their husbands. This relegates women's property rights concerns to the arena of inheritance and succession law (which is covered by the Domestic Relations Act), and of course appeals to conservative interests in eliminating the threat which the co-ownership clause posed to the integrity of clan land and to the preservation of a patriarchal lineage in land ownership patterns. In regrouping and reflecting after the disappearance of the co-ownership clause, UWONET and the ULA have considered ways of broadening their approach to women's land rights beyond the co-ownership proposal, and have also found support in unlikely places. Even the Queen of Buganda, Sylvia Nagginda, has been willing to criticise publicly – in her International Women's Day statement for 2000 – the way customary law so profoundly limits women's property ownership rights (Olupot 2000). Coming from a representative of one of the country's most entrenched clan-based institutions, her statement provides some indication of the broadening sense of unease amongst women about the way the NRM government and top leadership have reneged on their promises to women.

References

Kharono, E. (1998) 'Feminist Challenge to the Land Question: Options for Meaningful Action – a Concept Paper', paper presented at African Gender Institute, University of Cape Town, 1998.

Ofwono-Opondo, J. Kakande, and J. Bakyawa (1998) 'Spouses to Co-own Land', *New Vision*, 26 June 1998.

Okumu Wengi, J. (1994) *The Law of Succession in Uganda: Women, Inheritance Laws, and Practices: Essays and Cases*, Kampala: Women and Law in East Africa.

Olupot, M. (2000) 'Nabagereka Decries Gender Imbalance', *New Vision*, 8 March 2000.

Ovonji-Odida, I. (1999) 'Women's Land Rights and Uganda's 1998 Land Act: Threats and Opportunities for Women's Security of Tenure', presented at DFID Delegate Workshop on Land Tenure Policy in African Nations, Sunningdale Park Conference Centre, UK, 16-19 February 1999.

Ministry of Water, Lands and Environment (2000) 'A Study on Land, Gender, Poverty Eradication: Is There a Case for Spousal Co-ownership of the Primary Household Property?' Prepared for the Ministry by I. Ovonji Odida, F. Muhereza, L. Eturu and L. Alden Willy.

Tripp, A. M. (2002) 'Conflicting Visions of Community and Citizenship: Women's Rights and Cultural Diversity in Uganda', in M. Molyneux and S. Razavi (eds.), *Gender, Justice, Democracy and Rights*, Oxford: Oxford University Press.

ULA (1997) 'Open Letter to the Minister of Lands, Housing and Physical Planning, on the Proposed Land Bill of 1997', Uganda Land Alliance, Publication No. 3 (undated).

UWONET (1997) 'Women and Land Rights in Uganda: a Documentation of Women's Views and Suggestions on Land Issues in Uganda and the Proposed Land Bill: a Report of Findings of the Preliminary Study Undertaken by Uganda Women's Network', Kampala.

—— (1998) Proposed Amendments on the Land Bill 1998: Submitted to the Parliament of the Republic of Uganda by UWONET and UWOPA.

Notes

1 The authors wish to recognise the support provided by a number of people, including Winnie Byanyima, MP for Mbarara Municipality, and Dominica Abu, former Chairperson of UWOPA and MP for Moyo.

2 The Uganda Land Alliance is a consortium of non-governmental organisations that conduct advocacy on issues relating to land. Formed in 1995, its mission is to ensure that land policies protect the rights of the poor and that the poor retain access to and ownership of land.

3 Uganda Women's Network (UWONET) is an advocacy and lobbying coalition of national women's NGOs, institutions and individuals in Uganda, founded in 1993. UWONET aims at transforming the unequal gender relations in society by promoting networking, collective visioning and action among different actors working towards development. The members of UWONET are: the Association of Women Lawyers in Uganda; the Uganda Media Women's Association; Action for Development; the Association of Uganda Women Doctors; Women Engineers, Technicians and Scientists in Uganda; the Uganda Women's Finance Trust; the Uganda Women Parliamentarians' Association; the Forum for Women in Democracy; the National Association of Women's Organisations in Uganda; and the Department of Women and Gender Studies, Makerere University.

4 Since 1995, the lobby group that has campaigned for women's land rights has been drawn from a broad range of development organisations and women's groups, including the Uganda Women Lawyers Association – FIDA(U) – Action for Development (ACFODE), Akina Mama wa Afrika (AMWA), Action-Aid-Uganda, Oxfam-UK and Uganda Media Women (UMWA), some of which belong to ULA, UWONET or both.

5 Forum for Women in Democracy is an NGO for women politicians. ULA and UWONET actually raised the funding and organised the workshop but asked FOWODE to organise it in order to increase the numbers of parliamentarians who would attend. The strategy worked, as almost all MPs attended, a record.

6 The Land Act, 1998, defines *mailo* as 'a system of land tenure regulated by customary rules which are limited in their operation to a particular description or class of persons'. *Mailo* land, under the same provision, refers to 'the holding of registered land in perpetuity and having roots in the allotment of land pursuant to the 1900 Uganda Agreement' (Section 2, Land Act 1998).

7 *Bibanja* holders refer to persons holding user rights, not title, on *mailo* land. These were originally the customary users on feudal land before colonial rule.

8 For example, the Ministry of Gender's research on Women and Inheritance (1994–6) and Okumu Wengi (1994).

9 The Bill provided for land management bodies at parish, district and national level: Parish Land Committees, District Land Boards and a Land Commission.

10 The Land Commission and District Land Boards were to have a mininum membership of five persons, while the Parish Land Committees were meant to have four members each.

11 Kampala, Kibaale, Lira, Luwero, Mbale and Mpigi.

12 The Netherlands Development Organisation – (SNV)-Uganda – and Konrad Adenauer Foundation.

13 The methods used included a time trend analysis to establish the historical trends in land distribution and political changes since colonialism; mapping to identify social relationships in relation to demographic characteristics and economic status; and impact flow charts to establish the impact of interventions like the land agreements, and the Uganda constitution in relation to land ownership and land rights.

14 The Ministry of Lands carried out consultations in conjunction with ULA in late 1997.

15 Among special interest groups receiving recognition and protection of rights in the 1995 constitution are persons with disability, the aged, children, youth and women. Third generation rights are group-based rights (minorities, children, women, indigenous peoples), that have been distinguished from civil and political rights (first generation), and economic and political rights (second generation).

16 This advocacy began around 1990, when FIDA(U) hosted a national workshop for women leaders on the Domestic Relations Bill.

17 The coalition membership is drawn from NGOs including ISIS-WICCE, FIDA(U), EASSI, ACFODE, Akina Mama wa Afrika, LAW-Uganda and UWONET, as well as the Department of Women and Gender Studies, Makerere University.

7

Democratising Local Government: Problems and Opportunities in the Advancement of Gender Equality in South Africa[1]

LIKHAPHA MBATHA

The South African women's movement has made tremendous gains in increasing the representation of women in national and provincial government since the advent of democracy in 1994. And yet, despite the widespread recognition that local government is the site at which citizens experience the state at the most direct level, political parties and gender activists alike tend to neglect the extent and quality of women's representation at this level of government. One marker of this neglect is the difference in gender representation at different levels of the state immediately following the advent of democracy. Compared to the highly acclaimed 29 per cent representation of women at national level, women constituted only 19 per cent of local government councillors in 1995/6. This sharp disparity led to a new round of advocacy and political action in the run-up to the 2000 elections, leading to an increase in the representation of women to 28.2 per cent.

While notable in itself, the gain in formal representation has tended to overshadow other important questions about the extent to which policy formulation and service delivery can be made more responsive to the needs of women. To a much greater extent than national policy, local government determines the kinds of access women have to basic services, the extent to which services relating to women's gendered household responsibilities are prioritised in budgetary terms, whether services such as water and electricity are delivered in ways that take account of and validate the knowledge that is gained from these responsibilities and, particularly importantly for rural women, how land is to be used. Although increasing women's access to representation is a key mechanism to increasing women's decision-making power in these areas of policy, there has been relatively little research on the institutional, political and cultural conditions under which women councillors at the local government level work. This chapter questions the gendered constraints on women councillors, the extent to which they can be effective in representing women's interests and the relationship between women councillors and women's organisations in the community.

The chapter is based on research on two local councils, both of which are newly demarcated municipalities that were created in 1993 as part of the new democratic structure of local government. The urban Kempton Park–Tembisa Metropolitan Local Council (MLC) on the East Rand in Gauteng province is a combination of a former white municipality, with relatively good services and a large tax base, with the black township of Tembisa, which has large hostels housing former migrant workers.

The Greater Temba Transitional Representative Council (TRC) is a periurban council located on the outskirts of Pretoria and straddles two provinces, Gauteng and the North West. In preparation for the 2000 elections these councils were re-demarcated under the framework of the Local Government Municipality Structures Act 117 of 1998. The new councils have increased in size. After the 2000 elections, Temba Council was merged into the Greater Pretoria Metro Council, while the Kempton Park–Tembisa Council is now part of the Ekurhuleni Metro of Greater Germiston.

Under both the 1993 and 1998 demarcations, some areas within Temba Council have traditional authorities. As I will argue in the section on the history of local government reform, women's access to power and the extent to which they are seen as legitimate representatives in rural areas are highly dependent on the power and attitudes of traditional leaders. This is an issue that will be explored in some detail.[2]

The context of local government in South Africa

The design of local government in South Africa has been deeply embedded in the racial landscape of apartheid. Local government was structured along different institutional lines for each of apartheid's 'population groups'. In this context, a central goal of the negotiations process that preceded the transition to democracy in South Africa was to redesign a system of government that would be democratic, remove apartheid-based inequalities and, in a managed and stable manner, facilitate some degree of redistribution from wealthier and better-resourced municipalities to poorer municipalities. A substantial amount of research and political energy was consequently directed to the process of demarcations. The demarcation process concentrated on dismantling established municipalities and reviewing existing property relations with a view to deracialising them and prioritised issues of the economy, class and race over gender. One consequence has been to increase the size of councils to such a degree that local government is not particularly 'close to the people' in terms of accessibility and linkages between communities and their specific governing structures.

While the racial contours of the state were widely understood by the negotiators of the new structure of local government, considerably less attention has been paid to the ways in which the state, at different sites and differently over time, has regulated and reconstructed relations of power between women and men (Manicom 1992). For example, regulation of labour flows in the nineteenth and twentieth centuries was achieved with the collusion of black traditional leaders, resulting in a pattern of male migration to urban areas and female responsibility for subsistence production (Bozzoli 1983). The implication of both state and traditional leaders in the ordering of gender relations suggests that while women and men might share a common set of interests in deracialising the system of local government, there may be areas of local government design and practice over which women and men have different and possibly competing interests. In particular, there were early indications in the constitutional negotiation of 1991–4 that traditional leaders and rural women's organisations would disagree about the extent to which traditional authority should form the basis for rural local government.

And yet, in stark contrast to the manner in which institutions at the national and provincial levels had been negotiated, women's organisations and political parties were not part of the negotiating forums on local government. Although political parties had channels of communication to participating interest groups such as the South African National Civics Organisation (SANCO), women's organisations had almost no influence. Women's representation was a low priority in a context where there was tremendous competition for representation among business, residents' associations and ratepayers' groups. Even the ANC, which had used a 30 per cent quota for the national and provincial electoral lists, was not prepared to use a quota for its local government electoral list. Neither was progressive civil society, represented in the negotiations by SANCO, necessarily a committed champion of women's interests as, despite rhetoric about gender equality, the organisation's leadership was male-dominated. Robinson (1995: 10) notes that as a result, gender issues were not addressed in any detail. Although the negotiations were constituted with a formal commitment to non-sexism, therefore, there was no obligation on the negotiators nor were there avenues to lobby for the implementation of this commitment. The restructuring of local government has been governed by the Local Government Transition Act (Act 209 of 1993). The Act is emphatic about the need for integration of a society previously fragmented by apartheid, and about the importance of a developmental strategy inclusive of all communities. It uses gender-sensitive language and encourages the representation of women in local government bodies, although it does not prescribe the mechanisms through which this could be secured. Although the Act emphasises the integrated development planning framework (Act 117 of 1998: s 23)[3] which conceivably implies the participation of all in the planning of councils' activities, in practice it fails to respond to local needs efficiently and effectively. Integrated development planning implies, among many other things, technical support for local councils through capacity-building and confidence-building programmes, which are particularly needed by women councillors if they are to participate effectively in councils. The LGTA has also been criticised for its failure to define clear boundaries for powers and functions between provincial legislatures and local governments.

The LGTA defined a three-phased restructuring process (Fick 2000: 27). In the first phase, there were elections for new councils in 1995/6, within a framework provided for by the Act in preparation for the transitional local government. For purposes of stability, and until a final framework could be agreed upon, the apartheid structure of the cities, including existing municipal boundaries, was retained. In the second phase, temporary councils (known as transitional local councils) established by Local Government Negotiating Forums (LGNFs) took responsibility for local government functions. The LGNFs were made up of equal numbers of representatives from statutory bodies (those bodies previously part of the local authorities) and non-statutory bodies (those interest groups who had not been part of the apartheid authorities). While this secured the participation of a range of interest groups, not least traditional leaders, the Act provided no guarantee of women's representation on these structures. There was also no structure outlined for the constitution of councils in rural areas – there, provincial governments were to decide on what form of local government was most appropriate (Zondo 1995: 22). The result in rural areas was that traditional leaders were given tremendous powers over a relatively lengthy period of transition. The interim phase was to last for five years and new legislation crafted by the Government of National Unity during that period would inaugurate the final third phase.

Perhaps the most important gender-biased consequence of women's lack of representation in the negotiations was the creation of a system of mixed ward-based proportional representation for the interim phase. Unlike national and provincial elections, the PR quota was to be used to ensure fair racial representation. This was an important intervention, given that the retention of the basic apartheid municipal demarcations and council structure would otherwise result in the disproportionately high representation of white citizens. Nevertheless, the complete inattention to gender resulted in heavily male-dominated councils being elected under this system (Robinson 1995). Following the 1995 elections, only one in five councillors was a woman, and only one in ten ward councillors; and there were significantly fewer women in elected positions in local government than in national government (Gender Advocacy Programme 2000).

Cutting across the process of re-designing local government was the process of finalising a new and democratic constitution that would set the benchmark for democratic practice in South Africa. The constitution was adopted in 1996 with a comprehensive Bill of Rights with extensive equality provisions and a positive obligation on the state to ensure women's participation in decision making. Local government is required to be democratic, participatory and accountable, and to promote sustainable social and economic development. The constitution gives local government the power to deal with a wide range of issues, from regulating and providing services to formulating development plans. Chapter 7 of the constitution provides for the establishment of three different categories of municipalities within councils: a Metropolitan Council with executive and legislative powers in some of the areas under it (category A municipality), a Non-Metropolitan Council (category B) which shares municipal executive and legislative powers with a category C municipal council within which it exists. Category C municipalities are District Councils. These have legislative and executive powers in more than one municipality.

An important exclusion from the competencies of local government is control over land, which is designated as a national competence. As I will discuss below, this has very important implications for women's ability to increase their economic and social power. The constitution clearly gives scope for local government to act as an agent of transformation, but the reality is that localised power entrenches existing interests in social and cultural arrangements and continues to undermine the ideals of the constitution. In this chapter I explore the intersections between women's relative lack of social and cultural power and their effectiveness in the public realm through interviews with women councillors.

Women's mobilisation and advocacy

Historically women have played a very important role in community-level politics, and were a crucial part of the creation of an urban civics movement from the late 1970s. The civics movement was a grassroots social movement that protested against high rentals and services costs imposed by local councils, and opposed the apartheid state itself (Adler and Steinberg 2000). Women's participation in this movement enhanced the view that women were politically active in greater numbers at the local rather than the national level. In rural areas, women's participation in political activism has been less prominent. Rural women fought together with men against the forced removals imposed by the apartheid state. Although this process revealed to women the need for organising as a force to fight subordination, rural women have been less likely to challenge male authority than their urban counterparts. Women have been constrained from participating in gender-based struggles as most have no formal employment or source of cash income that does not depend on their migrant-worker husbands. In 1986, however, a Rural Women's Movement was started in the Northern Transvaal, that sought to challenge the exclusion of women from participation in rural community structures and later expanded its vision to include challenges to male authority within the family (Goldblatt and Mbatha 1999). The RWM also lobbied for change in women's legal status, in particular women's inheritance rights and the customary law of marriage.[4] During the negotiations for a new democracy, women organised under the banner of the Women's National Coalition (WNC) to ensure that their needs and interests would be addressed. The Women's Charter for Effective Equality, developed by the WNC in 1994, concretises women's needs and problems and calls for their participation in all government institutions, including local government.[5]

Given this history, women's lack of representation in the local government negotiations was a matter of some concern to women's organisations and to some progressive NGOs. The Urban Sector Network held a workshop in 1993, just prior to negotiations, where proposals were made to equalise the impact of service delivery on women and men, and for institutional arrangements that would facilitate women's participation. However, none of these proposals were taken up by the Local

Government Negotiating Forum (Robinson 1995). Later the Rural Services Development Network (RSDN), a network of organisations working in rural areas, also began to lobby for the inclusion of women's needs on the agendas of local councils.

However, the most sustained lobbying efforts have been conducted by the Gender Advocacy Programme (GAP), a Cape Town-based initiative. GAP was galvanised into action by the process leading up to the formulation of the White Paper on Local Government in 1998 where, once again, it seemed that the issue of gender would be marginalised. GAP critiqued the Green Paper on Local Government for omitting to address gender adequately. The organisation highlighted the document's failure to mention gender mainstreaming as a local government responsibility. It argued that this constituted a major contravention of the constitution and of government's policy commitments – underscored by commitments made with regard to CEDAW and at Beijing – to making government gender-sensitive. GAP argued that local government is particularly well placed to contribute meaningfully in transforming social, racial and gender relations among men and women in communities. Addressing the failure of political parties and the LGNFs to increase women's political representation, GAP recommended first a quota reservation of seats by all parties for women and, second, that if the mixed system of ward and PR was retained, gender considerations should be applied to top up numbers in councils. In addition, it argued that the quota should be supported by capacity-building programmes and financial support for independent women candidates (Gender Advocacy Programme 1997). GAP's proposals were crucial in the process of legislative reform, winning support from the ANC for a 50 per cent quota of women on PR lists for local elections. An ongoing concern for all political parties is that a statutory quota might undermine the freedom of both political parties and voters to exercise democratic choice with regard to their representatives. Largely as a consequence of the interventions of GAP and its alliance of women's organisations (including the Commission on Gender Equality) the Municipal Structures Act (1998) requires that 'every party must seek to ensure that 50 per cent of the candidates on the party list are women and that women and men candidates are evenly distributed through the list' (Item 11(3) of the Municipal Structures Act, 1998). Not quite a statutory quota, the provision nevertheless sends out a strong message in support of women's representation.

GAP acted as the crucial lever for women's organisations in the policy process. It coordinated research and convened workshops that included women's organisations, political parties and women politicians.

It launched a massive national education campaign around the slogan 'Put women in their place ... COUNCIL!'. GAP aimed to provide platforms that would hold political parties accountable for their policies, but also sought to enhance women's capacity to make decisions in their own interests. In its public campaigns, GAP advised women to ensure that party lists included women candidates and that the number of women representatives constituted half the number of constituency candidates (Van Donk 2000: 4–11).

The lobbying process described above identified a number of facilitating factors and constraints on women's effective representation, which I will consider below. These include the mechanisms that structure access to representation, such as the electoral system and the exigencies of demarcation, the social and cultural conditions within which women politicians work, the institutional cultures of local government, political party support for women representatives, and skills and expertise.

Getting women into local government: the numbers

The campaigns of women's organisations to get more women into local government had a considerable impact on the 2000 elections. There was a dramatic improvement in the number of women elected both as ward candidates and as PR candidates, although predictably most parties had more women on their PR lists than on their ward lists. Overall, women constituted 34 per cent of all party list candidates, with the ANC – the only party to use a formal quota – placing 46 per cent of women on their list (Pottie 2001: 3). In Gauteng province, 43 per cent of councillors elected on PR were women (ibid.: 4). Women performed significantly poorer as ward candidates, winning only 16.9 per cent of ward seats across the country (ibid.: 5). The difference between the PR and ward mechanisms is dramatically apparent in the KwaZulu–Natal province, where women won 34.3 per cent of seats through the party list but only 12 per cent of ward seats (ibid.: 5). Three women stood for mayoral positions (one for the ANC and two for the Democratic Alliance) but none were successful.

The guideline of 50 per cent representation advocated in the Municipal Structures Act and the fact that the ANC used a quota for women on its lists appear to have had interesting knock-on effects. Three parties – AZAPO, the Inkatha Freedom Party and the United Christian Democratic Party – had over 30 per cent of women on their PR lists, and women in the Democratic Alliance were highly represented in seats at Metro ward level (48 per cent of all DA seats) (ibid.: 3).

These figures represent a significant shift in party political commitment to increasing the number of women on their electoral lists, although the reluctance to front women as candidates in the ward seats remains a barrier to women's effective participation and to the development of strong relationships between women councillors and their constituencies.

Representation and accountability: the effect of the electoral system

One of the central factors impacting on women's representation is the electoral system. As Hassim shows in Chapter 3, gender activists in South Africa were alert to the opportunities provided by the PR with List system and exploited these to great effect in the 1994 and 1999 national elections. Local government elections were conducted under a different and more complex system, and were driven by different considerations.

In the local government elections of 1995/6, ward and PR systems ran parallel in both metropolitan and non-metropolitan areas. The PR system accounted for 40 per cent of the total seats while the ward system constituted 60 per cent. The Municipal Structures Act changed this system. From the 2000 elections onwards, the number of ward councillors was to be equal to PR councillors in a council in both metropolitan and non-metropolitan areas. According to this law, councillors in both metropolitan and local councils with wards must be elected according to a system of proportional representation from party lists and direct representation from wards. This means that registered voters in both metropolitan and non-metropolitan areas with wards continue to have two votes, one for ward and another for the party by proportional representation in a council.

In a local council with no wards, all the councillors are elected from the party lists according to a system of proportional representation. A voter still has two votes in a council that has no wards. In this case one vote is for the party in the council while the other vote is for the District Council representative. District councillors are elected from party lists for councils without wards and from areas that fall under the district management areas. There are different role expectations for the different types of councillors. Ward councillors have the responsibility to communicate with communities and to act as the liaison between the council's executive committee and the community. The PR councillor, on the other hand, is the watchdog of the council whose responsibility is to ensure that the council is implementing policies and that communities are aware of the local council's duties. Information collected from Temba shows that communities are not aware of these divisions of responsibilities between councillors. However, they do expect that all women councillors, regardless of how they are elected, should be responsible for addressing women's needs.

The system of closed party lists for proportional representation in councils is not ideal in terms of creating effective linkages and accountability between councillors and constituents. In a study conducted by the CGE, community members complained about parties imposing politicians on them and demanded that party nominees be appointed in consultation with supporters. They argued that councillors nominated by the party without consultation often lacked good qualities for serving the community and tended to be more accountable to the party than to communities or party members and supporters within the municipality (CGE 2000: 54). A study of rural communities in KwaZulu–Natal found that many women did not know who their local councillors were, and in one case a candidate that women in a community had selected was left off the list in favour of a candidate from outside the community (Motala 2000: 19). Complaints about councillors' failures to deliver on party commitments or promises were common on the Lesedi radio station, which broadcasts in the areas covered by this study. Research conducted for this chapter suggests that some of the women elected through PR lacked capacity to explain their council's responsibilities and problems to the communities. For instance, we asked a woman councillor from Temba to explain her responsibilities to the community to us and we found her explanation questionable. In the absence of concrete proposals and clear guidelines about the relationship between representatives, constituents and political parties, there is confusion about what constitutes proper accountability to constituents. In practice, councillors are either political party representatives or independents. If they are party representatives, they represent the vision of their parties in the council and are bound to vote in support of the line adopted by the party.

The success of the electoral system in terms of addressing women's concerns is also dependent on the extent of political parties' commitment to gender equality. Although all parties have made formal commitments (Gender Advocacy Programme 2000), only the ANC is prepared to use a quota and almost all have no explicit policy proposals that reflect a deep understanding of women's needs in particular communities (CGE 2000: 54). Without explicit commitments, women councillors, many of whom are inexperienced in the art of policy making, find it difficult to develop meaningful programmes that are implementable. The

197

CGE argues that some of the political parties' manifestos confuse strategies with principles, while others make statements that contradict their commitments (CGE 2000). For example, there is a common commitment among all parties to poverty alleviation, but none show how poverty alleviation strategies would benefit women. Gender-neutral language and programmes fail to recognise the disproportionate burden of poverty borne by women.

Traditional leaders and changes in local government in rural areas

Traditional leaders have a vested interest in ensuring that local government design does not radically change their customary roles, entrenched under apartheid, in determining land allocation and usage and making decisions about the nature and quality of service delivery to communities. The constitution provides for 10 per cent representation of traditional authorities on councils in areas where there are traditional authorities. According to the White Paper on Local Government, areas under traditional authority belong to category B municipalities. Within this category, the roles of traditional authorities include lobbying different spheres of government to promote the interests and development of communities in these areas. But traditional authorities are divided about whether to accept this arrangement, with some traditional leaders lobbying to increase the number of seats reserved for them in local councils and to broaden the responsibilities they are allocated within municipalities. From the concerns expressed in areas where there are traditional authorities it became clear that some community members support the current system of local government and question the future of the institution of traditional authorities (National Workshop on Rural Governance: Local Government, Traditional Leaders and Women, National Land Committee Offices, Braamfontein, 30 July 2000).[6] Most traditional authorities, however, are concerned about government interference with the boundaries of the constituencies and the intrusion on their conventional authority over economic and political decisions in these areas. They see the government's process of delineating municipalities as a strategy to usurp their powers, and view with suspicion the government's strategy of joining rich and poor areas together under one council to spread resources and speed up service delivery (Local Government Municipality Structures Act 117, 1998).

The traditional authorities' objection to the introduction of democratic councils in these areas has strained relations between councillors, government and traditional authorities. In some communities living in areas where there are traditional authorities, residents want the areas to be converted into townships – that is, residential areas without traditional leaders – as they doubt traditional authorities' developmental capacity (Interview: woman councillor, Temba, July 2000). Both male and female elected councillors in these areas also complain about the condescension and contempt with which they are treated by traditional authorities (*ibid.*). However, women face a particular constraint in that there is no established custom of female authority in community decision making. Although the institution of traditional authorities relies on female regents during periods when the male heir is either too young or is in some way incapacitated, these female regents are still believed to be incapable of holding office as a traditional authority. In some exceptional cases, however, with the support of their families female regents with aspirations to a political role have identified local councils as an area where they can legitimately participate. The queen of the Basotho in Qwa-Qwa, Free State Province, stood for local government elections in 2000 as a representative of the ANC. She won and was made a mayor of the council in her area. Because the institution of traditional authorities has not clarified women's participation in the structure, women family members of traditional authorities may sometimes find loopholes that facilitate their participation in representative government.

Organisations working with women in areas where there are traditional authorities were critical of the draft White Paper on Traditional Leaders and Traditional Institutions. They argued that the Department of Local Government was more concerned with accommodating traditional authorities than with the interests of ordinary citizens, and that the Department focused on placating these authorities at the expense of the communities living in these areas. The draft document was criticised for failing to grapple with the legitimacy of the institution of traditional leadership and the extent of its jurisdiction within a democracy. The premise of the draft White Paper is that traditional authorities and their institutions have legitimacy and enjoy the support of community members. However, community organisations point out many cases of conflict between councils and traditional authorities which delay development and service delivery, and make women continue to suffer by having to walk long distances for water and other services.

The Rural Services Development Network and the National Land Committee indicate that provision of basic services such as water, health care and road building and maintenance are not satisfactory in areas under the jurisdiction of traditional authorities (report at the National

Workshop on Rural Governance, 2000). Developmental projects identified by elected councils fail to find support among most traditional authorities because of the tug-of-war between traditional authorities and councils over proper authority. Where projects do find support with the traditional authorities, these agreements are made by men. Perceptions that women are not capable of serving as councillors and that women's participation in government is 'uncultural' marginalise the potential contribution of women councillors. These attitudes are problematic and justify community concern about the future of the institution of traditional authorities in a democratic country. Traditional authorities fail to show the loss they are likely to endure if women's participation in governance as traditional authorities is formalised.

Women's participation in councils

Both councils studied for this chapter are relatively small. The Kempton Park–Tembisa Council is made up of 30 representatives, of whom 15 are from the ANC. Out of the seven women in the council, three are ANC members, one is a Democratic Party member and three are from the New National Party (NNP). Only three of these seven women are black, but the deputy mayor is a black woman. The Temba Council is made up of 11 representatives, with women still constituting a minority of four. All councillors but one (independent candidate) in the Temba TRC are ANC representatives. Despite the ANC's use of a quota for women on its list, women were less successful in this council. Although disappointingly low, black women's representation is also an important achievement if one takes into account their inexperience and the cultural obstacles blocking their participation.

Following the 2000 elections, Kempton Park–Tembisa became part of Ekurhuleni Metro[7] and now forms part of a big council made up of 178 councillors, of whom 51 are women. The ANC has 99 councillors in this council while the Democratic Alliance (DA)[8] has 53 and the remaining 26 belong to different parties. Most of the women occupying seats in this council are PR candidates. More than 35 (20 ANC, 15 DA) women councillors in Ekurhuleni Metro are PR candidates,[9] while more than 14 women councillors (ten ANC, four DA) won their seats from the wards. This means that, unlike the national pattern described above, women have accessed the Ekurhuleni Metro almost equally through proportional representation and ward.

Although women's numbers in local councils are increasing they are still low in comparison with the male numerical domination of councils, committees and executive councils. The Kempton Park–Tembisa MLC's executive council is made up of seven men and one woman – the deputy mayor. There were four women to three men in the Temba executive council because the Chief Executive Officer (CEO) of the council was a woman. The CEO of the relatively affluent municipality of Kempton Park Tembisa MLC is a man.

Factors impacting on women's effective participation in councils

Although the electoral system may facilitate increases in women's representation, it cannot be a guarantee of the effectiveness of women councillors in articulating women's interests in decision making. The conditions for effectiveness are set by rather more intractable factors: cultural norms and expectation of women's roles, the openness of debate within local councils and the kinds of hierarchies that exist within local government, as well as the relative skill of individual councillors.

First, family expectations and household responsibilities act as a barrier to women's effective participation. The few women who are council members continue to live in families where a woman's primary work is believed to be in the home rather than the council. Female councillors continue to bear the responsibility of assisting children with homework and preparing evening meals for the family. Although councillors in South Africa are paid relatively well, they are not expected to be full-time employees. This can be seen as a facilitating factor for women's participation as it allows women to combine household responsibilities with public activities. However, council meetings are usually scheduled for the late afternoon and take several hours. This schedule accommodates councillors who are in full-time employment elsewhere, but fails to acknowledge women's gendered responsibilities. Some of these problems would be addressed by making childcare facilities available. Some analysts have argued that child bearing and rearing are social responsibilities for which women should be compensated or for which facilities should be provided by the state. But few councils – and neither of the two studied here – provide childcare for councillors and civil servants.

Women councillors have suggested that the limitations on their time as a result of their household responsibilities have given rise to myths about their ability to perform council duties and that these are used to limit women's opportunities within the council. Arguments about women's cultural roles are used inconsistently – or rather, they are used to achieve the consistent effect of marginalising women. A pregnant woman, for example, cannot use her condition as an excuse for failing to attend meetings or perform duties. It is quickly pointed out that she chose to be a councillor. Although it is easy for some men to prioritise work over family life, this is not always easy for women with the responsibility to look after children, the sick and the aged. In the national Parliament, a critical mass of women representatives was crucial in ensuring that matters such as hours of sitting and childcare were addressed by Parliament as an institution. The small number of women in local councils has inhibited such strategies; their concerns are simply ridiculed as 'women's problems' by male-dominated councils.

Women also have interests that are fundamentally different, which often makes it hard for them to work together. These differences in the council are compounded by class, colour and party interests. In Temba, PR women councillors complained about the woman ward councillor who would not allow the PR councillor any say about the communities in her ward. In Kempton Park–Tembisa, women were divided on priority projects. One group wanted to prioritise a crèche for residents of Tembisa. Women councillors from former white-only municipalities with infrastructure could not identify a crèche as a need. They therefore failed to support the efforts of the Tembisa women councillor to put the needs of her community on the council agenda. It may be that if the numbers of women in councils were higher, women's differences would not be so magnified.

Failure on the part of women councillors to participate in the discussions of the council is another problem. A central obstacle is the attitude of male councillors, who adopt dominant and subordinating attitudes towards women. Women councillors from Temba said that men question women's capacity for assuming responsibilities such as heading council committees. According to these women councillors, the council has to develop a policy dedicated to addressing gender bias in councils. They also identify this bias as one of the factors that discourage them from seeking more senior positions on council committees. In Temba the women councillors are quiet throughout the process of the council, even when important service delivery problems are being discussed. The quietness of women councillors does not go unnoticed by their male counterparts, as evidenced by the informal discussions at the end of one meeting we attended. At the meeting, residents' complaints to the council about water and electricity bills were discussed. 'Why did you not say something? Were the issues not important to you?' a male councillor asked. It was the fifth year of the council's term of office, but women council members were still not comfortable expressing their concerns during the council meetings.

The same observation was made during the council meeting of 11 July 2000 in Temba. Women councillors did not make concrete suggestions except to second motions. When asked to explain this behaviour, they blamed their ineffective participation on their male counterparts. One woman councillor said that 'men in the council laugh and interrupt our contributions'. Despite the ANC male councillors' apparent concern about women's silence, their practice of belittling women's contributions was not addressed by the party, the mayor or the deputy mayor. The mayor, in particular, is responsible for ensuring that councillors respect one another's views during the course of meetings, and for restricting interruptions and comments capable of inflicting an inferiority complex on others. It is highly unlikely that such behaviour would have been tolerated had it been white councillors laughing at black councillors.

The use of the English language in council meetings was also found to be an inhibiting factor, as the women we interviewed were less fluent in English than in indigenous languages, and less comfortable than men with the use of English for official business. The choice of English as the language of official discussion is understandable in Kempton Park–Tembisa because the council is racially mixed and representatives speak different languages. On the other hand, the use of English in Temba, where the council is mainly black and councillors can use another common language (Zulu) to communicate is exclusionary. Although the chairperson of the Temba Council said he expresses himself better in English and does not prohibit the use of other languages in meetings, in practice it is not easy to answer a question posed in English in any other language. Women councillors claimed they were prevented from participating by the use of English as the language of the meeting.

Councillors' training

The problems faced by women councillors are not all gender-specific; many (including language) are common to all new councillors. The movement of a large number of black people into local government in 1995 highlighted the huge disparities in knowledge of how government works and how policy is made between white and black councillors. Although at the national government level the lack of direct knowledge of government was somewhat compensated for by the experience of oppositional politics, the majority of local councillors had not participated at high levels in political organisations. As a result, there has been considerable emphasis in NGOs and in government on providing training to overcome historical disadvantages. Adequate training in areas such as what the roles of councillors are, how budgets should be drawn up and how democratic councils should be run also falls within the framework of the integrated development planning process that underpins the government's vision of developmental local government. GAP's submission to the Green Paper on Local Government emphasised the particular importance of providing training to women. 'Training' is thus a buzzword in the empowerment lexicon and it is worth exploring the gendered nature of access to and ability to utilise training in the local government sector.

Although we did not set out to assess the impact of training provided to councillors, training needs kept cropping up during interviews. This was surprising because our respondents confirmed that training was provided by the South African Local Government Association (SALGA), a government organisation, and by non-governmental organisations such as the Women's Development Foundation (WDF). The aim of training for both organisations was to improve councillors' participation in councils. Councils have an obligation to provide training for capacity-building purposes in line with the provisions of the Skills Development Act (28 of 1999, section 81) and the Local Government Municipality Systems Act (B27-2000, section 63). This view is also supported by the White Paper on Local Government.

Both training organisations had their own agendas on how to train local councillors and the content of the training to be provided. However, their plans did not always coincide with the training needs of councillors. Those interviewed claimed that they need training on procedure to conduct meetings, confidence building and raising issues in councils' meetings. 'Training was provided on some of the issues. But because we were new, we did not know the right questions to ask. We have since identified our needs. We have already approached the MEC for local government to assist in this respect,' said a woman councillor from Temba. This comment shows that the training provided was adequate – but was one-off, or came too early in the term of office of the councillor in question. She herself, on the other hand, made no effort to deal with the problem by notifying the organisation responsible about her need. Women councillors felt that training should be needs-based and ongoing, rather than the one-off training around predetermined issues identified by the trainers. There appears to be no assessment of whether there is any improvement of performance in the areas where training has been provided.

Women councillors in particular felt that they needed to acquire skills and confidence, and saw training as a structured tool to achieve this. Information we collected from Temba shows that only one of the women on the council had studied up to the final year of school (matriculation), and that this lack of formal education was a barrier to reading, understanding and responding to complex policy documents and budgets. The women councillors struggled to absorb the training that was provided and did not feel confident even about participating in training exercises. Existing training programmes expect them to grasp all the required skills in a day or a week. Councils such as Temba did not have a training programme or a proposal articulating councillors' needs to form the basis for training.

Training institutions also have a policy of providing training by representation. This means that one local councillor attends training provided by WDF on a particular aspect, with the expectation that the skill acquired will be shared with other councillors on return from the training. The 'trickle down' policy (as it is often called) fails to achieve its intended results in that it is not always possible to share skills. Some of the councillors who attended these courses felt inadequate to pass on the skill acquired through training. Some of them did not write reports to be used as a resource by others.

Councils also failed to use the opportunity of attending courses productively because they did not always nominate the appropriate councillor to attend the training. Men nominated each other. Women councillors from Temba nominated men even to attend training workshops specially organised for women councillors because they felt inadequate to act on the council's requirement that those who attended courses should produce reports. The Kempton Park–Tembisa Council did not have a policy of providing special training for women councillors. Professional training was offered to all personnel. There is no special training on issues relating to gender relations or those issues affecting women and men as members of the different groups.

Party support enjoyed by local councillors

One of the key values of the PR system in promoting women's representation is the ability that it provides political parties to overcome traditional obstacles to women's participation in government. This is underscored by the legislative advocacy of equal representation, and by the use of a quota by the ANC. In this context, the ongoing support of political parties is vital if increased numerical representation is to be the lever for substantive representation. Without ongoing party political support, there is no protection for women representatives from powerful localised interest groups (or indeed individuals) who do not believe that women have a place in government.

Kempton Park–Tembisa was divided into 18 wards for the 1995/6 local government elections. The ANC and NNP won eight wards each, and the remaining ward seats were won by an independent candidate and the DP. Men were the candidates in all the eight wards won by the ANC. NNP women councillors won two ward seats. Although the NNP representatives interviewed say that the party policy does not spell out support for women candidates at local level, from the numbers it would seem that the party clearly supports women. The ANC also had a ward seat occupied by a woman in Temba.

The ANC (partly through the use of a quota) and the New National Party (without the use of a quota) both had an equal number of women councillors in the Kempton Park–Tembisa council. Talking about party support, the deputy mayor (ANC) said it made a huge difference to her. Like other women councillors interviewed in both councils, the deputy mayor said she enjoyed more support from her party than from male colleagues in the council. Nevertheless, party bias constitutes one of the main problems for women's numerical under-representation in councils. Women councillors say parties are biased towards male candidates, if not always in the selection of candidates then certainly in terms of who they viewed as capable and important. They blame deep cultural biases against women's participation in public politics for this. Also, while party leadership might support women, male councillors who are not part of the leadership might express bias in their day-to-day dealings with women which undermines the official party 'line'.

Distinctions between PR councillors and ward councillors are considered to be significant: greater legitimacy attaches to ward councillors, who are seen to be 'true' representatives of 'the people' as opposed to the party (Telela 2000: 40). Interviews with women councillors suggest that as long as the PR component of the electoral system is in place, parties may prefer this route as a way to demonstrate their commitment to women's representation. Women receive less encouragement to stand for ward seats, possibly because the party fears its chances of election would be jeopardised by cultural biases against women. Yet even in Temba, where the ANC enjoyed an absolute monopoly of the council, two of the three women councillors were PR rather than ward representatives. In its campaigns for women's representation in the 2000 elections, GAP encouraged women voters to be critical of how parties chose their electoral lists. It suggested that one important marker of a party's commitment might be the extent to which it supports women standing for ward seats, together with the issues a party focuses on when canvassing and campaigning for support to be elected (Gender Advocacy Programme 2000). One of the difficulties posed was whether women councillors should primarily represent women or their communities. 'All community members elected me. Why should I focus on women's needs only?' asked a woman ward councillor from Temba.

The Kempton Park–Tembisa respondents were divided on whether the PR system has been useful for communities. Some prefer the focus on the party rather than the individual because it does not leave room for personal conflicts between powerful local actors. These respondents say they are comfortable to choose a party but uncomfortable with the party representative. Where voters were not comfortable with the party representative, they say they chose independent candidates. Other community members are against the system of closed party lists because it does not always tell the voter who is being chosen. The CGE report shows that there is a strong possibility of changing the parallel or dual system of voting in local government, partly because of dissatisfaction on the part of civil society (CGE 2000: 4).

Communities need to be supported in exercising their voting right adequately. From the high turn-out of women for national elections, it can be deduced that awareness was raised on the importance of their vote and what it might mean if the vote was withheld. However, the failure to improve the practical aspects of the voting process forces women to make a choice between having to queue to vote and queuing for water or medicines for a child or a sick parent. Shortening the process enables women to do both.

Women councillors and the articulation of policy interests

As Goetz and Hassim (2002) have noted, there are still considerable hurdles to be cleared in both Uganda and South Africa to ensure that the increase in the number of women representatives translates into policy leverage for women. In this regard there are two challenges facing women in local government: institutional transformation to allow women's voices to be validated and women's interests to be routinely addressed in policy making (Goetz 1998); and the creation of linkages between elected representatives and constituencies of women who would be able to challenge existing patterns of resource allocation (Kabeer

1994). In South Africa, although the notions of participation and trans-formation have been placed at the core of the local government framework, women councillors have not yet effectively addressed these challenges. Subethri Naidoo, one-time gender coordinator for SALGA, argues that women representatives 'have not had the kind of impact on service delivery issues at local government level that one would antici-pate' (2000: 49).

The reasons for the slow pace at which gender equality is integrated into policy at the local level are manifold. As the discussion above has argued, women councillors have been dealing with the institutional shock of the restructuring of local government – the large-scale incorpo-ration of previously excluded groups into the system of governance – and the somewhat nebulous (although no less real in its effects) barrier of male undermining of women's roles in public decision making. Budgets for 1995/6 were set before the elections and all councillors were engaged in a rubber-stamping exercise (Telela 2000). Between 1995 and 2000, councillors have had to rapidly acquire knowledge of the technical aspects of government as well as learning to work with white colleagues who were vastly more knowledgeable about the rules and procedures of councils. New councillors have found that municipalities 'are often un-prepared or not equipped to change institutional or bureaucratic pro-cesses, out-dated procedures, and to cope with challenges to policy or to accept demands that they re-think budget priorities (Naidoo 2000: 47).

Women councillors in the two councils studied nevertheless believe that they make a difference to the kinds of issues that are raised and have begun to represent the particular interests of women. Most argued that they focused to a much greater extent than men on community needs and interests in their campaigning, in part because of their own personal experience of local services (councillor from Temba). Another councillor pointed out that she felt more comfortable participating in projects relating to health as they 'primarily focused on women's issues'. Similarly, women councillors from Kempton Park–Tembisa were more prominent in committees dealing with social welfare and health. Three of the Kempton Park–Tembisa committees – welfare, *masakhane* (literally translated to mean 'together let us build our nation/community'), and gender – were headed by women.

Although women councillors expressed frustration, they said they were capable of placing women's concerns on the local council's agenda. For most councillors interviewed, women's economic indepen-dence was a major policy goal to strive for during their term of office. But the interpretation of 'economic independence' was fairly restrictive.

Women councillors from Temba saw economic projects like knitting and sewing as a vehicle through which they could emancipate women. For these councillors, assisting communities to put up a knitting project by passing on ideas on how to secure funding in the council's area was part of their agenda of representing women's interests. Income-generating programmes are a limited strategy for women's empowerment. They make women dependent on funding rather than giving them an independent source of income. Most are small-scale programmes with low productivity, which do not meet the objective of generating enough income to provide women with economic independence. In addition, they are not properly appraised in terms of the marketability of the products. Finally, the capital invested is too low to be of benefit to poor people, who expect to reap profits from the income-generating programme on the first day of implementation.

A woman councillor from Temba, whose objective was to ensure that women in the municipality benefit from the local council's policy of outsourcing services, said: 'I confronted the council for its failure to award women contracts when awarding tenders by forcing the council to account by discussing the process they follow in awarding contracts.' According to this woman, failure on the part of the council to give work to women contractors increases unemployment rates among women in the municipality. Although it became clear that women contractors did not possess the expertise required by the council, drawing the council's attention to the needs of women, in this councillor's view, signals an attempt to push women's concerns up the agenda of the local council.

There have been some attempts to create linkages between women representatives and women's organisations. In Kempton Park–Tembisa, the ANC Women's League made violence against women an issue in the 2000 elections. One of the councillors, a retired nursing sister, carried through this commitment by making it an issue for the council, which established a gender committee chaired by the deputy mayor. According to the chairperson, women councillors are supportive of the programme – for once, across colour and class. The council as a whole is supportive of measures intended to deal with crime and violence. Liaison measures between the police and the council are in place.

Conclusions

This chapter has examined the extent and effectiveness of women's representation in two local councils in South Africa. It has shown that descriptive representation is an important marker of the extent to which a political system is able to accommodate women as citizens, particularly in the context of entrenched conservative cultural norms that are biased against the political participation of women. In this context, the numbers of women in government are a reflection of whether democratic political parties are prepared to use their electoral strength to break cultural barriers. In South Africa, as this chapter points out, the ANC has set a benchmark for democratic participation that has had important knock-on effects within the political system as a whole.

However, the chapter also reveals the difficulties that face women once they are in government. Women are less likely to occupy important seats in the executive structures of local councils, are less likely to be supported in their work by their peers and by their political parties, and are frequently the object of distrust by constituents and ridicule by their male colleagues. Due to women's low representation in councils, they are spread thinly in the different committees of the council, which prevents them from providing support to each other or from developing effective strategies. The failure to integrate structures, community participation, plans and budgets by the department responsible for local government and by councils, and the negative impact all these have on the local government's vision of development, have been highlighted.

Local government is an interesting arena in which to test the extent to which women will become effectively integrated into the democratic system and the extent to which the women's movement will begin to shape policies and service delivery. Given that the majority of women's organisations in South Africa are small and localised, the most likely terrain on which they can influence government is at the community level. Linkages between these organisations and the almost equally isolated women councillors in local government are surely vital to make democracy meaningful.

References

Adler, G. and J. Steinberg (2000) *From Comrades to Citizens: the South African Civics Movement and the Transition to Democracy*, Basingstoke: Macmillan.

Bozzoli, B. (1983) 'Marxism, Feminism and South African Studies', *Journal of Southern African Studies*, 9, 2.

CGE Report (2000) 'Election Network: Local Government', Braamfontein, 28 February.

Fick, G. (2000) 'The Importance of Equality to the Sphere of Local Government', *Agenda – Empowering Women for Gender Equity*, 45: 27–39.

Gender Advocacy Programme (1997) 'Submission for the White Paper on Local

Government on Gender', mimeo, November.

—— (2000) 'Gender Politics at Local Level', *Agenda – Empowering Women for Gender Equity*, 45: 13–17.

Goetz, A. M. (ed.) (1998) *Getting Institutions Right for Women in Development*, London: Zed Books.

Goetz, A. M. and S. Hassim (2002) 'In and against the Party: Women's Representation and Constituency Building in Uganda and South Africa', in S. Razavi and M. Molyneux (eds.), *Gender Justice, Development and Rights*, Oxford: Oxford University Press.

Goldblatt, B. and L. Mbatha (1999) 'Women's Rights – the Maintenance and Customary Marriages Act', *Indicator*, 16, 3: 77–9.

Kabeer, N. (1994) *Reversed Realities*, London: Verso.

Manicom, L. (1992) 'Ruling Relations: Rethinking State and Gender in South African History', *Journal of African History*, 33.

Motala, S. (2000) 'Rural Women Demand Meaningful Representation in Local Government', *Agenda – Empowering Women for Gender Equity*, 45: 18–21.

Naidoo, S. (2000) 'The Integrated Development Plan: a Framework for Women's Mobilisation around Service Delivery', *Agenda – Empowering Women for Gender Equity*, 45: 45–53.

Pottie, D. (2001) 'Women and Local Government: by the Numbers', *Update*, 9, Johannesburg: Electoral Institute of Southern Africa, 12 April.

Robinson, J. (1995) 'Act of Omission: Gender and Local Government in the Transition', *Agenda – Empowering Women for Gender Equity*, 26: 7–18.

Telela, R. (2000) 'Advancing Women in Power: Rosalee Telela Speaks to Gawa Samuels and Gertrude Pheko-Mothupi', *Agenda – Empowering Women for Gender Equity*, 45: 40–4.

Van Donk, M. (2000) 'Local Government: a Strategic Site of Struggle for Gender Equity', *Agenda – Empowering Women for Gender Equity*, 45: 4–12.

Zondo, Ntomb'futhi (1995) 'Rural Women Pessimistic', *Agenda – Empowering Women for Gender Equity*, 26: 22–4.

Notes

1 This study is based on nine in-depth interviews with women councillors, two discussion groups of both men and women councillors, one-to-one, in-depth interviews randomly selected with women members of the community, and group interviews with women members of the communities in the chosen areas (these involved 40 people from the two areas). The information generated through one-to-one interviews and group discussions was complemented by information generated through Radio Lesedi (an SABC programme with slots to discuss local government and its problems). The information was collected between 1999 and 2000.

2 The study used a range of diverse sources. In the case of Kempton Park–Tembisa the 1998/9 annual report of the council was studied to support the information collected. In addition, information from Radio Lesedi on local government programmes, issues and concerns from the points of view of both local councils and the community nationally has complemented this research. The station broadcast live meetings convened in different areas with

a view to exposing problems experienced by councillors and community members. Community members were able to accuse councillors face to face over failures to deliver services. The meetings also gave councillors an opportunity to explain certain things and to show community members the importance of attending council meetings. Apart from these meetings, the Minister of Local Government Affairs was interviewed live by the station on the impasse between traditional authorities and local government. The station gave civil society spokespersons an opportunity to ask the Minister questions related to local government. During the last four weeks before the 2000 elections, this radio station invited all political parties to come and talk about their local government manifestos.

3 Section 23 of the Municipal Structures Act No 117 of 1998 provides that municipal planning must be developmentally oriented, while section 26 provides that the municipal long-term development plan and internal transformation needs must be reflected in budget allocations. The existing level of development must also be assessed. For example, if the council has communities without access to basic services, these must be identified.

4 For example, rural women use money remitted by husbands to buy livestock. It was only in November 2000 that the law repealing their minority status was passed. Before the end of 2000, women in the rural areas had no power to sell livestock unassisted, even if it was for purposes of sending a child to school.

5 The Women's Charter categorises women's needs into 12 articles. The most relevant one for local government purposes is Article 1, which provides for similar treatment of women and men. The article indicates that equality between men and women would often require 'distinction to be made', although such distinctions should not disadvantage women. See also Article 5, dealing with Development, Infrastructure and the Environment.

6 The issue of traditional leaders and local councils was a matter of interest to the Rural Services Development Network, the National Land Committee and the Rural Women's Movement (these are umbrella bodies with affiliates in many rural areas).

7 The Metro Council includes Kempton Park–Tembisa, Edenvale, Springs, Germiston, Benoni, Boksburg, Nigel and Brakpan.

8 The former white parties – the New National Party (NNP) and the Democratic Party (DP) – joined forces as the Democratic Alliance in preparation for the local government elections of 2000.

9 The total number of PR candidates for Ekurhuleni Metro in 2000 was about 88.

8

Gender Equity and Local Democracy in Contemporary Uganda: Addressing the Challenge of Women's Political Effectiveness in Local Government

JOSEPHINE AHIKIRE

In 1998, over 10,000 women were elected to local government in Uganda. This was the result of affirmative action measures put in place in the first local government elections held since the 1995 constitution of the Republic of Uganda decreed that one third of positions on all local councils would be reserved for women. This represents a tremendous increase in the numbers of women in local government from the one reserved post (Secretary for Women) in the earlier Resistance Council[1] system of local government. The increase of women in local government has also taken place in the context of decentralisation, which has involved the transfer of administrative, fiscal and financial powers from the centre to the locally elected district and lower councils.

This chapter focuses on questions of gender equity and local democracy. The concern is to situate women's participation in local politics within the broader process of democratisation in Uganda, with democratisation seen, as Gordon White puts it, not as a relatively sudden rupture or rapid transition, but as a process of institutional accumulation, built up gradually like layers of coral (1995: 32). The chapter will analyse the ways in which a substantial numerical increase of women in local government affects not just the articulation and promotion of gender issues in local politics, but also the character and conduct of local politics. This is an inquiry into the extent to which the visibility and presence of women in governance translates into the transformation of political culture and space, and greater politicisation of inequalities in gender relations. Women local councillors' experiences are examined to highlight the constraints and opportunities they face. The instruments at their disposal are analysed in view of the expanded space for their participation in local government. Experiences and perceptions of male politicians and citizens in relation to gender issues are also studied.

213

The chapter is based on a study of two districts selected for the purpose. One is Mukono, located in the central region, east of Kampala. The other is Kabale, located in south-western Uganda, bordering on Rwanda. Mukono is one of the biggest districts, relatively well endowed with natural resources which include Lake Victoria and soils suitable for horticulture and coffee growing. Commodity-processing industries and proximity to the capital city are among its other assets. Kabale, on the other hand, is a small district with a weak resource base. In the past it has thrived on cross-border trade and smuggling between Rwanda and Uganda, but this trade has since lost impetus due to political instability.

Decentralisation in the 1990s – institutionalising women's access to local government in Uganda

Decentralisation and women's increased numerical representation in local government have no obvious causal relationship. There is scepticism even about the bare democratic potential of decentralisation, about its much-touted capacity to promote broader popular participation and efficient service delivery. Griffith warns us that 'power at the local level is more concentrated, more élitist and applied more ruthlessly against the poor than at the centre' (1981: 225). As far as patriarchal social relations are concerned, this observation could have far-reaching implications for women's capacity to advance their interests in a context of political decentralisation.

Critics of decentralisation have tended to view it principally as a project of mobilising the public to support the central government, rather than a project of building genuine popular control over decision making (Mutizwa-Mangiza and Conyers 1996). Current decentralisation initiatives by the NRM government in Uganda could well be analysed in this sense – some argue that decentralisation is being implemented in order to deepen the government's hegemony (Mamdani 1988, 1994). Alternatively, as Doornbos (1999) argues, decentralisation can be seen as a reflection of the depth of external (donor) involvement with the process of policy formation in independent countries of the Third World, where decentralisation is part of the political conditionalities attached to foreign aid.

While the influence of donors and state inclination to political expediency cannot be entirely discounted, it is important to underline the fact that Uganda's history of turmoil, mass struggle and reconstruction has a lot to tell us about the nature of decentralisation today. The inclusion of women and other groups such as youth and people with disabilities through specific reservations is part of broader reforms introduced in the aftermath of the civil war. Hence, the present local government system is largely based on the Resistance Council (RC) system that was first established by the National Resistance Army during 1981–5. The RC system is based on village councils in which one seat was always reserved for a Secretary for Women. However, the recent significant expansion of women's representation in local government has happened within the context of decentralisation, not *because* of it.

The current system of local government, though based on the RC system, brings major changes too. The RCs have been transformed into more conventional local government units, known as Local Councils (LCs). The apex of this system of local government is the district and there are no intermediate levels between the national and district-centred local government. Under the district are four lower levels of local government (LC1–4), and the LC3 is a body corporate.[2]

According to the Local Governments Act 1997, councils and committees are constituted by elected representatives. At the village level, or LC1, there are ten positions on the executive committee, as illustrated in Box 8.1. The ten executives are elected by adult suffrage (by queueing up behind candidates in a public forum) and four of them must be women.

While explaining how it was decided which of these positions should be taken by women, the Chairperson of Kanjuki LC1 (Mukono district) noted that according to the list provided, there were already two female-identified positions: the Chairperson of the Women Councils and the

---

Box 8.1 Positions on the Village Council (LC1) executive committee

1 The Chairperson
2 Vice-Chairperson (also Secretary for Children Welfare)
3 General Secretary
4 Secretary for Information, Education and Mobilisation
5 Secretary for Security
6 Secretary for Finance
7 Secretary for Production and Environmental Protection
8 The Chairperson of the Women Councils at the village level (also Secretary for Women and Public Health Coordinator)
9 The Chairperson of the Youth Council at the village level (also Secretary for Youth)
10 The Chairperson of the Organisation for Persons with Disabilities at the village level (also Secretary for Persons with Disabilities)

Vice-Chairperson. The latter position was seen as appropriate for a woman because of its extra mandate as Secretary for Children Welfare – a sex-typed concern. His identification of the other seat also follows a logic about female attributes and appropriate activities. The positions of either Production or Information also tend to go to women. Another interesting pattern that is developing is a tendency for women to be assigned the seat of the Secretary for Finance. Reasons for this will be discussed below.

At the parish level (LC2) all village executive committees in a parish form an electoral college and elect a parish executive committee. In relation to women councils, youth councils and persons with disabilities (PWDs), this means that there is another parallel election to establish the relevant chairpersons at parish level.

At the sub-county level (LC3) there are direct elections. The Chairperson is elected by adult suffrage on a secret ballot. The other councillors are elected by lining up behind the candidate of choice. Here, the mechanism to include women follows a different pattern. Whereas there are established positions for which candidates run in the village and parish elections, and one third of these positions have to be assigned to women candidates, the election of councillors at the sub-county level is based on a ward representative system. Women may run as ward representatives, of course, but a new set of seats have been designed specifically for them. These seats are formed by grouping together existing wards to constitute another one third of seats in the local council. Separate elections for these additional seats are held after the 'normal' ward-based elections. Box 8.2 shows how the number of women councillors is established for a LC3.

As shown in the Bukinda case, all ward, youth, and PWD representatives are considered to constitute two thirds of a council, and now a number of women are added to constitute a new total. Women can also run for the normal parish seat but only a few women have stood and won. The reservation for women has generally been misunderstood, so that now it is often assumed that women have to wait their turn and run for their specially designated seats, rather than contest what are increasingly assumed to be 'men's' ward seats.

At the county level (LC4), the directly elected representatives of the sub-county level (LC3) constitute the electoral college from which an executive committee for the LC4 is elected.

The election of the District Council (LC5), the highest authority of local government, follows the same pattern as the sub-county. At these levels, the 30 per cent quota for women as well as the more limited

---

Box 8.2 *Inclusion of (one third) women in LC3 councils: the case of Bukinda sub-county, Kabale district*

There are 6 parishes in Bukinda sub-county. The LC3 council consists of:

      6 men to represent the parishes

      2 representatives of people with disabilities – 1 male and 1 female

      2 youth representatives – 1 male and 1 female

      1 Chairperson

Sub-total: 11 people. This is now held to constitute two thirds of the council.

      5 women are added to constitute the remaining one third of councillors

---

reservations for youth and PWDs are effected through separate elections. The youth representatives, a male and a female, are elected through the National Youth Council system, while the PWDs are elected through their National Union of Disabled Persons (NUDIPU). In the Local Governments Act 1997 it is stated that the District Council shall consist of:

a) The District Chairperson;

b) One councillor directly elected to represent each electoral area of a district;

c) Two councillors, one of whom shall be a female youth, representing the youth in the district;

d) Two councillors with disabilities, one of whom shall be a female, representing persons with disabilities;

e) Women councillors forming one third of the council such that the councillors elected under paragraphs (b), (c) and (d) shall form two thirds of the council (Part III [11])

Box 8.3 (page 218) illustrates how this formula works out for the District Council of Mukono.

Justifying this unusual arrangement, the Deputy Speaker of Mukono District Council (a woman) said:

> Reservations for women within the existing constituencies would have meant that some sub-counties would be forced to have a woman as their representative. That would again be dictatorship and suffocation of democratic right of choice (Interview, November 1999, Mukono district).[3]

217

Box 8.3 Inclusion of women at district level: Mukono district

Mukono District: 32 sub-counties and 5 town councils

           37 members (34 men and 3 women who stood for the general
           sub-county seat)
           2 members for people with disabilities – 1male and 1 female
           2 youth members – 1 male and 1 female
           1 District Chairperson

Sub-total: 42, taken as two thirds of council

           21 women added (as a third of 63)
           37 constituencies reorganised to create 21 women's constituen-
           cies, taking into account population and size of sub-counties

---

This matter generated much contention in Constituent Assembly debates on the formulation of the constitution. The chairperson of Committee Four (which dealt with local government), Mr Kateenta Apuli, moved an amendment that one third of the membership of each local government council should be women (CA proceedings, March 1995: 3704). The reactions to this amendment ranged from lukewarm to outright objection. Brigadier Kyaligonza moved a motion to oppose the amendment. He argued that since affirmative action had been enshrined in the constitution, there was no rationale for a one-third provision. He said:

> Women as their rights should have equal participatory democracy. After all they are the majority, and in our national objectives, Mr Chairman, national objective No. 9 it is already mentioned in Clause (3) that all people in Uganda shall have access to leadership position at all levels subject only to the constitution and other laws in Uganda. Mr Chairman, the rationale for favouring this group the committee is regarding as marginalised, is unreasonable on the grounds that women or all citizens have equal rights to compete in leadership positions (CA proceedings, 30 March 1995: 3707).

Another member had similar concerns:

> I find this particular provision as an excessive and detrimental approach to what has been dubbed affirmative action (CA proceedings 30 March 1995: 3707).

Women members of the CA rallied to protect the clause on women's representation in local government since it was on the verge of being deleted. Jeninah Ntabgoba reacted thus:

Thank you Mr. Chairman ... . I start with a heartache in reply to Brig. Kyaligonza who hides behind the support of the marginalised group according to his references and then he ends up abusing women's rights at the same time ... . I would like to inform the Hon. Kyaligonza that any forum without women will come out without sound results, therefore, this one third is not a big fraction to scare him. In fact, I would ask him to increase the number (CA proceedings, March 1995: 3707).

Winfred Masiko submitted that though participatory democracy might sound virtuous, it has not delivered much when it comes to real life and there have to be specific instruments to enable women to participate in levels of governance, particularly at the local level. Victoria Ssebagereka, adding to Masiko's submission, said that instead of one third, it should have read 'at least one third', a more emphatic encouragement to women to move from the position of non-participation to being part of the decision-making process.

The debate developed into a stand-off between men and women and very few men supported the amendment. One male member, who had been part of the committee that recommended the provision, reversed his position and said that having heard from the floor, he thought that the committee might have been too generous or too inconsistent (CA, March 1995: 3714). Despite the stiff resistance, the amendment was passed and the one-third representation for women was enshrined in the 1995 constitution and subsequently operationalised by the Local Governments Act 1997. This relative success can be attributed to the unity and activism of the women in the CA, and women's organisations, as well as the lobbying and identifying of some men as allies.

Implications of the 'add-on' method of reserving seats for women

There has been a relative shift in mainstream feminist scholarship from outright dismissal of the capacity of the state to achieve gender equity, to a position that makes room for engagement with and within the state. Beyond the debate on autonomy and fear of cooption (Goetz 1998; Oloka-Onyango 1998), there is the question of mechanisms to address structural imbalances. The importance of the state stems from the state's capacity to generate social legitimacy for gender equality. The state is an arena for bargaining between interest groups, and hence women's interests must be articulated within that space (Goetz 1998). Therefore, rather than reject the space created for women in state

219

structures as cooption, one is compelled to take a stance that includes both the need for women to be part of the governing entity and a consciousness at the same time of the limitations of the state, and of the need to cultivate other arenas of interest aggregation and bargaining. In Uganda the inclusion of women in local government leadership has been embedded within the constitution in explicit terms. The Article (180 2 (b)) stipulating the one-third reservation for women in each local government council is justified by Articles 32 and 33 of the same constitution, which seek to accord to women full dignity and equality with men, and to give women the right to 'affirmative action for the purpose of redressing the imbalances created by history, tradition or custom'.

The method of reservation in Uganda raises a number of questions about the objective of increasing the numbers of women in politics. Of all the special groups identified in the constitution as requiring assisted access to political space, it is only women that are *not* elected on the basis of group representation. The youth representatives are elected by the electoral college derived from the Youth Council structure, and likewise the PWDs are elected from NUDIPU. More problematic still is the fact that the election of women representatives at sub-county and district levels, the two major pillars of the LC structure, takes place as a separate exercise from elections to ward seats. This highlights the 'afterthought' character of the provision of an additional 30 per cent of seats for women.

In Uganda, the election for women councillors is very much an 'add-on', such that normal constituencies hold their regular elections and then return some time later to vote for women councillors. As reported in local newspapers, these women's polls in many places flopped owing to a lack of quorum and new dates had to be set. In the case of Mukono, voting failed to take off because 'voters shunned polling stations' (*Sunday Vision* 19 April 1998). After rescheduling three times, the Electoral Commission decided to endorse all results, including those where there was failure to raise quorum.[4] According to the *Sunday Vision* (19 April 1998), voters shunned the polls for women councillors because they were tired of voting. There were simply too many elections: 'They voted for the President, MPs and even LC3 chairmen. Even tomorrow they are supposed to vote.' The official line was that poor voter education accounted for the low turn-out. Other views were that men thought it was only women who were supposed to vote for their fellow women; and yet another view was that women district councillors were to blame because they did not do as much campaigning as men (*ibid.*). These views demonstrate voter ambivalence about the legitimacy of women councillors, and confusion about the constituencies they represent. Although the women who experienced the problem of lack of quorum tended to cite the practice of voting by queuing in public as the underlying explanation for low voter interest, the fact is that the 'women elections' were both legally and symbolically assigned low significance. The electoral law and the practice of the elections itself placed women in a different status from other subjects of 1998 elections.

Voters are not the only ones confused by the new system – it is also misunderstood by local council leaders themselves. While it is stipulated that women councillors are to be elected by universal adult suffrage (by queuing up), the general view seems to be that women were to be voted for by some special electoral college. It is also assumed that women representatives are not required to canvass for votes as do candidates for ward seats. For instance, the view of the Chairperson, Kabale District Council, was that it is mass adult suffrage that makes a politician – which most women in the District Council are not (Interview, April 2000, Kabale district). The LC3 Chairperson of Bukinda sub-county in Kabale district equally asserted 'kyenda bareke abakazi batutuke nkabandi', meaning that women should also be left to tussle it out and sweat like the others (that is, men) (Interview, April 2000, Kabale district). The general view is that women sailed through the easy way and have therefore not proved themselves, which has negative implications for their legitimacy as local leaders. That the means by which women's representatives come to sub-county and district councils is misunderstood and derided even by local council chairmen demonstrates not just gender bias and lack of interest but also a serious structural weakness in their mode of inclusion.

The mode of inclusion of women in Uganda has not challenged the problem of voter preference for male candidates – no voter is obliged to choose a woman as his or her 'main' representative, because they may have their regular representative *plus* a woman representative. Local politicians are charged with the responsibility of making decisions relevant to their area of jurisdiction and in this way their 'representativeness' is more direct and tangible than, for instance, that of politicians at the national level. The new system which makes women represent an artificial cluster of wards – drawn together just for the purpose of giving a platform to a woman representative – deprives the women councillors of a chance to become representative of a genuine constituency. The 'add-on' woman suffers from a lack of legitimacy. It is not clear who or what she represents. The women's representativeness

221

is not as immediate or as tangible as is that of the mostly male ward councillors. This means that the quality of representativeness – which is important in local politics – has retained a masculine character. Women have been concentrated in minor positions of local government. At a conference on Ugandan Women in Politics, the Minister of Local Government, Bidandi Ssali, asserted that despite increased participation of women, they had not attained positions with the capacity to increase their ability to influence policy. As can be seen from the figures he presented (Table 8.1), the most powerful position in local government, the LC5 Chairperson, is always male.[5] Two major emerging trends are evident: one is that there is a marked difference between appointed and elected positions. Women are faring better in appointed positions, which implies that people's preferences have not changed fundamentally. Second and perhaps most relevant to local-level politics is the feminisation of the deputy role.[6] Ssali's count of 40 female deputy district chairpersons out of 45 may reflect a situation where women are getting closer to the seat of power but, in reality, there is a consistent trend emerging in local government that mirrors marriage arrangements – the male as the head and the female as his deputy. Besides, the District Vice-Chairperson is not selected through the ballot box but nominated by the chairperson, breeding a patron–client relationship. The only legitimating moment is that the nomination has to be approved by two thirds of all members of council (Local Governments Act 1997, Part III, 19: 1).

It should be observed that the 'add-on' system in Uganda was to a

Table 8.1

Elected positions

	No. councillors	Male	Female	Female %
LC5 Chairperson	45	45	0	0
LC5 Vice-Chairperson	45	5	40	89
Mayors	14	14	0	0
LC3 Chairperson	860	841	9	1

Appointed positions

	No. councillors	Male	Female	Female %
Chief Administrative Officer	45	39	6	13
Town Clerk	63	62	1	2
Resident District Commissioner	45	35	10	22

Source: Bidandi (1998).

large extent conceivable due to the 'no party' system, viewed as a *de facto* one-party system by its opponents. The principle of individual merit and the absence of systems for party campaigning means that candidates contest elections as individuals. The system of campaigning on individual merit rather than party platforms points to lack of political society in terms of formal political organisations, and hence serious gaps in the articulation of interests. It makes it more difficult to campaign on broader matters of policy and principle – such as gender equity concerns.

The advantage of the add-on system is that women candidates experience less antagonism and hostility than they would if they were unseating incumbent male candidates or threatening other male candidates. This is because the inclusion of women does not necessarily force a redefinition of the polity. In spite of the deficiencies noted, it is also possible that within this very ambiguity could also lie the opportunity for women in Uganda to build up political legitimacy over time. In South Africa, as shown in Chapter 7, the closed-list PR system makes women candidates heavily dependent on the party. When people are voting for the party and not the particular candidate, there is an element of political capital lost on the part of the individual candidate. For women, this may be significant because when party conditions change, the clout of individual women can equally be lost. On the whole, though, the mechanics of women's inclusion in Uganda's local government are inhibiting – despite the evident increase in the number of women in councils. We now proceed to look at some of the gendered experiences and the potential for gender equity and local democracy.

Gender and local politics: the experience of elections

Asked whether she would stand for re-election in the next round of local government elections, a woman councillor in Kabale District Council had this to say: 'I would be willing but I am afraid. Voters expect a lot of money and I am still indebted' (Interview, April 2000, Kabale district).

The financial constraint was aired by all women interviewed. Contrary to the general view that women did not have to canvass for votes, women feel they have faced a major problem with voters holding them to ransom during the campaign period. It seems that the electorate have been made to learn that it is only during the campaigning and voting period that they can benefit materially from their representatives. This weighs heavily on women, especially the poor. Although this could be said of poor men, too, women face this problem in a unique way, partly because of the way in which they are elected.

The election of women councillors has a unique feature in that while all other councillors are representatives of some constituency, the women are legally defined in their biological being as *women* councillors. There is no converse description for men as 'men councillors', for instance. This, combined with the way campaigning is based on 'individual merit' and not a party programme of policies and ideas, concentrates voters' attention on the femininity – not the policies – of the woman candidate.

This feature of women's campaigning experience emerged from the testimony of a number of women councillors. In Mukono, for instance, one woman councillor said that at the campaign podium she had to kneel for the electorate. She asserted that: 'If you don't do it you stand to lose. They say *omukyala tatusamu kitibwa*, meaning "this woman does not respect us"' (Interview, September 1999, Mukono district).[7] Campaigns are attended by people of all ages and walks of life, but it is by kneeling that women demonstrate a desirable subservience, to the men in particular. It appears that women have to assure voters of their propriety as women, demonstrating culturally appropriate forms of feminine behaviour, in spite of the fact that this conventional femininity is contradicted by their engagement in politics. In a discussion, one male councillor argued that a candidate kneeling for votes is not an experience particular to women alone. He submitted that even men are required to do 'funny things', such as dancing and even kneeling. But, unlike men, women candidates are under specific pressures to prove that they are 'still' women. Socially submissive acts required of candidates, particularly women, tend to be more pronounced in the case of local government elections, indicating the stronger grip of traditional attitudes at the local level.

Women in the councils

The visibility of greater numbers of women in councils has an unquestionable impact on the observer. In Mukono, for instance, the mandatory one-third add-on, plus three women who won seats through the general ticket, as well as the fact that women held both the female youth and PWD seats, accords women considerable numerical significance as it makes 24 women out of a total of 63 councillors, or over 30 per cent of the District Council. Women's presence therefore breaks up the male character of this public assembly (see Box 8.4).

Box 8.4 *The District Council (DC) meeting – Mukono district*

It is approximately 2.30 pm. And the councillors are finishing up with their lunch (a heavy one). Everybody is in a jovial mood.

People slowly take their seats and the sergeant-at-arms breaks the after-lunch informal conversation by announcing the entry of the Speaker. It is the Deputy Speaker, a woman. There is some murmur and laughter in the room, but seriousness quickly takes its place as the Deputy Speaker walks powerfully to take her seat. This is the Mukono District Council meeting on 11 November 1999.

The meeting is conducted in the Luganda language.

The Clerk to Council then announces the order of the opening rituals. He announces that they will start with the national anthem, 'Ekitibwa kya Buganda',[8] and a prayer.

The Deputy Speaker, in an impressively audible voice, announces that the Speaker is on travel abroad. She congratulates all the people on the Kabaka's wedding which took place in August and makes several announcements including the death of Mwalimu Julius Nyerere, the former President of Tanzania and a well-respected African leader, and that of the wife of the Speaker: her last funeral rites were to take place in January. Here she makes a slight mistake and says 1999 instead of 2000. There is loud murmuring and the speaker comments, 'Now I know that you are all attentive,' regaining her grip on the meeting.

The meeting proceeds with the address by the District Chairperson, who mostly dwells on the issue of headquarter offices for the district. He gives a very elaborate history of how the current offices occupied by the district were confiscated from the Buganda kingdom during the regimes of Obote and Amin, and how Mukono, despite its fame and glory, does not have a district headquarters. He then announces that the construction of the district headquarter building is under way (at a total cost of 4.2 billion shillings) although it has been beset by problems in the initial stages. Moving ahead, the Chairperson also comments on the urge within certain quarters to press for the subdivision of the district and emphatically relays a resolution by the executive that the subdivision of the district was not timely in view of the impending national referendum on political systems. He also talks about the issue of service delivery, which has proved to be a thorny one, particularly in this era of decentralisation. Other items on the agenda are debated: they include quarterly reports by the Secretary of Finance and Administration.

The floor is open and the first to stand is a woman councillor who supports the motion in question and then thanks the executive for services, particularly improved roads in her sub-county. As the meeting progresses into issues of finance and accountability, women appear to have been phased out. Some are evidently dozing off.

Though punctuated by the somewhat expected 'slip of the tongue' – frequent reference to the Speaker as a 'he', using the unusual combination 'Ssebo[9] Madame Speaker' – it is, on the whole, a sober and well-managed meeting. The highly sophisticated manner in which Luganda is employed could eventually change the culture of politics from an élitist exercise where points are scored merely on one's capacity to speak English, to that in which more substance is required of a politician.

The significant and important question to pursue is about the impact of these women on political debates and policy making. The prevailing impression of women's performance is that they generally are most visible when it comes to giving a vote of thanks. This has been coined the 'thanking syndrome'. The other impression is that women generally do well in recalling what was discussed and agreed in previous meetings. One will always hear submissions from women such as *nzijukkira luli*, implying, 'I remember we agreed in a certain meeting.' The major point expressed by several informants was that the women councillors still lack a proactive strategy. In other words, women have generally been good at supporting motions rather than sponsoring them. They point to what was agreed earlier, but do not initiate a particular political agenda.

With regard to Kabale District Council, there is a general view that women councillors are still timid and reluctant to speak. One of the woman councillors said that even when some women are specifically called upon, they just keep silent and wait until after the meeting to grumble. The Chairperson could only remember about four women who had ever said something in council. The district as a whole is riddled with intense religious polarisation between Catholics and Protestants. It is said that the District Council, once elected, had to spend a whole year in wrangles that did not allow normal council business to proceed, whereas other councils in the country had elected standing committees and begun to conduct business. In this context, it can be argued that the religious dimension has tended to overshadow many other identities and interests that could have emerged. The evaluation of women in this context as being fearful and silent may have to take into consideration the very business being conducted by the District Council.

A key arena for advancing interests is the process of agenda setting for the District Council meeting, ensuring that particular issues get to the order paper. It was noted that this process is very intricate and does not make room for the majority of the women's expressed agendas such as the provision of loans to women. This explains the frustration of a number of women about low perceived levels of effectiveness in councils. However, it is also important to acknowledge the fact that measures of effectiveness are largely gendered. While women's expressed agendas, or what they would like to achieve in council, are specific to minute development problems, male councillors tended to cast their agendas in gesturally broad phrases that refer to 'serving my people', participation in decision making, influencing decisions for development, improving leadership in the area, etcetera. The grandiose agendas of male councillors indicate a gap between women and men in terms of self-perception and general evaluation of effectiveness.

There is hardly any space in the DC for discussing immediate community concerns such as developing one's own community and getting loans for women. In one of the meetings, the Chairperson denounced the tendency of many councillors to take the issue of service delivery at a personal level. He reiterated the fact that people find it easy to say that there is no service in the district and yet schools, roads, health centres and improved seeds were all in place. He went on to urge councillors to identify themselves with the shared development goals of the district. For instance, if there is a road being improved in one's area or a school being renovated, one is to say *tukoze* ('look, we have worked') instead of seeking to claim personal credit for bringing a programme or project to one's own ward. He posed a question: 'Programme *eyiyo weka onogyija wa?*' meaning, 'Where will you get your own programme as a person?' The urge to make councillors take on identity as district politicians could have two contradictory effects. On the positive side, it helps representatives, especially women, to claim legitimacy from their respective communities. The negative side of it, however, could be that the community is robbed of the opportunity to make leaders accountable.

The other view is that issues are dealt with informally through lobbying and simply sail through at the time they are tabled formally in the District Council meeting. In Mukono, it was noted that cases of conflicting views in the LC5 were very rare because positions are generally agreed on beforehand. The Deputy Speaker of Mukono asserted that women in the council sometimes had good ideas but these could not be accommodated. She said: 'In many cases you find that a woman brings up an idea which is entirely hers. She has not sold it to anybody.' This could also reflect demands on women's time such that they are not able to 'combine business and pleasure' as men do in bars and other social arenas. Furthermore, voluminous documents (such as materials for meetings) are sent to them and, more often than not, are not read owing to practical constraints of time as well as (for some women) poor capacity to interpret technical reports. It was noted earlier that the LC5 meeting in Mukono is conducted in Luganda, whereas English is spoken during District Council meetings in the much more remote area of Kabale. This could also contribute to the silencing of women and other groups who may not be able to speak English well enough to perform in such a forum. The Speaker for Kabale District Council actually permitted people who might find it difficult to speak English to make their contributions in the local language (Rukiga). But this does little to encourage non-English speakers. It is hard to imagine them making an intervention in a debate from which they have been excluded because they cannot follow the language. Further, since English is regarded as a superior language, people who make their contributions in Rukiga are likely to be ridiculed or assigned low status. In either case, it has been observed that contributions made in local languages are generally not taken seriously and will tend not to appear in the record of council meetings.

Some observers acknowledge that, as relatively new entrants in the system, women are at a disadvantage in council debates. One of the Mukono district officials observed that women have to confront men who have been long in the business and are more seasoned and sophisticated (Interview, April 1999, Mukono district). This sophistication is not necessarily in terms of the substance of what the men have to say but rather the kind of legitimacy they claim, which determines how what they say and do is received and validated. Some observers suggest that women tend to be overwhelmed by the fear of making mistakes. 'For some women, to stand up and talk is an uphill task and yet the mode of politics tends to privilege those who just talk, even when they do not have much content,' the Community Development Officer went on to assert.

Of particular significance is the generally held view that that the District Council women are generally less educated than their male counterparts. Levels of education are regarded as influencing how different individuals act, particularly in a forum such as the District Council, since education also determines levels of exposure. In general discussions, education was given as the major determinant of the difference between men and women councillors. Table 8.2 captures education levels for a number of women and men councillors in Mukono district.

According to Table 8.2, the differences between women's and men's education levels are not so significant as to justify the view that there are major disparities between the two. Almost the same proportion of women as men had completed some form of schooling up to secondary school graduation (27.2 per cent of women and 25 per cent of men).

Table 8.2 Levels of education of District Councillors, Mukono

	Men		Women	
	No.	%	No.	%
PLE	1	2.8	2	9.1
O Level	5	13.9	3	13.6
A Level	3	8.3	1	4.5
Certficate	4	11.1	5	22.7
Midwife	0	0	1	4.5
Teacher	2	5.6	1	4.5
Diploma	13	36.1	8	36.4
University	6	16.7	1	4.5
Postgraduate	2	5.6	0	0
Total	36		22	

Source: District records.

Table 8.3: Occupations of District Councillors, Mukono

	Men		Women	
	No.	%	No.	%
Peasant	1	2.7	4	19.0
Farmer	8	21.6	7	33.3
Secretary	0	0	2	9.5
Teacher	4	10.8	3	14.3
Business	3	8.1	3	14.3
Social worker	2	5.4	1	4.8
Engineer	2	5.4	1	4.8
Lecturer	1	2.7	0	0
Accountant	1	2.7	0	0
Fishmonger	2	5.4	0	0
Technician	1	2.7	0	0
Administrator	7	18.9	0	0
Marketeer	1	2.7	0	0
Cashier	1	2.7	0	0
Magistrate	1	2.7	0	0
Retired	2	5.4	0	0
Total	37		21	

Source: District records.

Not as many had been to university as men, but just as great a proportion had undergone some other form of post-secondary school training. The major difference between the men and women is in the range and diversity of their occupations. From the table it can be observed that over 50 per cent of the women work in the agricultural sector, as opposed to 24 per cent of the men. The men work in a wide range of socially respectable, formal sector and lucrative occupations, while the

229

women are clustered in a limited range of traditionally female sectors, reflecting the lack of opportunities open to them.

Addressing women's perceived deficiencies in the District Council: the women's caucus in Mukono district

'They are very powerful women but there is no concerted effort,' observed a Community Development Officer (Interview, April 1999, Mukono district). This notion is widespread in Mukono. Beyond the evident recognition for women's political capabilities, the statement hides an implicit criticism based on an expectation that women councillors be united. However, there has not been much evidence that women have worked together strategically, at least not in this first term in which there have been greater numbers of women in local office.

In 1999, the women District Councillors in Mukono made a decision to form a caucus. They sought to offer mutual support to each other and to use the caucus to build the skills of women who have demonstrated a weak capacity in public tasks, particularly public speaking. One of the more experienced female politicians in the district commented that women often come unprepared to the District Council meeting and raise flimsy ideas. She suggested that women tend to present unresearched information such as, for instance, claiming that a number of bags of cement meant for a certain school in their sub-county were stolen, when they have no idea how many bags of cement were stolen, or who stole them. A district officer in Mukono commented that 'the bad thing with women councillors is that they tend to present hearsay' (Interview, April 1999, Mukono district).

In the initial meeting held in June 1999 to discuss the *modus operandi* of the women's caucus, there was a strong conviction that in the District Council meetings women councillors had in most cases been used by male colleagues as vote fodder – in other words, to support male-sponsored motions. It was felt that women had not had any major impact on issues that they could call their own. In nominating a committee to draft the constitution of the caucus, the major point stressed was that there was a need to spell out the women representatives' agenda, how to pursue it, and to be clear on what the measures of success would be. The caucus however never went beyond the first meeting. Subsequent meetings were convened but failed to realise quorum. Though women in councils are beginning to focus on their capacity and effectiveness as politicians, they have yet, in Mukono at least, to work together effectively to establish a set of shared concerns, or to advance these in council meetings.

Secretary for Finance: where does the power lie?

As noted earlier in this chapter, the post of Secretary for Finance at district and lower council levels has tended to go to women. This is an intriguing phenomenon. Finance is normally regarded as a key arena of power, and is therefore a seat one would expect to be jealously guarded by men. Why is finance becoming feminised despite its apparent centrality? How are women using this centrality, if it exists? Or, has the power shifted elsewhere? Or is this an indication of women's growing political effectiveness?

The Secretary for Finance in Mukono tells of her experience where fellow women councillors came over to congratulate her after a number of meetings because she had performed 'beyond the expectations of many' (Interview, November 2000, Mukono district). In a discussion in August 1999 at Ngogwe sub-county (Mukono), where the Finance Secretary is also a woman, there were conflicting views about why finance had become identified as a woman's post. Some argued that women were less prone to embezzling, and some that women were still naïve in issues of finance, and hence not able (or clever enough) to hide irregularities; some, however – especially women – argued that women were inclined to be more concerned with development than men.

Interviews with sub-county officials and politicians on the subject of women's political effectiveness produced assertions as to women's growing impact. Most commonly, male officials pointed out that women councillors had initiated a number of projects. LC3 Chairperson Busana (Mukono) asserted: 'Women are far ahead of the youth' (August 1999). He noted that women leaders had initiated projects such as rearing goats for milk, piggeries and vegetable growing. In this sub-county women had even applied for space to establish a market and the matter had been received positively by the council, and was put under consideration. Apart from the infantilising practice of always comparing women with the youth, there are some emerging local discourses that call for much more nuanced examination. At a general level, women are said to be more inclined to development owing to their role in society as mothers, but we need to go beyond these essentialising assertions to a more critical analysis of what is going on.

Views on the appropriateness of putting women in charge of finance signify essentialised notions of womanhood. But they also, perhaps, provide an opening for building women's effectiveness in local government. Efforts by a feminist NGO – the Forum for Women in Democracy (FOWODE) – are building on this by developing tools to help women politicians analyse local budgeting and spending from a gender-sensitive perspective. The finance aspect signifies subtexts emerging around local notions of womanhood.

Making sense of womanhood in local public politics

The essentialist notions of women's greater propensity to manage money carefully – supporting their appointment to Secretary of Finance posts on Local Councils – brings us to the question of the meaning of womanhood and its positionality in local politics.

The gender identity of woman councillors seems to be forefronted in politics in a way that manhood is not. In one of the sectoral committee meetings in Mukono, two councillors, a male and a female, were holding a conversation during the lunchbreak. As the Chairperson, a woman, proceeded to take her seat and call the meeting to order, she joked to the two councillors: 'Beware, that is somebody's wife.' This was a light-hearted warning to the men not to overstep social boundaries. The woman councillor responded by saying, 'I thought I was a councillor.' But as if to respond to this 'gender role revision lesson', she quickly abandoned the discussion with her male colleague and took her seat. The joke evidently made both councillors conscious of their respective gender roles, underlying the significance and salience of marriage and womanhood in local politics particularly.

The salience of conventional marital status takes different shapes at different times in relation to women in local politics. In times of elections and campaigns, marital status was perhaps the single most important area on which questions posed to women focused. If a woman was not married, questions were raised about her moral probity. If a woman was married, questions were raised about her geographical origin and that of her spouse. This was because women marrying into the area could be seen as less legitimate candidates than those born locally. Incidentally, widows seem to be spared such questions.

In a one-day workshop organised in December 2000 to present findings of this research to the councillors in Mukono, one of the comments made about constraints on women was the fact that men tend to treat female councillors (symbolically) as their wives – as persons in their service. Female councillors are sometimes expected to serve food at functions. While it is generally observed that members of the council, and particularly the executive, are very supportive of women, men are still holding on to being served. One of the highly placed women in the District Council asserted:

We are big people. Fine. But when it comes to food, men still feel that we are women and we should serve them. They will always call the nearest woman around to serve food. If the District Chairman calls you to serve, you have to go because you would not like to embarrass him in public (Interview, November 1999, Mukono district).

Women in the executive committee of Mukono have brought the issue of food serving to the attention of the executive members. The male members initially wanted to brush it aside as an irrelevant issue to the committee, but the women insisted that, as a matter of policy, food at district functions should be served by support staff. When the question was put to different people, there were varied views: there were those who did not see anything wrong in women leaders serving food; others speculated that serving at such important gatherings may help one to build social and political capital. Others argued for the necessity of this practice, saying that political heavyweights at such gatherings have to be served by somebody they trust, since there can easily be people with motives to poison them or do other harm. In Kabale, the problem of requiring women councillors to serve at mealtimes does not even arise. There are district staff who are supposed to perform such tasks.

Whether the motive behind the practice of women politicians taking on domestic service roles is to build political capital or to protect the visitors, it reflects a tendency for society to seize every opportunity possible to facilitate women's backsliding into domesticity.

The identity of wifehood works in contradictory ways, though. With regard to taxation, we see wifehood being invoked by both men and women in very interesting ways. The question as to whether women leaders pay tax is normally answered by the observation that if women are just housewives, they are not required to pay tax. In one of the discussions in Mukono (November 1999, Kanjuki village, Mukono district), men especially tended to argue 'abakyala baffe bafumbo' – 'Our women are just housewives', and hence not earning a taxable income. In other words, within the discourse on tax, women have a collective identity of wifehood that shields them from paying graduated tax, seen as a male duty. Women councillors were defending their immediate economic position in avoiding tax-paying responsibility. But the long-run impact could be a reinforcement of the construction of womanhood as an economically dependent, secondary social position.

Most women did not seem to perceive any danger in this. In a focus group discussion in Bukinda, Kabale, most women asserted that if gender equality meant paying tax, then it could as well wait. The comment emerged in a discussion about how the NRM government had accorded women a voice and the liberty to make money and hence make autonomous decisions. One vendor of second-hand clothes said: 'Ery'iraka ryayeenda ribure tugarukye tuvigiire, kwonka tindi hamushoro' – 'The voice can go. We can as well return to whispers, but I am not in for tax' (Group discussion, April 2000, Bukinda, Kabale district). Quite a few women, however, argued that tax increases one's legitimacy or respectability as a citizen. The deputy mayor of Kabale municipality also suggested that it would be good for women to pay tax. Being called empa mushoro (taxpayer), in her view, is a very significant aspect of citizenship and belonging, and it also legitimises one's right to make demands at local and even national levels.

The issue of women paying tax is still a latent one. Some districts had proposed to introduce graduated tax for women household heads, but the Minister of Local Government intervened and stopped it. In Kabale it had been suggested that women pay an annual flat rate tax of 2,000 Uganda shillings,[10] but this was immediately opposed and it was stopped. According to the Kabale deputy mayor, 2,000 shillings is petty cash that every woman can raise in a year. In her view, women are already doing a lot in areas such as farming, handicraft and animal rearing. But the major contestation may lie not in the amount of money but rather in the principle that women are not supposed to pay tax. Since tax policy is an enormously important issue in decentralised local government and local politics, and is key to raising resources for local service delivery, it is essential that it be analysed in a critical manner. In relation to the question of women paying tax, there are several crucial factors to consider.

First is the fact that, although graduated tax is seen as predominantly the responsibility of male income earners, it is essentially a tax on the whole household, or what in colonial times was referred to as hut tax. The whole household contributes to it. This comment was made by the people who participated in a focus group discussion held at Kanjuki (LC1) in Kayunga sub-county, Mukono district (November 1999). Men argued that assessment of tax is based on household resources – for instance land acreage, crops grown, animals reared – and these are based on the labour of men and women, including children (since they also form part of the household labour resource, especially in rural areas).

On age and seniority

Women councillors mentioned that the community still views a woman in public politics as Nalukalala – meant to imply 'irate woman', one with experience of the world. Only older women who have gone through the full cycle of child rearing were said to be free to venture into the world of public activity. A scan of the age structure of the councillors of Mukono district shows that men and women were found in similar proportions across age groups, as Table 8.4 below shows.

Table 8.4 Age structure of Mukono District Councillors

Age group	Male	Female	Total
25–29	2	1	3
30–34	6	5	11
35–39	5	8	13
40–44	7	4	11
45–50	4	3	7
51–55	2	0	2
56–60	3	1	4

Source: District records.

Most men and women were concentrated in the age range of 35–50. However, age has different implications for men and women. Age, especially in a rural context, is mediated by such factors as education and age of marriage, which means that a married person of 30 would be *socially* older than a school-going man or woman at the same age. Married women of 35 are regarded as old, justifying the argument that only old women find it easier to go into public politics. What is interesting, however, is that while the women are conceived of as socially older, that status does not work into the logic of local politics to accord them greater legitimacy and authority.

On Dress

One of the issues that have featured prominently in the discourse on women in local politics is dress. Women at the national level, particularly the Vice-President, have been under close scrutiny for their sartorial choices.

What seems to be happening in Mukono district is that the scrutiny is even more specific. For women to be respected as leaders, they have to be seen to be wearing appropriate dress. Here, what is 'appropriate' has not been left to the discretion of the women, but rather to tradition. The *gomesi*, a traditional dress for women in Buganda, is the expected attire. The *gomesi* is almost compulsory for women if they want to be listened to in election campaigns or any other important function, otherwise a woman will be taken to have appeared in public virtually naked (or *bukunya* in Luganda).

One of the women District Councillors argued that one of the things that people tend not to approve of in relation to women politicians is indecent dress. She asserted that some women were in the habit of wearing very short dresses or skirts with very high slits, and this was tarnishing the image of women politicians (Interview, April 1999, Mukono district). Actually it was found that this statement referred to only two women, but they had caused so much outcry that it was to be explicitly stated that women councillors should wear *gomesi* at all official functions of the district. Indeed, at one of the DC meetings attended, only one woman councillor was not wearing a *gomesi*. As she walked to the meeting venue she asked: '*Abatayambadde gomesi oba tunatuula tutya? ba nakyalo be Mukono tobamanyi?*' – 'How will those of us not wearing *gomesi* sit? Don't you know these villagers of Mukono?' (Informal conversation, November 1999, Mukono district).

The analysis of the contestation over dress leads one to pose questions about the construction of political space. It points to processes of seeking ideologically to contain women in public space and to cater for the moral panic that seems to see danger in the increased participation of women in the 'outer world'. Although there are minimum standards for men, particularly when they are attending the District Council meeting, here the semi-official consensus is that one should be what is generally regarded as smart. This could be a matter of simply wearing a clean shirt with or without a necktie, or a safari (commonly known as a Kaunda) suit, or a full suit, or a jacket and necktie.

Gomesi has become a signifier of women's propriety in local politics, the situation in Mukono seems to be culturally specific. In Kabale, the issue of dress has not become a visible public issue.[11] Looking at the age of most of the women, wearing *gomesi* could well be part of their daily practice already, because it is the dress for most functions in Kiganda culture. But it can be argued that there is something more than tradition at stake because, if this were just about tradition, men equally would be required to wear *kanzu* (the traditional dress for men). The way in which women conspicuously appear in the *gomesi* has an implicit bearing on the ways in which masculinity and femininity are expressed in local politics. It is acknowledged that once a woman is clad in this decent dress, she is supposed to walk, stand and even look about in a particular way, while holding part of it and taking particular care that the dress stays in place (Ahikire 1998). There is definitely some amount of energy and time required in walking gracefully and keeping the dress in place, not forgetting the constant adjustments that one has to make on the sleeves and belt. What then strikes the observer is that the uniformity in the way the women dress, coupled with the nature of the dress itself, tends symbolically to drift them away from the business-like realm of important decision makers.

Concluding remarks

The space that has been created in local government, particularly in relation to women, may have contradictory impacts. The relative isolation and lack of perceived legitimacy of women politicians, and the failure so far to advance any gender equity agenda in local assemblies, suggests that women councillors need a support system in terms of civil society organisation, where women's associations can support women councillors and press them to advance a gender equity agenda. This is in view of the fact that women cannot merely be assumed to represent women's interests and, even if they were able to do so, women's interests are so varied that for them to filter into the policy process, there is a need for more organisation and coalescence to process those interests. For gender issues even to find their way onto the order paper of the District Council requires much more than individual effectiveness. Civil society action is needed to raise and refine policy suggestions, since women councillors cannot be expected to bring unprocessed issues and concerns to the councils.

Women councillors feel inadequately equipped with skills for public office. While there is a role for the support services provided by NGOs, these should not focus on women alone, but rather on local political systems, because the fact that women may fail to fit in also stems from the patriarchal character of the systems in place. In other words, the yardsticks for adequacy also need to be reviewed. Also, technical support is needed, not by women alone, but by local government councillors in general, in terms of building capacity to engage with technical reports and documents.

It would be naïve to think that women's interests are somehow severed from centres of local domination. Nevertheless they might represent alternative perspectives on leadership. In some cases women have been said to be more inclined to concentrate on feedback to the community and close concern with local development problems. In this way the numerical increase of women on councils could engender more responsive local governance and politics. On the whole, it can be argued that the space created for women's participation, though riddled with inconsistencies, and seemingly rigged to underline women's latecomer and secondary status, could all the same hold the potential for transforming local-level politics. The visibility of women has, in some way, meant that gender relations have to be confronted in public discourse. Even in instances where gender equity is ridiculed, or seen as a threat to society, there is a great potential for change as women continue their journey from oblivion and silence.

References

Ahikire, J. (1998) 'Of Dress and the Mind', *Arise*, 23 (a women's developmental magazine published by ACFODE, Kampala).

Awori, T. (2000) 'Women in Decision-making Positions in National and Local Level Public Office in Uganda', report prepared for FOWODE, Kampala.

Bidandi, S. (1998) 'Accounting to Women: Reducing the Gender Gaps in Local Government', paper presented at the First National Conference on Ugandan Women and Politics, organised by FOWODE, 24–26 June, Kampala.

Ddungu, E. (1989) 'Popular Forms and the Question of Democracy: the Case of Resistance Councils in Uganda', Kampala: Centre for Basic Research, Working Paper No. 4.

Doornbos, M. (1999) 'Globalisation, the State and Other Actors: Revisiting State Autonomy', in J. Martinussen (ed.), *External and Internal Constraints on Policy-making: How Autonomous Are the States?* Occasional Paper No. 20, Institute of Development Studies, Roskilde.

East African Initiatives (1998) *East African Initiatives, No. 4.* Kampala: East African Sub-Regional Support Initiative for the Advancement of Women.

Goetz, A. M. (1998) 'Women in Politics and Gender Equity in Policy: South Africa and Uganda', *Review of African Political Economy*, 76.

Griffith, K. (1981) 'Economic Development in a Changed World', *World Development*, 9, 3.

Longwe, S. and R. Clarke (1990) *Woman, Know Your Place*, Lusaka: Zambia Association for Research and Development.

Mamdani, H. (1988) 'Democracy in Today's Uganda', *New Vision*, 20 December.

Mamdani, M. (1994) 'Africa Was Highly Decentralised', *New Vision*, 20 December.

Mutizwa-Mangiza, N. D. and D. Conyers (1996) 'Decentralization in Practice, with Special Reference to Tanzania, Zimbabwe and Nigeria', *Regional Development Dialogue*, 17, 2: 77–93.

Oloka-Onyango, J. (1998) 'Governance, State Structure and Constitutionalism in Contemporary Uganda', Working Paper No. 52, Kampala: Centre for Basic Research.

White, G. (1995) 'Towards a Democratic Developmental State', *IDS Bulletin*, 26 2.

UWONET (1997) 'Vote in the Local Council Elections: Understanding the Local Government Act and Local Council Elections in Uganda', booklet developed in conjunction with the Civic Education Department of the Electoral Commission.

UWONET (1998) 'Documenting Women's Experiences in Local Council Elections', Kampala: UWONET.

Notes

1 The spread of the RC system countrywide itself dates back to 1986 when the NRM government came to power. The institution of the RCs emerged in the course of the guerrilla war and started within the war zones as a process to ensure popular participation and possibly the population's support for the guerrilla movement. When the NRM took over power, the RC system was generalised for the whole country. Every village community was organized into a Resistance Council (RC) with the Village Council as RC1, Parish RC2, Sub-county RC3, County RC4, and the District, RC5. In each RC, there was a Resistance Committee to be elected from the members of the RC, constituting the Chairperson, Vice-Chairperson, the General Secretary and Secretaries for Women, Information, Youth, Finance, Defence and Mass Mobilisation (see Ddungu 1989, for a detailed exposition of the RC system).

2 In the case of urban councils, a city is equivalent to a District, while Municipal Councils and Town Councils are equivalent to the sub-county.

3 All interviews were conducted on the basis of anonymity. Each quotation from an interview therefore only indicates the respondent's position in local government, and the date and place of the interview.

4 The UWONET documentation of women's experiences in Uganda's Local Council and local government elections states that 'on the whole, elections for district women councillors were a flop countrywide. Originally these elections were gazetted for Saturday, 18 April, but due to the failure to raise a two-thirds quorum in many parts of the country, the Electoral Commission postponed the exercise to 19, then to 26 April and finally to 17 May 1998. The postponement, however, did not yield better results either, but instead caused a lot of confusion to the candidates and the voters .... Many monitors reported that elections in many parts of the country went ahead without realising the quorum because the electoral officials insisted that they would never raise the legally stipulated quorum' (UWONET 1998: 48).

5 One woman contested the seat in Hoima district and lost (Awori 2000). For the mayoral seat of Kampala City, one woman contested but won 0.5 per cent of the votes cast (East African Initiatives 1998).

6 This phenomenon is replicated in the majority of lower councils throughout the country (Official, Decentralisation Secretariat).

7 In Kiganda culture, kneeling is a sign of respect. It tends to be heavily gendered, however, when it becomes a rule for women to kneel for men and this replication of the cultural arrangement in politics means that women were symbolically 'put in their place' (Longwe and Clarke 1990).

8 The anthem of Buganda.

9 A Luganda word for 'Sir'.

10 Graduated tax ranges from 8,000 to 80,000 shillings. Most people in rural areas other than public servants would be in the range of 8,000 for the poor, to 40,000 for the local rich. Most public servants pay 80,000 regardless of the salary scale.

11 In part this could be culture-specific in that there are major differences between Buganda, where Mukono district is located, and the rest of Uganda. Historically, Buganda had a long tradition of aristocracy that also had refined and institutionalised traditions, including those of dress.

Index

abortion 62, 102

accountability, and access/presence/influence levels of public engagement 7-8, 29-31, 39-48, 55-9, 71-3, 85, 110; administrative 29, 31-2, 39, 41, 61-5, 67, 69, 73-4; answerability and enforceability 30-2, 34, 39, 64, 67, 72-3; and civil society 45-8, 69, 75; for bias 33, 68; and constituency of women 6, 40-1, 46, 52-3, 57-8, 73, 82-5, 88, 91-6, 99-101, 103-4, 118-21, 131, 133, 196-7, 207-8, 221-2, 224; for capture of public resources 32-3, 68; consumerist model of 63; electoral 49, 51-3, 58, 115; and feminism 53; financial 7, 20-1, 32, 48, 60-1, 67, 69, 72, 75; horizontal 67-8; informal 69; institutions and xi, 5-6, 18, 29, 40-1, 68-71, 73, 184, 197, 207; internal and external 45-7, 99, 103; judicial 29, 31-2, 39, 61, 70-1, 73, 94; on land issues 168, 184-5; legal 32; to local communities 20-1, 25, 168, 192, 196-7, 227; moral 94-5; of Parliament 184; of parliamentary committees 64, 75; pluralism and 15-16, 26, 135; and policy making 5, 40-1, 184, 197, 207; power relations distort 34; and representation 115, 196; proportional representation and 98; in the sexual contract 37-8; and the state 4, 20, 62; and women's movement 5-6, 26, 14, 46-7, 53, 57, 94-5, 184-5; and women's voice 34-5, 39, 48, 73

Action for Development (ACFODE) 116, 186n, 187n

ActionAid–Uganda 186n

AEB 105

affirmative action 1-2, 4, 9, 11, 13, 17, 35, 38, 50, 53, 56, 58, 74, 79n, 87, 110-11, 114, 118-20, 122, 133-4, 136, 173, 213, 218-20

Africa, one-party states in 14; women's experience of the state in 10, 16, 63, 68; women's movement chooses autonomy in 60; women representatives in politics 52, 64

African Christian Democratic Party 105

African National Congress (ANC) 13, 17, 22, 83-6, 90-3, 97-8, 101-3, 105, 108n, 134, 142, 146, 148, 151, 155, 190, 194-5, 197, 199-200, 205-6, 210; Deployment Committee 98; Emancipation Commission 148-9; Women's Caucus 93, 101-2, 153, 155; Women's League (ANCWL) 13, 99, 107n, 148, 209

aged people 187n, 207

Agenda 91

agriculture 65, 67, 168-9, 181, 190, 214, 230, 234; coffee 214; subsistence production 190

aid/donor agencies 112, 125, 171, 176, 182, 214

Akina Mama wa Afrika (AMWA) 186n, 187n

Amin, Idi 112, 116, 225

Andhra Pradesh 48

Ankole 164

Apuli, Kateenta 218

Argentina 29, 36, 51-2, 55, 60, 62; Consejo Nacional de la Mujer 62; Ley de Cupos 62

Australia 56, 90, 142

authoritarianism x, 2, 11, 17, 49, 60, 62, 73, 82, 123, 136

Ayume, Francis 175

Azanian People's Organisation (AZAPO) 87, 105, 195

Babihuga, Winnie 127, 134

Baganda people 23, 112, 130, 133, 236-7, 240n

Banda, Hastings 44

Bangladesh 25, 52, 65, 74, 142

Banyankore people 130

Basotho people 199; Queen of 199

Benin 68

Besigye, Colonel Kiiza 129, 139n

Bidandi Ssali 222-3

Bigombe, Betty 117, 131

black consciousness 144

Black Sash 153

Bosman, Frances 146-7, 158

Brazil 48, 66, 70

budgets/expenditures/revenues 7, 20-1, 32, 48, 60-1, 67, 69, 72, 75, 103, 114, 128-9, 154, 157, 188, 194, 204-5, 208, 210, 225, 231-2

Buganda kingdom 112, 114, 128, 164, 176, 185, 225, 235-6, 240n; Kabaka of 112, 225; Queen of 185

Bukinda LC3 221

Bukinda sub-county 216-17, 221, 233

Bunyoro kingdom 164

bureaucracy 6-7, 11, 30, 34-5, 39-41, 48, 60-7, 69, 73-4, 82, 95, 114, 118, 129, 141-2, 145, 157-8, 179, 182; national machineries 11-12, 30, 35, 62, 67

Burkina Faso 52

Busana, Chairperson 231-2

business associations 44-5, 63, 190

Byanyima, Nathan 138n

Byanyima, Winnie 127-9, 131, 134-5, 182

CALS 212n

Camerer, Sheila 148, 158

Canada 142

Cape Province 147-8, 153-4

Cape Town 145, 151, 194

Carolus, Cheryl 98, 108n

caste 9, 33, 36-7

centralisation/decentralisation 6-7, 12-13, 15, 20-4, 39, 51, 53-4, 58, 62, 71-2, 75, 88, 90, 97, 99, 103, 213-15, 225, 234

children, childbirth 9; childcare 64, 91, 96, 108n, 201, 207; Children's Statute (Uganda) 180; constitutional rights of 187n; custody of 32, 61, 127, 150; labour by 234; land rights of 165, 167, 170, 177, 180; maintenance support for 150, 157; orphans 131; rearing of 9, 201